POLITICS AND
POPULATION CONTROL

POLITICS AND POPULATION CONTROL

A Documentary History

Kathleen A. Tobin

GREENWOOD PRESS
Westport, Connecticut • London

Library of Congress Cataloging-in-Publication Data

Tobin, Kathleen A., 1957–
    Politics and population control: a documentary history / Kathleen A. Tobin
        p. cm.—(Documentary reference collections)
    Includes bibliographical references and index.
    ISBN 0–313–32279–1 (alk. paper)
        1. Population policy—History—Sources. 2. Birth control—History—Sources.
    I. Title. II. Series.
    HB883.5.T63 2004
    363.9—dc22   2003055490

British Library Cataloguing in Publication Data is available.

Library of Congress Catalog Card Number: 2003055490
ISBN: 0–313–32279–1

First published in 2004

Greenwood Press, 88 Post Road West, Westport, CT 06881
An imprint of Greenwood Publishing Group, Inc.
www.greenwood.com

Printed in the United States of America

The paper used in this book complies with the
Permanent Paper Standard issued by the National
Information Standards Organization (Z39.48–1984).

10 9 8 7 6 5 4 3 2 1

CONTENTS

Contents

Contents

INTRODUCTION

The history of population is the history of mankind. For that reason alone it is impossible to paint a picture of what this book is about in just a few pages. But here is a prelude: It is about birth rates, movement, family economies, regional economies, and global economies. It is about womanhood, agricultural production, military conflict, and babies. It is about colonies and about color. It is the human story.

Population, which is in essence the simple result of the most intimate of human acts, has drawn the attention and commentary of authorities at the highest level for centuries. These authorities were concerned about numbers of people and their location. They were concerned about the capacity to feed them. They were concerned about their means of production and means of employment. They were concerned about their racial makeup, their intelligence, their health, and their drain on society. They were concerned about their sexual behavior and their methods of child rearing. They were concerned about threats to the ecosystem. And ultimately, each of these concerns helped to shape population policy.

But every prescription—every proposed solution—has been steeped in controversy. Few experts have agreed on the sources of the problem, or even the degree to which there was a problem. In turn, they rarely came to an agreement about what should be done. But it is striking to discover that fundamental notions regarding population have remained with us for hundreds of years. It is my intention to present to the reader a broad sample of writings reaching back to the eighteenth century to illustrate developments and universal concepts addressing population. Some of the documents come from historical figures who are well known for their population theories. Others come from less remembered spokespeople who nonetheless had a significant impact on policies of their day. Still others come from rather famous people in history who held surprising views on population.

In initially researching and writing on various aspects of birth control, I came across some fascinating documents. In early versions of my first book, *The American Religious Debate Over Birth Control, 1907–1937*, I found it very difficult to choose short passages from the primary sources. They were so rich, and each word lent meaning to the entire human story of population. My editors insisted that my quotes be brief, and my own interpretation more extensive. I complied. But I promised myself to produce a work one day that would allow readers to see more of the documents themselves. In subsequent research I found so many documents that I decided I could best tell the story by including as wide a selection as possible. It is my hope that the reader will seek out the original sources in order to gain a more comprehensive understanding of what each author had to say.

Historians value primary source documents as important pieces of any historical puzzle, but I believe they hold tremendous value for the nonhistorian as well. Of course it is essential to examine them within some framework—within some degree of context—in order to make sense of their intent and their significance. For that reason, I have attempted to provide at least a short introduction to each selection. But it is important for readers to find their own meaning in each of them.

I originally came to the subject of birth control with the understanding that it was an issue of women's rights, and the first histories of birth control in America that I read introduced activist Margaret Sanger and others in a very favorable light. However, upon further study, particularly of primary sources, I came to understand the birth control movement as something far more complex. In fact, I can generally conclude that if contraception were solely a matter of a woman's right to reproductive choice, it never would have been legalized. At least not in the early decades of the twentieth century. What appealed to lawmakers was its greater potential to address social and economic ills.

Growing up in the 1960s, I was made aware that a so-called population explosion threatened the world's resources and the future of the planet as we knew it. The numbers were shocking. So, in fact, long before I began researching any aspect of population policy, I had had embedded in my mind a vision of global metropolises and developing nations teeming with people for whom there were no provisions. Numbers were what needed to be addressed, and the numbers could never stabilize without international birth control programs. Above all, I understood the situation, and all of the related commentary that emerged, to be a recent development in human history. But it soon became clear that the fear of numbers and their impact on resources had existed for centuries.

These are just a few of the assumptions that are challenged as the result of more deep and broad examination of the topic of population policy. There are more. In order to demonstrate the complexity of the subject, while clarifying it at the same time, I have placed documents into the following categories: resources, economics, eugenics, race, colonialism and imperialism, war, nation and migration, religion, children and family, gender and sexuality, technology, and numbers. Each of these has played a significant role in shaping the way we have come to understand population. From the mid-eighteenth century to the present, they have influenced policy from a local to an international level.

Perhaps the greatest difficulty in putting this work together was in making decisions regarding the placement of each document. Most of them could be placed into any one of a number of categories. For example, Darwin addresses resources as well as race; Roosevelt addresses gender as well as economics; Sanger addresses sexuality as well as children; and so on. I did my best. In the end, the collection offers a wide spectrum of issues that are related. It was my intention to include a variety of treatises, essays, speeches, articles, and passages from books, scholarly journals, and periodicals that represent any one of a number of perspectives on population. The collection I am presenting here is by no means exhaustive, but it is my hope that the reader will find it enlightening.

1

Resources

Concern over global population and the world's resources is often perceived as a very recent development in human history. In fact, the connection between population and resources was outlined in one of Thomas Malthus's first works. Enlightenment philosophy based on rational and mathematical principles warned that population numbers were increasing more rapidly than could be sustained by available resources. Concerned primarily about food supply, population theorists also warned of future scarcity of fuel and housing supplies (primarily wood) and other raw materials. Nineteenth-century critics of Malthus and of others making similar arguments pointed to technological advances in agriculture as evidence that such claims could no longer be substantiated.

Malthusians countered such arguments, maintaining that while technology might improve the quantity of food supply, the quality of food being made available to the masses of poor might be questionable. In addition, they argued that the potential for agricultural production was not limitless, while population growth clearly seemed to be. Twentieth-century concepts of progress suggested that man did have the potential, through advances in science and technology, to combat hunger and feed all of the world's people adequately. However, the arguments that focused on resources gained momentum during the 1960s and 1970s, as the environmental movement strengthened. Environmentalists of previous decades had directed their efforts toward conserving natural resources, often for the benefit of stable social and economic progress for any one nation. The new environmental movement, however, warned of the poisoning of the planet brought on by human progress. Post–World War II modernization had introduced rapid industrialization into regions where it had not existed before, as well as the mass consumption of petroleum and chemical-based products that produced longer-lasting and more toxic by-products. At the same time, the world was experiencing unprecedented population growth in the developing world, along with desires to bring modern technology and an improved standard of living to even the most underdeveloped of regions. Unless there was significant population control, environmentalists feared for the health of the planet and its people.

DOCUMENT 1.1: Rev. T. R. Malthus, *An Essay on the Principle of Population; or, A View of Its Past and Present Effects on Human Happiness; With an Inquiry Into Our Prospects Respecting the Future Removal or Mitigation of the Evils which it Occasions,* **6th ed. (London: John Murray, 1826, pp. 1–9)**

The Rev. Thomas R. Malthus was not the first population theorist, but he has made the greatest impact in the modern world in the area of population theory. Before publishing his first *Essay on the Principle of Population* in 1798, Malthus had been aware of related arguments already made by various economists of his day. However, it was his work that opened the floodgates for comment and debate. In subsequent editions, Malthus noted that his point of view regarding the scarcity of resources and the natural tendency toward population growth had in fact been outlined at least as early as the time of Aristotle and Plato. In this edition, he defends his position more intently, citing the work of Benjamin Franklin and others who also wrote on population. Still, Malthus, whose namesake the Malthusians and neo-Malthusians are, will be recognized as the father of population theory. His arguments are viewed as being based in mathematical reasoning and projections common in the Enlightenment, and his recommendations for moral restraint are representative of notions of the perfectability of humankind that prevailed among his contemporaries. In this first chapter, he lays the groundwork for the relationship he sees between resources and population.

The principal object of the present essay is to examine the effects of one great cause intimately united with the very nature of man; which, though it has been constantly and powerfully operating since the commencement of society, has been little noticed by the writers who have treated this subject. The facts, which establish the existence of this cause have, indeed, been repeatedly stated and acknowledged; but its natural and necessary effects have been almost totally overlooked; though probably among these effects may be reckoned a very considerable portion of that vice and misery, and of that unequal distribution of the bounties of nature, which it has been the unceasing object of the enlightened philanthropist in all ages to correct.

The cause to which I allude, is the constant tendency in all animated life to increase beyond the nourishment prepared for it.

It is observed by Dr. Franklin, that there is no bound to the prolific nature of plants or animals, but what is made by their crowding and interfering with each other's means of subsistence. Were the face of the earth, he says, vacant of other plants, it might be gradually sowed and overspread with one kind only, as for instance with fennel; and were it empty of other inhabitants, it might in a few ages be replenished from one nation only, as for instance with Englishmen.

This is incontrovertibly true. Through the animal and vegetable kingdoms Nature has scattered the seeds of life abroad with the most profuse and liberal hand; but has been comparatively sparing in the room and the nourishment necessary to rear them. The germs of existence contained in this earth, if they could freely develop themselves, would fill millions of worlds in the course of a few thousand years. Necessity, that imperious, all-pervading law of nature, restrains them within the prescribed bounds. The race of plants and the race of animals shrink under this great restrictive law; and man cannot by any efforts of reason escape from it.

In plants and irrational animals, the view of the subject is simple. They are all impelled by a powerful instinct to the increase of their species; and this instinct is interrupted by no doubts about providing for their offspring. Wherever therefore there is liberty, the power of increase is exerted; and the super-abundant effects are repressed afterwards by want of room and nourishment.

The effects of this check on man are more complicated. Impelled to the increase of his species by an equally powerful instinct, reason interrupts his career, and asks him whether he may not bring beings into the world, for whom he cannot provide the means of support. If he attend to this natural suggestion, the restriction too frequently produces vice. If he hear not, the human race will be constantly endeavouring to increase beyond the means of subsistence. But as, by that law of our nature which makes food necessary to the life of man, population can never actually increase beyond the lowest nourishment capable of supporting it, a strong check on population, from the difficulty of acquiring food, must be constantly in operation. This difficulty must fall somewhere, and must necessarily be severely felt in some or other of the various forms of misery, or the fear of misery, by a large portion of mankind.

It may safely be pronounced . . . that population, when unchecked, goes on doubling itself every twenty-five years, or increases in a geometrical ratio.

The rate according to which the productions of the earth may be supposed to increase, it will not be so easy to determine. Of this, however, we may be perfectly certain, that the ratio of their increase in a limited territory must be of a totally different nature from the ratio of the increase of population. A thousand millions are just as easily doubled every twenty-five years by the power of population as a thousand. But the food to support the increase from the greater number will by no means be obtained with the same facility. Man is necessarily confined in room. When acre has been added to acre till all the fertile land is occupied, the yearly increase of food must depend upon the melioration of the land already in possession. This is a fund, which, from the nature of all soils, instead of increasing, must be gradually diminishing. But population, could it be supplied with food, would go on with unexhausted vigour; and the increase of one period would furnish the power of a greater increase the next, and this without any limit. . . .

If it be allowed that by the best possible policy, and great encouragements to agriculture, the average produce of the island could be doubled in the first twenty-five years, it will be allowing, probably, a greater increase than could with reason be expected.

In the next twenty-five years, it is impossible to suppose that the produce could be quadrupled. It would be contrary to all our knowledge of the properties of land. The improvement of the barren parts would be a work of time and labour; and it must be evident to those who have the slightest acquaintance with agricultural subjects, that in proportion as cultivation extended, the additions that could yearly be made to the former average produce must be gradually and regularly diminishing. That we may be the better able to compare the increase of population and food, let us make a supposition, which, without pretending to accuracy, is clearly more favourable to the power of production in the earth, than any experience we have had of its qualities will warrant.

DOCUMENT 1.2: William Godwin, *Of Population. An Enquiry Concerning the Power of Increase in the Numbers of Mankind, Being an Answer to Mr. Malthus's Essay on That Subject* (London: Longman, Hurst, Rees, Orme, & Brown, 1820, pp. 463–467)

William Godwin was one of the first to discount Malthus's work with detailed arguments. In 1820, he published his own essay addressing population, throughout which he criticized Malthus. He spends much of the book disputing population figures, and then goes on to attack Malthus's assertions regarding resources and food supply. The following selection outlines Godwin's thoughts on scarcity.

There lurks an ambiguity under the term "means of subsistence"; and, but for that ambiguity, I conceive that Mr. Malthus's doctrine upon this head could never have been listened to for a moment.

The earth is, in a liberal point of view, the "means of subsistence" to man; and, till her prolific bosom has been exhausted, and her soil has been so cultivated, that the store of provisions she is able to afford can be no further enlarged, there can be no danger to free and unshackled, and at the same time civilized man, on the score of the means of subsistence.

In another, and a very restrained sense, the provisions actually collected from the surface of the earth, may be called our "means of subsistence"; and in this sense Mr. Malthus always chooses to understand the term.

If this ambiguity had been attended to, every one would have felt the absurdity of talking of "population pressing hard against the limits of the means of subsistence," in any intermediate period, till the "whole earth had been cultivated like a garden."

To place this fact in a more striking point of view, let us set apart from each other the two great modes of the existence of man, the civilized, and the savage state. For the present I will confine myself to the former.

Civilized man, is man not living upon the wild fruits of the earth, or the wild animals of the field, but for the most part upon that which is matured by human industry. Here therefore every man that is born into the world, is a new instrument for producing the means of subsistence, in the sense of provisions; and every member added to the numbers of the community, is a new instrument for increasing those means.

The basis of civil society, at least as it exists in those countries with which we are best acquainted, will be found in the truth of this proposition, that man in society is capable of rearing a greater quantity of provisions than is necessary for his won subsistence. Till this was the case, all mankind were shepherds or husbandmen; and if the case had not been altered, such we must for ever have remained.

It is to this supererogatory power in man, that we are indebted for all our improvements, our refinements, and elevation. The result has been the dividing the members of civil society into two great classes, the one, who are employed in rearing the fruits of the earth, and the other, who live in idleness, or who are employed in other kinds of industry, not immediately connected with the production of food.

How profound therefore the absurdity of talking of "population pressing hard against the limits of subsistence," till the earth, and the different parts of the earth, have been "cultivated like a garden"!

Let us look to the continent of North America, whose real or fabulous history has had the shame to give birth to Mr. Malthus's hypothesis. There, we are told, every man considers each additional child that is born to him, as so much added to his wealth, to his means of subsistence, or rather to his means of indulgence and of accumulating a moderate fortune. There, it has over and over again been pretended, the population doubles by procreation only, in fifteen, twenty, or five-and-twenty years. There, we are assured, the number of inhabitants in 1749 was one million, and at the present hour is ten millions. (I grant the increase; but I deny that there is such a progressive and permanent increase from procreation only.)

Why is all this? For one simple reason. Because on the continent of North America there is a vast quantity of productive land, yet uncultivated, which may be had *gratis*, or at a low price, so as to be, with a little patience and industry, within the reach of every man to obtain.

It is clear therefore, that, so long as there is in any country cultivable land, yet unapplied to the purposes of human subsistence, or not yet improved to those purposes to such a degree as is easily within the reach of existing science and skill, population may be checked, but it is not checked by any thing that is connected with a paucity of the means of subsistence. In other words, till the whole earth has been cultivated like a garden (for the power of such cultivation is in proportion to the number of human beings naturally capable of agricultural labour), or till some one of its considerable portions has been so cultivated, and the inhabitants will not be persuaded to seek their fortune elsewhere, there can be no cause, inherent in the nature of things, why population should not go on to increase, to any extent to which it has the power of increasing.

Nothing therefore can be more insolent, or more groundless, than to talk to an unportioned man, who has come into the world in obedience to the great laws of nature, and without his own consent, of his having come into a "world, where every thing is appropriated." Appropriated indeed it is, but not to the wisest and most honest purposes, not to purposes most conducive to the diffusion of human happiness. He has only to lift up his eyes, and survey our heaths and our forests, our parks and our pleasure-grounds, and he must see that the world is not appropriated, as the simple, but never to be confuted, laws of nature direct us to appropriate it. I am not now enquiring whether the appropriation made by the institutions of society has or has not good reasons to defend it: but I say, that as long as that appropriation operates in its present form, population is not kept down by the want of the "means of subsistence."

DOCUMENT 1.3: David Booth, *A Letter to the Rev. T. R. Malthus, M.A. F.R.S. Being An Answer to the Criticism, On Mr. Godwin's Work On Population, Which Was Inserted In The LXXth Number of the Edinburgh Review: To Which Is Added An Examination of the Censuses of Great Britain and Ireland* (London: Longman, Hurst, Rees, Orme, & Brown, Paternoster-Row, 1823, pp. 63–64)

David Booth questioned contemporary arguments based on the teachings of Malthus that population growth at the existing rate threatened food supply. Booth argued that supply did not pose a problem as much as distribution did. He also pointed out that population theorists based their works on the premise that the population of the poor must be checked. Booth added that the population among the rich should be checked as well. By the first few decades of the nineteenth century, population theories were viewed as classist, and critics noted that the rich consumed more of a nation's resources than did the poor.

We know very little of the past, and nothing at all of the future history of the human race. Whether on the whole their number be at present increasing or diminishing, I will not pretend to determine. We amuse ourselves and others with speculations on the subject; but, with respect to a solution of the problem, I suspect that we have not advanced a single step, since it occupied the pens of Wallace and of Hume. For centuries, at least, there seem to be sufficient room and sustenance upon this globe for all its probable inhabitants; and I see no necessity of legislating for eternity until we are certain that man, in this world, is eternal. While food can be procured by industry, the sole evil to be conquered is its unequal distribution. If there be any principle in man which will render the many for ever the slaves of the few, it is from their masters alone that we can expect amelioration; and these, perhaps, may listen to our lectures on political economy, especially if they tend to foster their prejudices and flatter their passions; but if, by the gradual improvement of intellect, the many shall ever be able to govern the few, we may safely leave it in the hands of those new governors to provide for their own subsistence. But even should they be improvident, what would our laws avail? Those future legislators would laugh at our checks upon their population. That all men have not now food in abundance, is the consequence of misrule. I will not say that this misrule may not be necessarily permanent in every human society; that the mass of mankind, active rather than reasoning beings, may not for ages to come, as in ages past, deceive the hopes of the philosopher; and that the best form of government that can be devised, must, like the mushroom, partake of the corruption from which it springs: should this, unfortunately, be true, the inequality of distribution must be perpetual; but this is not your principle; for it acts independently of the amount of population, the pressure upon subsistence being caused by a combination of ignorance and despotism.

Were I an absolute monarch, and at the same time convinced of the truth of your principles, I would take care that the *checks* upon population should press *at least* as heavily upon the rich as upon the poor.

DOCUMENT 1.4: Friedrich Engels, "Outlines of a Critique of Political Economy" (1844), in *Marx and Engels on Malthus: Selections from the Writings of Marx and Engels Dealing with the Theories of Thomas Robert Malthus*, ed. Ronald L. Meek (London: Lawrence and Wishart, 1953, pp. 57–58)

Friedrich Engels would become most famous for his works on economics, particularly those produced in collaboration with Karl Marx. However, here his critique of Malthus and other population theorists centers on resources. Malthusian population theory used mathematical and scientific principles of the Enlightenment to measure and predict the capacity for food supply. A few decades later, Engels countered with contemporary notions embracing more modern technology. To Engels, "The productive power at the disposal of mankind is immeasurable." This line of reasoning was essential to discussions of population and resources into the twentieth century. Also essential in his perspective is the claim of uneven distribution of resources, which supported his general condemnation of uneven distribution of wealth.

The struggle of capital against capital, labor against labor, and land against land, drives production into a state of feverish activity, in which all natural and reasonable relations are turned upside down. No one capital can stand up against the competition of another if it is not brought to the highest pitch of activity. No one piece of land can be profitably cultivated if its productivity is not constantly being increased. No one worker can hold his own against his competitors if he does not dedicate all his strength to his work. No body, in fact, who enters the competitive struggle can endure it without the greatest exertion of his strength, without the abandonment of all truly human purposes. The consequences of this hypertension on the one side is necessarily exhaustion on the other. If the fluctuations of competition are small, if demand and supply, consumption and production are almost equal to one another, then in the development of production a stage must ensue in which there is so much superfluous productive power in existence that the great mass of the nation has nothing to live on, so that people starve to death from sheer abundance. England has already been in this crazy situation, in this truly absurd condition, for a considerable time. If the fluctuations of competition become stronger, as they necessarily do in such a state of affairs, then we have the alternation of prosperity and crisis, of overproduction and stagnation. The economists have never been able to understand this crazy state of affairs, so in order to explain it they thought up the theory of population, which is just as nonsensical, indeed, even more nonsensical, than this contradiction of the coexistence of wealth and poverty. The economists did not dare to see the truth; they did not dare to understand that this contradiction is a simple consequence of competition, because if they had done so, their whole system would have collapsed.

For us the explanation of the matter is easy. The productive power at the disposal of mankind is immeasurable. The productivity of the land can be infinitely increased by the application of capital, labor and science. "Overpopulated" Great Britain, according to the calculations of the ablest economists and statisticians, could be so developed in the course of ten years as to produce sufficient corn for six times its present population. Capital increases daily; labor power grows together with population; and science masters natural forces for mankind to a greater extent every day. This immeasurable productivity, administered consciously and in the interests of all, would soon reduce to a minimum the labor falling to the lot of mankind; left to competition, it does the same, but only within the limits imposed by the contradiction. One part of the land is cultivated according to the best methods, while another part—in Great Britain and Ireland thirty million acres of good land—lies waste. One part of the capital circulates with phenomenal speed, while another part lies inert in strong-boxes. One part of the working population works fourteen, sixteen hours a day, while another remains unemployed and idle, and dies of hunger. Or this coexistence of idleness and activity gives way to another pattern: today trade goes well, demand is very considerable and everyone is working, capital is turned over with wonderful speed, agriculture flourishes, the workers work themselves sick—then, tomorrow, stagnation comes on the scene, agriculture is no longer worthwhile and whole stretches of land remain uncultivated, capital becomes paralyzed in the middle of its course, the workers are unemployed, and the whole country suffers from surplus wealth and surplus population.

The economists cannot regard this account of the matter as the correct one, for if they did, as stated above, they would have to abandon their whole system of competition; they would have to acknowledge the stupidity of its antithesis between production and consumption, between surplus wealth and surplus population. But in order to bring these factors into harmony with theory—since the facts themselves could not be denied—the theory of population was invented.

DOCUMENT 1.5: Achille Loria, *Contemporary Social Problems: A Course of Lectures delivered at the University of Padua*, trans. from Italian by John Leslie Garner (London: Swan Sonnenschein & Co. Ltd., 1911, pp. 64–67)

In the following selection, Italian economist Achille Loria, too, notes that Malthusian theory was grounded in classism. Marxism appealed to Loria, and it is evident in his criticism of prevailing population theory. Very importantly, he reexamines fears of scarce resources and a threatened food supply through a twentieth-century perspective. Following decades of rapid technological advancements in agricultural production, short food supply seemed almost a problem of the distant past. The emergence of the United States as an essential supplier of food to the world proved to Loria that Malthus's philosophy should be reexamined.

Among the social doctrines which have filled our century with learned controversies and philosophical arguments, none has found more valiant supporters and more determined adversaries than Malthus's theory of population. Received at first with enthusiasm and later bitterly denounced, it has continued, up to the present time, to be the object of serious investigations and erudite discussions. The reader, therefore, will not be surprised, if, before examining certain more important questions, I devote some time to a discussion of a theory which has found both devoted defenders and bitter enemies.

The doctrine may be summarized in a few words:

The number of beings who may exist at any time, says the pastor of Hailey-bury, clearly is rigorously determined by the amount of provisions at their disposal; consequently if, at a certain moment, there is only food enough for one hundred persons, and a hundred and one are born, some will necessarily suffer from deficient nourishment. This lack of equilibrium between population and food is a constant and inevitable phenomenon in life, and not a rare or hypothetical one. For while the amount of food available increases very slowly, owing to the decreasing productivity of land which has been long cultivated, and to the diminishing returns from capital too often turned, population, owing to the uncontrollable instinct implanted in every organic being, increases with unabated energy. The increase in the supply of food therefore follows at best an arithmetical progression, while that of population follows a geometrical one.

This disproportion between the increase in agricultural products and the increase in the number of human beings occasions a chronic excess in the number of mouths to be fed. Some of those who come into the world, finding no place at the banquet of life, are condemned to hunger and death—this law of nature therefore is the first cause of poverty, of the unequal distribution of wealth, and of social discord. This lack of balance is not, therefore, as radical writers maintain, the result of human institutions, of the creation of privileges, and of the existence of property; but it is a natural and eternal phenomenon, a manifestation of the Divine Will, to which man must yield, unless he heroically resolves to extirpate the evil by abstaining from reproducing his kind.

It is not difficult to understand why this doctrine was enthusiastically welcomed by the wealthy proprietors, since it offered them valuable and unexpected support. The poignant contrast between their opulence and the poverty of the masses may have aroused in them some scruples, some indistinct feeling of remorse; and the new theory came most opportunely to dispel these clouds and to relieve the rich of all responsibility for pauperism, since it had been found to be necessary, and inexorably imposed by both natural and divine laws.

Malthus even advised them not to endeavour to find means to lessen the suffering, and he bade them stay their hands when a generous impulse or a sudden fear disposed them to offer help. "Charity," exclaims the pastor-economist, "why, that is absurd!" When the poor find they can count on the obolus of the rich they will cast aside the last scruple, which keeps them from marriage and procreation, and the greater the excess of population over the food supply, the greater will be the increase in poverty. Therefore away with all philanthropic societies, all organizations, and all laws intended to increase wages, for a rise in wages immediately impels the labourer to marry and procreate, which means a further extension of the curse of a super-abundance of mouths to be fed. Institutions which extend or increase the well-being of the people, which ameliorate their lot, are, therefore, harmful and reprehensible, since they render an excess of population still more certain. The working classes ought not to look to others for any betterment in their condition; they can secure it without external aid and prevent poverty simply by avoiding the shafts of Cupid—according to Townsend, another English clergyman, equally as well versed as Malthus in the science of population, therein lies the salvation of the labouring man. Is it surprising that this doctrine was acclaimed by the rich and furiously attacked by the poor and their champions?

DOCUMENT 1.6: William Graham Sumner and Albert Galloway Keller, *The Science of Society* (New Haven, Conn.: Yale University Press, 1927, pp. 45–48)

This selection by William Graham Sumner, a former professor of political and social science, and Albert Galloway Keller, professor of the science of society (both at Yale University), is representative of neo-Malthusian observations of the early twentieth century that assumed a so-called law of population. But Sumner and Keller also incorporate the teachings of Charles Darwin, which suggest that a scarcity of resources leads to competition, which in turn leads to advancements in culture.

The ratio between numbers and land is something that plants and animals cannot alter. If their increase is such as to press heavily upon their food-supply, the only possible immediate outcome, apart from migration, is such elimination of numbers as will leave the survivors provided for. Over a long period, structural adjustments might take place which would enable more individuals to live upon the same area; but even so the immediate mortality would be little if at all decreased. Animal and plant life tends to increase up to the limit of the supporting power of the environment; it cannot advance beyond that deadline. The case of man is different; he is an animal with superior capacities for speed adjustment which enable him to operate upon the numbers–land ratio. By the invention of various methods of getting more food out of the land, he virtually increases that term of the ratio, a feat which allows of a rise in human numbers. We call these adjustments of his the arts of life, or, briefly, the arts. When they deal directly with the extraction from nature of the prime necessities of life, chiefly food, they include the instruments and processes of hunting, herding, and tillage, all of which are, directly or indirectly, ways of exploiting land. And men can also operate upon the other term of the ratio, for they can practise limitation of their own numbers. This is generally put into operation, not so much to avoid the worst as to maintain a standard of living that is traditional, or to attain to a higher one. Thus the arts are seen to be operating upon the land-side of the basic ratio, and the standard of living upon the man-side.

The foregoing considerations may be gathered up, prior to analysis, into a law of population. Numbers vary directly with the arts and inversely with the standard of living. To align this law of human population with the one which covers the case of plants and animals, all that is necessary is the proviso that the modifying arts and standard of living shall remain constant—thus: Population tends to increase up to the limit of the supporting power of the environment (land), on a given stage of the arts, and for a given standard of living. This is, it will be noted, simply a more explicit rendering of the bare man–land ratio. The rest of this chapter will be devoted to the disclosure in finer detail of the ways by which men have altered the terms of that ratio through the development of the arts of life and of the standard of living. It should never be lost to sight that those alterations have taken place through the evolution of folkways and mores, for both the arts and the standard of living belong among these basic adjustments. . . .

The question of numbers is paramount in the organic world. Successful adjustments are those permitting of numbers, while dwindling species are approaching extinction. The same is true in the societal range. The sum of men's adjustments to their life-conditions is their culture, or civilization. These adjustments, it has been seen, are attained only through the combined action of variation, selection, and transmission. There must be numerous and frequently recurring variations for selection to operate upon, if the process is to work out into a high degree of civilization; and this cannot be, unless there are many individuals present who are striking out on various tentatives in the realization of interests. Variation calls for numbers. Nor can selection appear in full vigor unless the competition is keen. Selection, too, demands numbers. And the products of selection cannot attain to any extended transmission, so as to spread both lineally to subsequent generations and laterally to contemporaries, unless there is some density of population. Civilization is therefore a function of numbers in contact. On the other hand, numbers cannot increase greatly unless the adjustments to life-conditions are successful, especially those that have to do with the food-quest. . . .

Population among tribes of low civilization is sparse; such people are not succeeding in the struggle for existence because they have not developed culture, and their lack of numbers halts that development. Their degree of societal adaptation is not high enough to allow of a reduction of the death-rate by an augmentation of the food-supply and of protection from the elements and from violence. Here is a case of the supporting and interlocking action of societal factors: Population fails to increase because culture is backward, while at the same time the arts do not improve with any promptness by reason of lack of numbers. Even upon a low stage of the arts, however, civilization has been capable of development where the natural supporting power of the environment has allowed of considerable numbers despite the backwardness of culture. The first foci of civilization were precisely where environmental conditions combined to favor numbers and the contact of numbers: in river-bottoms of the warmer temperate sections of the Old World—in China, India, Assyria, and Egypt. Numbers made possible the development of the arts; then the arts improved to support a still larger population; then the added numbers, in turn, stressed the arts to further advance. Thus the process rolled up on itself. An advanced civilization and a relative density of population are destined to occur conjointly.

DOCUMENT 1.7: Warren S. Thompson, "Population Pressure in Japan" (*Eugenics* 3, October 1930, pp. 363–364)

Warren S. Thompson is one of the most recognized demographers of the mid-twentieth century. Working for the Scripps Foundation for Research in Population Problems, he presented this paper at the Conference on Immigration Policy in New York City, March 27, 1930. He gives special attention to Japan, which the West saw as demonstrating clearly imperialist tendencies. Many argued that the desire to invade other lands lay at least in part in the need for resources to sustain a growing population. An island nation,

Japan had limited space for agricultural development. In addition, Thompson's essay reflects twentieth-century consumption of additional raw materials such as iron ore and coal.

The fact that Japan is growing very rapidly at the present time makes one ask, then, what means is Japan going to use for the support of these people? When we come to examine the economic situation in Japan, it appears that the population is growing much faster than any visible means of support. Japan is a poor country from the standpoint of its economic resources. . . . When you ask the Japanese what they are going to do, the reply is, "Well, we don't have the land, but we are going to emulate the example of Great Britain and become the manufacturing and commercial center of the Far East." That is being talked about a great deal. On the face of it, it seems we must again ask, on what basis are they going to develop this intense commercial and industrial life that will enable them to support a growing population such as they have now? I cannot see that there is any answer to that question at present. Japan is a poor country from every standpoint. The amount of coal that is available in Japan would last us probably a year, maybe two years. The amount of iron ore that is available would not supply us for a year unless we developed far better methods of reducing and use than we have already developed.

When one understands Japan's poverty in the essential resources for the support of her people, one will comprehend much more readily a great deal of her policy with regard to Manchuria, because Manchuria has many of the things that Japan is in very great need of.

DOCUMENT 1.8: Dr. Paul R. Ehrlich, *The Population Bomb* (New York: Ballantine Books, 1971, pp. 26–44)

The first half of the twentieth century continued to bring improvements in agricultural technology, but many of them proved harmful to the environment. In addition, a new trend in unprecedented population growth was under way. Increased life expectancy in the developing world contributed to what was termed a population explosion by the 1960s. Biologist Dr. Paul Ehrlich was responsible for much of the attention paid to the population explosion. His warnings were harsh, and he was instrumental in influencing population policy. Here, he describes some current and future destruction of the planet's ecological system due to modern technology and unchecked population growth.

It is fair to say that the environment of every organism, human and nonhuman, on the face of the Earth has been influenced by the population explosion of *Homo sapiens*. . . . Ecologists—those biologists who study the relationships of plants and animals with their environments—are especially concerned about these changes. They realize how easily disrupted are ecological systems (called ecosystems), and they are afraid of both the short- and long-range consequences for these ecosystems of many of mankind's activities. . . .

In short, when we pollute, we tamper with the energy balance of the Earth. The results in terms of global climate and in terms of local weather could be catastrophic. Do we want to keep it up and find out what will happen? What do we gain by playing "environmental roulette"? . . .

The causal chain of the deterioration is easily followed to its source. Too many cars, too many factories, too much detergent, too much pesticide, multiplying contrails, inadequate sewage treatment plants, too little water, too much carbon dioxide—all can be traced easily to too many people.

Of course, a smaller population could eventually destroy the ability of the planet to support sizable numbers of human beings. This could occur through the profligate use of weapons as diverse as chlorinated hydrocarbon insecticides or thermonuclear bombs. But with a human population of, say, one-half billion people, some minor changes in technology and some major changes in the rate of use and equity of distribution of the world's resources, there would clearly be no environmental crisis. Equally, regardless of changes in technology or resource consumption and distribution, current rates of population growth guarantee an environmental crisis which will persist until the final collapse.

DOCUMENT 1.9: Tadd Fisher, *Our Overcrowded World: A Background Book on the Population Crisis* (New York: Parents' Magazine Press, 1971, pp. 186–210)

Here Tadd Fisher reaffirms population concerns as they relate to food supply. Not only were policymakers concerned about the environment, they were also concerned that the modern world might be reaching its capacity for food production. At the same time, demands for land redistribution in poorer regions of the world were viewed as socialist threats in this era of the Cold War. In this piece, Fisher argues that such land reform measures would contribute to even lower productivity.

If world population growth rates had not rocketed upward so alarmingly after World War II, poor Malthus might soon have been left to rest in peace. But as statisticians plotted population, economic, and agricultural trends, the lines on their graphs began to justify the long-dead English parson. By 1961, two of the most important lines had collided. Surplus grain stocks ceased expanding as they had been since 1953, and began to decline. Swift population growth and rising incomes have pushed the world demand for grain ahead of production. That was a matter of great moment. Grain is truly the staff of life for the world, but most especially for the developing nations.

Financially, farmers in developing countries rarely know what they can count on from one harvest to the next, since prices for produce fluctuate widely. Increased farm output calls for expensive farm inputs that peasants cannot afford unless they receive adequate compensation for their crops. Even if they could depend on fair and stable prices, they would need to borrow additional money to develop their farms properly, but credit is unavailable to most of them.

Developing nations could hasten progress by becoming more hospitable to foreign private investment in agricultural projects. Nationalism and ideology are ceasing to raise as many barriers as before, but many foreign agribusinessmen are wary of conditions that make such projects very risky in have-not nations. . . .

Undeniably the potential exists for feeding everyone in the world, plus a reasonable increase in numbers. The process of actually doing so is something else again. Man, land, and food stockpiles unhappily do not juxtapose in most of the world. While a far better balance between the three is possible, it will take more years to accomplish it than anyone today is qualified to estimate.

DOCUMENT 1.10: Alan Thein Durning, "The Conundrum of Consumption," in _Beyond the Numbers: A Reader on Population, Consumption and the Environment_, ed. Laurie Ann Mazur (Washington, D.C.: Island Press, 1994, pp. 42–43)

In this essay, taken from his work _How Much Is Enough? The Consumer Society and the Fate of the Earth_, director of the Northwest Environment Watch Alan Thein Durning points to modern levels of consumption as integral to any discussion of population. Though birth rates may be high among the poorest of the world, Durning argues that it is the consumer class that is responsible for most of the destruction of forests, the production of carbon dioxide emissions, the depletion of fuel supplies, the extinction of animal species, and the poisoning of water. While most historical population theories placed substantial blame for the world's ills on the poorer classes for their allegedly uncontrolled breeding, Durning is one of many observers of the late twentieth century who noted that it was the upper classes who caused notable problems through their consuming behavior.

The world has three broad ecological classes: the consumers, the middle income, and the poor. These groups, ideally defined by their per capita consumption of natural resources, emissions of pollution, and disruption of habitats can be distinguished in practice through two proxy measures: their average annual incomes and their life-styles. . . .

The gaping divide in material consumption between the fortunate and the unfortunate stands out starkly in their impacts on the natural world. The soaring consumption lines that track the rise of the consumer society are, from another perspective, surging indicators of environmental harm. The consumer society's exploitation of resources threatens to exhaust, poison, or unalterably disfigure forests, soils, water, and air. We, its members, are responsible for a disproportionate share of all the global environmental challenges facing humanity.

The consumer class's use of fossil fuels, for example, causes an estimated two thirds of the emissions of carbon dioxide from this source. (Carbon dioxide is the principal greenhouse gas.) The poor typically are responsible for the release of a tenth of a ton of carbon apiece each year through burning fossil fuels; the middle-income class, half a ton; and the consumers, 3.5 tons. In the extreme case, the richest tenth of Americans pump 11 tons into the atmosphere annually.

Parallel class-by-class evidence for other ecological hazards is hard to come by, but comparing industrial countries, home to most of the consumers, with developing countries, home to most of the middle-income and poor, gives a sense of the orders of magnitude. Industrial countries, with one fourth of the globe's people, consume 40–86 percent of the earth's various natural resources.

DOCUMENT 1.11: Timothy E. Wirth, "The Human Factor" (*Sierra* 80, September/October 1995, p. 78)

In 1995, Timothy E. Wirth, former Colorado senator and U.S. undersecretary of state for global affairs in the Clinton administration, responded publicly to congressional consideration of a foreign aid appropriations bill that would have eliminated funding for international population programs and significantly reduced sustainable-development assistance. Wirth based his population projections on recent trends, warning that the world's population could reach 15 billion by the end of the twenty-first century. But his most direct warnings addressed resources, noting that developing nations' raw materials were disappearing—not only because of high birth rates within those nations, but also because of continued demands by wealthier foreign nations. His comments also reflect contemporary understanding of the links between stable population growth and sustainable economic development that would keep in mind environmental protection.

[O]ur collective security can be diminished by the soils disappearing around the world and the decline of biological systems—the croplands, forests, grasslands, oceans, lakes, and streams—that support the world economy. Stated in the jargon of the business world, the economy is a wholly owned subsidiary of the environment. All economic activity is dependent on our global resources base. If the environment is finally forced to file for bankruptcy because it has been polluted, degraded, dissipated, and irretrievably compromised, the economy will go down with it. . . .

Some environmental challenges are spurred less by population growth than by large and wasteful consumption patterns. The appetite of the affluent countries for timber products is a menace to the forests of Malaysia, Indonesia, the Philippines, and Brazil, as well as Canada and the United States. The bulk of the underground water being drained away from our future flows into the shining cities of the "haves," not the parched lands of the "have-nots." Those same cities, and we who live in them, are the furnaces of global warming.

As these examples illustrate, our future hinges upon whether we can strike an equitable balance between human numbers and consumption and the planet's capacity to support life. It depends on whether the economies of the world, including our own, can meet the needs of today's generation without stealing from tomorrow's. Striking this balance is often referred to as "sustainable development," a concept rooted in a recognition of the reinforcing nature of economic, social, and environmental progress. . . .

The most important theme voiced in these gatherings is the need for the United States to set an example at home for others to follow.

2

Economics

The topic of economics has shaped population policy and population theory perhaps more than any other. Modern population theory was given birth during the latter part of the Enlightenment, when new economic theories embraced philosophies of a free market and opposed what were considered antiquated colonial mercantilist policies regulating trade for the good of the mother country. Responding to demands for an unregulated economy, theorists developed a new consciousness of the relationship between population and economic principles. Initially, concerns of so-called surplus labor fueled economic debates—fears that too large a laboring class would upset an otherwise stable economy. Prevailing notions that laboring-class couples tended to produce more children than they could afford intensified concerns. In addition, promoters of a free market economy opposed any kind of welfare assistance—as implemented under England's Poor Laws—claiming it encouraged the lower classes to have even more children.

Mid-nineteenth-century reformers called for changes ranging from increased poor relief to increased wages to economic revolution. Arguing that unbridled capitalism was to blame for much of the poverty that existed—primarily in Europe—reformers maintained that overpopulation did not so much pose a problem as did weak economic structures. On both sides of the argument, theorists looked at population as it related not only to the prosperity of an individual nation, but also to colonies and international business. In addition, discussions of population became fundamental to the microeconomics of the family as well as to the macroeconomics of the nation. As much of the world began to industrialize and urbanize, children were considered more of a financial burden, and families became smaller. By the end of the twentieth century, global economic concerns had drawn increased attention to the world's population, and eventually demands for stable birth rates and sustainable development were introduced at international conferences addressing population.

DOCUMENT 2.1 Jonathan Swift, *A Modest Proposal for Preventing the Children of poor People in Ireland, from being a Burden to their Parents or Country; and for making them beneficial to the Publick* (Dublin: S. Harding, 1729, pp. 5–7)

Though *A Modest Proposal* is considered among the best examples of satire in the history of literature, Anglo-Irish author Jonathan Swift did not intend it as humor; rather, he wrote it as a scathing attack on an English political economic system that left Ireland's poor living in squalor. In this tract he suggests fattening poor babies and feeding them to the wealthy as a solution for what was deemed excessive numbers of children among the poor.

The Number of Souls in *Ireland* being usually reckoned one Million and a half; of these I calculate there may be about Two Hundred Thousand Couples whose Wives are Breeders; from which Number I subtract thirty thousand Couples, who are able to maintain their own Children; although I apprehend there cannot be so many, under *the present Distresses of the Kingdom;* but this being granted, there will remain an Hundred and Seventy Thousand Breeders. I again subtract [*sic*] Fifty Thousand, for those Women who miscarry, or whose Children die by Accident, or Disease, within the Year. There only remain an Hundred and Twenty Thousand Children of poor Parents, annually born: The Question therefore is, How this Number shall be reared, and provided for? Which, as I have already said, under the present Situation of Affairs, is utterly impossible, by all the Methods hitherto proposed: For we can *neither employ them in Handicraft* or *Agriculture;* we neither build Houses (I mean in the Country,) nor cultivate Land: They can very seldom pick up a Livelyhood *by Stealing* until they arrive at six Years old; except where they are of cowardly Parts; although, I confess, they learn the Rudiments much earlier; during which Time, they can, however, be properly looked upon only as *Probationer;* as I have been informed by a principal Gentleman in the County of *Cavan,* who protested to me, that he never knew above one or two Instances under the Age of six, even in a Part of the Kingdom *so renowned for the quickest Proficiency in that Art.*

I am assured by our Merchants, that a Boy or a Girl before twelve Years old, is no saleable Commodity; and even when they come to this Age, they will not yield above Three Pounds, or Three Pounds and half a Crown at most, on the Exchange; which cannot turn to Account either to the Parents or Kingdom; the Charge of Nutriment and Rags, having been at least four Times that Value. . . .

I shall now therefore humbly propose my own Thoughts; which I hope will not be liable to the least Objection.

I have been assured by a very knowing *American* of my Acquaintance in *London;* that a young healthy Child, well nursed, is at a Year old, a most delicious, nourishing, and wholesome Food; whether *Stewed, Roasted, Baked,* or *Boiled;* and, I make no doubt, that it will equally serve in a *Fricasie,* or *Ragout.*

I do therefore humbly offer it to *publick Consideration,* that of the Hundred and Twenty thousand Children, already computed, Twenty thousand may be reserved for Breed; whereof only one Fourth Part to be Males; which is more than we allow to *Sheep, black Cattle,* or *Swine;* and my Reason is, that these Children are seldom the Fruits of Marriage, *a Circumstance not much regarded by our*

Savages; therefore, *one Male* will be sufficient to serve *four Females.* That the remaining Hundred thousand, may, at a Year old, be offered in Sale to the *Persons of Quality* and *Fortune,* through the Kingdom; always advising the Mother to let them suck plentifully in the last Month, so as to render them plump, and fat for a good Table. A Child will make two Dishes at an Entertainment for Friends; and when the Family dines alone, the fore or hind Quarter will make a reasonable Dish; and seasoned with a little Pepper or Salt, will be very good Boiled on the fourth Day, especially in *Winter.*

I have reckoned upon a Medium, that a Child just born will weigh Twelve Pounds; and in a solar Year, if tolerable nursed, increaseth to twenty eight Pounds.

I grant this Food will be somewhat dear, and therefore very *proper for Landlords;* who, as they have already devoured most of the Parents, seem to have the best Title to the Children.

DOCUMENT 2.2 Adam Smith, *An Inquiry into the Nature and Causes of the Wealth of Nations* (Washington, D.C.: Regnery Publishing, 1998, pp. 643–645)

Adam Smith is known as the father of free trade economics. His *The Wealth of Nations* rejected the colonial mercantile system, which placed trade regulations on colonists that would benefit the mother country. Rooted in Enlightenment philosophy, Smith's work asserted that there were natural laws of economics that would allow for prosperity and provide internal checks if left alone. Some criticized his discussions of population for some of the same reasons they would criticize Malthus, as Smith suggested that population and resources were integral elements in discussions of a balanced economy. Here he describes how population and resources shape colonial economic development.

The colony of a civilized nation which takes possession, either of a waste country, or of one so thinly inhabited, that the natives easily give place to the new settlers, advances more rapidly to wealth and greatness than any other human society.

The colonists carry out with them a knowledge of agriculture and of other useful arts, superior to what can grow up of its own accord in the course of many centuries among savage and barbarous nations. They carry out with them too the habit of subordination, some notion of the regular government which takes place in their own country, of the system of laws which support it, and of a regular administration of justice; and they naturally establish something of the same kind in the new settlement. But among savages and barbarous nations, the natural progress of law and government is still slower than the natural progress of arts, after law and government have been so far established, as is necessary for their protection. Every colonist gets more land than he can possibly cultivate. He has no rent, and scarce any taxes to pay. No landlord shares with him in its produce, which is thus to be almost entirely his own. But his land is commonly so extensive, that with all his own industry, and with all the industry of other people whom he can get to employ, he can seldom make it produce the tenth part of what it is capable of producing. He is eager, therefore, to collect labourers from all quarters, and to reward them with the most liberal wages. . . .

In other countries, rent and profit eat up wages, and the two superior orders of people oppress the inferior one. But in new colonies, the interest of the two superior orders obliges them to treat the inferior one with more generosity and humanity; at least, where that inferior one is not in a state of slavery. Waste lands, of the greatest natural fertility, are to be had for a trifle. The increase of revenue which the proprietor, who is always the undertaker, expects from their improvement, constitutes his profit; which in these circumstances is commonly very great. But this great profit cannot be made without employing the labour of other people in clearing and cultivating the land; and the disproportion between the great extent of the land and the small numbers of the people, which commonly takes place in new colonies, makes it difficult for him to get this labour; he does not, therefore, dispute about wages, but is willing to employ labour at any price. The high wages of labour encourage population. The cheapness and plenty of good land encourage improvement, and enable the proprietor to pay those high wages. In those wages consists almost the whole price of the land; and though they are high, considered as the wages of labour, they are low, considered as the price of what is so very valuable. What encourages the progress of population and improvement, encourages that of real wealth and greatness.

DOCUMENT 2.3 Thomas Chalmers, *On Political Economy in Connection With the Moral State & Moral Prospects of Society* (1832) (New York: Augustus M. Kelley Publishers, 1968, pp. 398–401)

From the early seventeenth through the eighteenth century, any proposal of government relief or assistance for the poor was met with tremendous opposition. Critics contended not only that it would disrupt the economic system, but that it would encourage the poor to have even more children. In the following selection, the Scottish evangelical Presbyterian minister Thomas Chalmers outlines such an argument. At the time of this writing, nineteenth-century social reformers were insisting that the industrial economy was creating new problems of poor housing, illness, injury, etc., which needed to be addressed, as the economy was generating enough capital to do so. Chalmers restates the old argument, which would continue through the twentieth century, that if given assistance, the poor would have no incentive to limit their family size.

1. The last topic which we propose to discuss, in this catalogue of expedients for the removal of want from the human family, and the secure establishment of a general prosperity and abundance in its place—is a legal and compulsory provision for the poor. It stands distinguished from all the former expedients, in one important particular. Its object is, not the creation, but the division, of wealth.

It is evident, that every levy upon property for the support of the indigent, trenches on the means of its owners for the employment and maintenance of the disposable population. There is no new provision created under such an economy. A part of the old provision is simply transferred, or withdrawn, from the sustenance of one class to the sustenance of another class. Every additional impost that is laid upon me in the shape of poor's rate, lessens my ability to support those industrious who are remunerated for their services by my expenditure. Supplies are provided for the destitute in one quarter of society, at the expense, not of my enjoyments alone, but of privations to those who minister these enjoyments in another quarter of society. And, accordingly, it has been well observed, that, for all the visible relief effected by a poor's tax, there is much of real though unseen poverty created among those, who have not yet entered within the territory of pauperism, but stand, a countless and untold multitude, around the very margin of it. The distress is not swept off from the face of the community. It is only shifted to another, and generally a far more deserving class of sufferers—to a mass of respectable families on the verge of destitution; struggling against the hard necessity of descending amongst the throng of sturdy applicants for a legalized charity; and all the more hopeless of relief, that the springs of gratuitous benevolence have been well nigh dried up, by the heavy impositions which the artificial or compulsory system has laid on the upper classes of society. It is thus, that, by a sort of festering and spreading operation, the sphere of destitution is constantly widening in every parish, where the benevolence of love has been superseded by the benevolence of law. Generally speaking, every year, or at least every decade of years, the pauperism, like a moral leprosy, makes a wider sweep among the families than before.

DOCUMENT 2.4 William Cobbett, *Surplus Population: and Poor-Law Bill. A Comedy in Three Acts.* (n.p., 1835, pp. 3–8)

The following passage is from the first of a three-act satire on nineteenth-century population policy. Its author, William Cobbett, was a popular English journalist and harsh critic of industrialized society. He was a champion of the working class and rural poor, who were marginalized as ignorant overbreeders and a drain on society. In this scene, Cobbett presents Squire Peter Thimble ("a Great Anti-Population Philosopher"), Mrs. Stiles (a farmer's wife), Betsey Birch (betrothed to Stiles's servant), and Sir Gripe Grindum (a county nobleman).

SCENE II.—A room at the Inn: SQUIRE THIMBLE sitting at a Table, covered with written papers and pamphlets.

SQU. THIMBLE [*Rising, and going to the window.*] Oh, God! Only look at that swarm of children! Why, this village of NESTBED is properly enough named; for it really resembles an ant's nest. It was high time to pass a *Poor Law Bill;* high time to pass a *Dead Body Bill;* high time, as my friend the *fellosofer* [whom Cobbett calls the *hell-featured brawling Scotch vagabond*] says, to put a stop to this "breeding of beggars" to swallow up the estates of the landlords; high time, as the Rev. Mr. CAPPER recommends, and as the Rev. Mr. LOWE practises, to separate man from wife, upon the same principle that farmers separate rams from ewes and boars from sows; high time, unless all of us *gemmen* and ladies, mean to go to work; high time, as the *"hell-featured brawler"* says, to put them on a *"coarser sort of food,"* unless we of the genteel orders have a mind *to go to work,* the bare thought of which makes the blood curdle in my veins!—But I wonder I do not hear from Sir Gripe, in answer to my letter, which he got by post yesterday. I know he is at the Hall, for the waiter saw him there last night.

SCENE IV.—A small parlor in the Farm-house: SQUIRE THIMBLE sitting before the fire, breakfast preparing.

SQU. THIM.　[*to himself.*] I don't much like his sending me here instead of receiving me at the Hall, but I dare say he will explain it when he comes.

MRS. STILES　[*Entering.*] Hope you will excuse our homely fare, Sir, but we'll give you the best we've got. [*Betsey, entering with the eggs, lets a couple of them roll off the plate upon the floor.*] What a deuce is the girl about! But [*turning to Squire Thimble*] I hope you'll look over it, Sir: She's going to be married tomorrow, and her head has been running upon that all the morning.

SQU. THIM.　*Married,* did you say! *Married!* That girl going to be *Married!*

MRS. STILES　Yes, Sir; They have been courting a long while, and they be desperate fond of one another.

SQU. THIM.　*Desperate, indeed!* But do you encourage such things, then!

MRS. STILES.　What things, Sir?

SQU. THIM.　Why, the coupling together of these poor creatures to fill the country with beggars and thieves.

MRS. STILES.　[*With warmth.*] I'm sure there isn't a better young man in the parish than Richard Hazle; and as for Betty Birch, young as she is, she shall make bread, butter, cheese, or beer, with any woman in the whole county, let the next be who she will. Beggars and thieves, indeed!

SQU. THIM.　Well, if these be good people, so much the more reason to keep them from being plunged into misery and . . .

MRS. STILES.　[*Interrupting him.*] Misery, Sir!

SQU. THIM.　Yes, and from adding to that great national disease the *surplus population.*

MRS. STILES.　Never heard of that disease before, Sir; we ben't troubled with't in these parts, though we have the small-pox and measles terrible bad sometime; and our poor neighbour, Chopstick, lost four as fine children last week as . . .

SQU. THIM.　So much the better! So much the better!

MRS. STILES.　What, Sir!

SQU. THIM.　Yes; so much the better. I say, and [*aside*] if it had taken you off too, it would have been better still. [*To her.*] Go, good woman, and tell the girl to come and speak to me.

MRS. STILES.　She's going to her mother's to get ready for her wedding; but I'll call her in for a minute. [*Exit.*]

Enter BETSEY.

SQU. THIM.　So, young woman, you are going to be married, I understand?

BET.　Yes, Sir.

SQU. THIM.   How old are you?

BET.   I'm nineteen, Sir, come next Valentine's eve.

SQU. THIM.   That is to say, you are *eighteen!* [*Aside.*] No wonder the country is ruined! [*To her.*] And your mother now; how old is she?

BET.   I can't justly say, Sir: but I heard her say she was forty some time back.

SQU. THIM.   And how many of you has she brought into the world?

BET.   Only seventeen, Sir.

SQU. THIM.   Seventeen! *Only* seventeen!

BET.   Seventeen now alive, Sir; she lost two and had two still-born, and . . .

SQU. THIM.   Hold your tongue! Hold your tongue. [*Aside.*] It is quite monstrous! Nothing can save the country but plague, pestilence, famine, and sudden death. Government ought to import a ship-load of arsenic. [*To her.*] But, young woman, cannot you impose on yourself "*moral restraint*" for ten or a dozen years?

BET.   Pray what is that, Sir?

SQU. THIM.   Cannot you keep single till you are about thirty years old?

BET.   Thirty years old, Sir! [*Stifling a laugh.*]

Enter SIR GRIPE GRINDUM.

SQU. THIM.   [*Rising.*] How do you do, Sir Gripe; hope I've the pleasure of seeing you well.

SIR G.   Very well, very well; but rather hungry.

SQU. THIM.   Draw up, then; here are plenty of eggs and butter.

SIR. G.   Yes, they think nothing of MALTHUS here.

SQU. THIM.   So it seems, for this young hussey is going to be married to-morrow, though she is only eighteen. Her mother has had, it seems, *only* twenty-one children; so that you'll have your parish finely stocked.

SIR G.   Married! [*Aside.*] What a beautiful creature it is!

SQU. THIM.   Yes, married; and she laughs at the idea of *moral restraint*.

SIR G.   I dare say she does. [*Aside.*] And so shall I too, if I can get her into my clutches.

SQU. THIM.   You may go, young woman; for I find I can do nothing with you. [*Exit Betsey.*]

SIR G.   [*Aside.*] But *I can* do something with her, I fancy. [*To Thimble.*] Yes, she may go for the present; but it is my duty, my bounden duty to my country, to prevent this marriage.

SQU. THIM.   To be sure it is. It is a duty of humanity, as well as of patriotism. But you must be quick, for she is to be married to-morrow morning.

SIR G.   To-morrow morning!

SQU. THIM.   Yes: and the farmer's wife approves of the match! Would it not be well to find the farmer, and talk to him about it?

SIR. G.   I shan't, but you may; and in the meanwhile, I'll go home and dispatch some business, and be with you again in an hour or so.

SQU. THIM.   Business! What *business?* He thinks that I did not perceive him staring at her. He has some scheme in his head. But no matter; anything is better than her having seventeen children. Why, 'tis littering, 'tis pigging, 'tis hatching, 'tis swarming, and if they are allowed to proceed at this rate, there won't be room for them to stand upright in the country. I'll go and find the farmer and see what I can make of him. [*Exit.*]

DOCUMENT 2.5 Karl Marx, *Wage Labor and Capital* (New York: New York Labor News Company, 1902, pp. 39–42)

Karl Marx is best known for the *Communist Manifesto*, in which he (with Friedrich Engels) describes the faults of industrial capitalism and outlines objectives for a socialist revolution. Marxist theory disputes Malthus's teachings on population, arguing that economic injustice, not overpopulation, causes poverty. In general, Marxists take issue with the term *surplus labor*, used widely in population theory. The following selection is not one of Marx's clearest essays, but in it he describes the relationship he sees between the laboring class and capital. Essentially, he argues that just as labor creates capital, the capitalist creates the laboring class. According to Marx, if there is an excess of labor, it is the fault of capitalism.

What is it that takes place in the exchange between capitalist and wage-laborer?

The laborer receives means of subsistence in exchange for his labor-power; but the capitalist receives, in exchange for his means of subsistence, labor, the productive activity of the laborer, the creative force by which the worker not only replaces what he consumes, but also *gives to the accumulated labor a greater value than it previously possessed*. The laborer gets from the capitalist a portion of the existing means of subsistence. For what purpose do these *means of subsistence* serve him? For immediate consumption. But as soon as I consume means of subsistence, they are irrevocably lost to me, unless I employ the time during which these means sustain my life in producing new means of subsistence, in creating by my labor new values in place of the values lost in consumption. But it is just this noble reproductive power that the laborer surrenders to the capitalist in exchange for means of subsistence received. Consequently, he has lost it for himself. . . .

Does a worker in a cotton factory produce only cotton goods? No. He produces capital. He produces values which serve anew to command his work and to create by means of it new values.

Capital can multiply itself only by exchanging itself for labor-power, by calling wage-labor into life. The labor-power of the wage-laborer can exchange itself for capital only by increasing capital, by strengthening that very power whose slave it is. *Increase of capital, therefore, is increase of the proletariat, i.e., of the working class.*

And so, the bourgeoisie and its economists maintain that the interest of the capitalist and of the laborer is the same. And in fact, so they are! The worker perishes if capital does not keep him busy. Capital perishes if it does not exploit labor-power, which, in order to exploit, it must buy. The more quickly the capital destined for production—the productive capital—increases, the more prosperous industry is, the more the bourgeoisie enriches itself, the better business gets, so many more workers does the capitalist need, so much the dearer does the worker sell himself.

The fastest possible growth of productive capital is, therefore, the indispensable condition for a tolerable life to the laborer.

But what is growth of productive capital? Growth of the power of accumulated labor over living labor; growth of the rule of the bourgeoisie over the working class. When wage-labor produces the alien wealth dominating it, the power hostile to it, capital, there flow back to it its means of employment, *i. e.,* its means of subsistence, under the condition that it again become a part of capital, that it become again the lever whereby capital is to be forced into an accelerated expansive movement.

To say that the interests of capital and the interests of the workers are identical, signifies only this, that capital and wage-labor are two sides of one and the same relation. The one conditions the other in the same way that the usurer and the borrower condition each other.

As long as the wage-laborer remains a wage-laborer, his lot is dependent upon capital. That is what the boasted community of interests between worker and capitalists amounts to.

If capital grows, the mass of wage-labor grows, the number of wage-workers increases; in a word, the sway of capital extends over a greater mass of individuals. Let us suppose the most favorable case: if productive capital grows, the demand for labor grows. It therefore increases the price of labor-power, wages.

DOCUMENT 2.6 J. M. Robertson, M.P., *The Economics of Progress* (New York: E. P. Dutton & Co., 1918, pp. 280–282)

The outbreak of World War I stimulated much population debate. Birth control activists were attempting to legalize contraceptives in Great Britain and the United States. Working in part on the grounds that this was a women's-rights issue, they also enlisted the support of neo-Malthusians. There was an upsurge in the neo-Malthusian movement, which claimed that population pressure contributed to the outbreak of the conflict in Europe. Here, J. M. Robertson, author of *Trade and Tariffs*, *The Evolution of States*, and *The Fallacy of Saving*, illustrates recent developments in Europe in light of birth rates. He contended that quality of population benefited a nation more than quantity, and that rational birth restriction would strengthen a nation's economy.

We have seen that in Germany the popular motive to limitation of births has been the desire for better life-conditions, partly backed by a notion that mere limitation of labour supply will give them a new advantage as against the capitalist employer. Here, however, they are met by the economic retort that limitation of labour supply will elicit further developments of machinery, and that the latter state of the workers will be no better than the first. There is here a twofold confusion, which it is well to clear up. In the first place, resort to machinery goes on continuously, whether the birth-rate is falling or rising. It went far, in the last century, when labour supply was ruinously redundant. The motive is always there. In the second place, as we have seen, limitation of births does not mean decline of net population. It is likely to be long before population is even stationary in our own country.

In France it became nearly so through the twofold pressure of heavy debt-burden, with relatively small increase in total production, and the determination of the mass of the people to maintain their standard of comfort. If in the future it should absolutely decline under the economic burden left by the war, that will simply mean that the people are again adjusting themselves to their load, seeking to maintain quality rather than quantity. The notion that this is a kind of national decay or "race-suicide" is a hallucination correlative with modern megalomania. Population often declined or became stationary for periods in France in old times, as indeed it did in England, where the net increase of population between the eleventh and the fifteenth centuries [sic] was extremely slow. It well might be, seeing that there, as in Europe generally, probably 75 per cent of the children born never reached maturity. For France as for all the other belligerent countries, however, there will arise a new fiscal problem, involving that of the considerate taxation of capital for the reduction of debt; and what will be sound policy for us will be so for her. In the future, the watchword of political progress will be the reduction of idle life simultaneously with the husbanding of life in general by the maintenance of good life conditions.

DOCUMENT 2.7 Dr. Martha Ruben-Wolf, "Birth Control in Soviet Russia," in *The Practice of Contraception: An International Symposium and Survey*, ed. Margaret Sanger and Hannah M. Stone (Baltimore: Williams & Wilkins, 1931, pp. 264–267)

Since the Enlightenment, the so-called laws of population had been discussed in relationship to a free market economy. Theorists generally debated whether population grew to meet supply or whether available resources could effectively meet the demands of a wealthy nation or a poverty-stricken populace. But the twentieth century introduced the modern notion of a planned economy. With the rise of Soviet Russia, new possibilities arose for population management within a controlled economy. Some of the most prominent birth control activists of the Progressive Era were socialists who warned that a surplus of children among the working classes served as fodder for the capitalist system, which would easily exploit them as factory workers. By the time of the publication from which the following excerpt is drawn, activist Margaret Sanger had abandoned much of her socialist teaching, at least publicly, but she included this piece by Dr. Martha Ruben-Wolf, who praises Soviet society for providing for the well-being of its members.

The new and special importance of the Soviet program for the prevention of conception is not as yet based on scientific contributions but on the general health policy. The grant of technical facilities for the study of contraception, the state organization of education work, the state production of preventives, and the free distribution of these (because the proletarian State recognizes assistance in the contraceptives as a social duty towards the needy classes) all this signifies tremendous progress in population control policy, as compared with the rest of the world. . . .

The Soviet Union adopts the attitude that the criterion of the wellbeing of a country is not the number of the population but the economic system. The Soviet Union believes that it cannot guarantee the happiness of its peoples by regulating the increase or decrease of population, but that it is its duty to ensure a contented life for the greatest possible number by economic measures. . . .

The Soviet birth policy, therefore, abstains consciously from regulating the number of births in any way. Its measures are guided exclusively by health considerations.

It recognizes the prevention of conception as a valuable weapon in the campaign against abortion, which is always an undesirable phenomenon. At the same time, it provides free facilities for abortion in order to substitute the far more hygienic skilled abortion for the harmful quack abortion.

Furthermore, it values the prevention of conception as an essential means for the realization of the spacing between pregnancies, which [is] necessary for the health of women.

Thirdly, it sees in contraception an important indirect means for the campaign against infant mortality.

These are the points of view which dictate the birth policy of the Soviets. Their aim is the health of the community.

DOCUMENT 2.8 John Maynard Keynes, "Some Economic Consequences of a Declining Population," in *The Collected Writings of John Maynard Keynes*, vol. 14, *The General Theory and After, Part II, Defence and Development*, ed. Donald Moggridge (London: Macmillan/St. Martin's Press for the Royal Economic Society, 1973, pp. 125–126)

John Maynard Keynes developed a modern economic theory rooted in the development of a mass market economy reliant on consumerism. Where economists of the past had addressed population in terms of agricultural and industrial growth, mass production depended on sustained growth of a mass market. During the Great Depression, Keynes warned of the dangers of a diminished market that would come as the result of birth restriction. The following is taken from a presentation given as a Galton Lecture to the Eugenics Society, London, on February 16, 1937.

An increasing population has a very important influence on the demand for capital. Not only does the demand for capital—apart from technical changes and an improved standard of life—increase more or less in proportion to population. But, business expectations being based much more on present than on prospective demand, an era of increasing population tends to promote optimism, since demand will in general tend to exceed, rather than fall short of, what was hoped for. Moreover a mistake, resulting in a particular type of capital being in temporary oversupply, is in such conditions rapidly corrected. But in an era of declining population the opposite is true. Demand tends to be below what was expected, and a state of over-supply is less easily corrected. Thus a pessimistic atmosphere may ensue; and, although at long last pessimism may tend to correct itself through its effect on supply, the first result to prosperity of a change-over from an increasing to a declining population may be very disastrous.

In assessing the causes of the enormous increase in capital during the nineteenth century and since, too little importance, I think, has been given to the influence of an increasing population as distinct from other influences. The demand for capital depends, of course, on three factors: on population, on the standard of life, and on capital technique. By capital technique I mean the relative importance of long processes as an efficient method of procuring what is currently consumed, the factor I have in mind being conveniently described as the period of production, which is, roughly speaking, a weighted average of the interval which elapses between the work done and the consumption of the product. . . . [T]he demand for capital depends on the number of consumers, the average level of consumption, and the average period of production.

DOCUMENT 2.9 John Kenneth Galbraith, *The Affluent Society* (Boston: Houghton Mifflin, 1958, pp. 27–35, 325–329)

Economist John Kenneth Galbraith is renowned for his observations on American prosperity of the post–World War II period. In this selection from his famous *The Affluent Society*, Galbraith analyzes the work of his predecessors, placing their theories in historical context. He ultimately concludes that poverty still exists, adding, however, that history has proven that the poor may well exist as a minority rather than the majority, as was traditionally believed. And he explains that the modern economist must reconsider previously held notions regarding the causes of poverty.

Any increase in the supply of food would bring, in Malthus' view, an increase in the number of people to consume it. Nothing but stark need limits the numbers who are propagated and who endure. As a result, men will forever live on the verge of starvation. . . . [P]eople might indefinitely protect their standard of living at a level above subsistence, and this would become all the more likely once both restraint and vice were abetted by effective contraceptive techniques. But as also with [David] Ricardo, Malthus' qualifications were lost in the sweep of his central proposition. This was the inevitability of mass poverty. . . .

Since most men had always been poor, it is hardly surprising that Malthus was on the whole unperturbed by his conclusions and that he did not feel called upon to propose any remedy. . . .

In the usual view, from the middle of the nineteenth century on, economists became more sanguine, even optimistic. England was the center of the influential discussion. She was in her great era of commercial and industrial expansion. Real wages were rising. There was a clear and apparently enduring margin over mere subsistence. In Western Europe and America the Malthusian horror was also receding, although it was still possible to suppose that this was the result of the fortuitous opening, all in a few decades, of the North American prairies and plains, the Pampas and the Veld, the New Zealand pastures and the endless Australian outback. . . . Only in the present century, as the relation between real income and the rate of population increase has become increasingly unreliable, has there ceased to be fear that the ghost of Malthus might return to haunt western countries as it still roams the villages of Asia.

DOCUMENT 2.10 "Declaration of Population Strategy for Development," *United Nations and Population, Major Resolutions and Instruments* (Dobbs Ferry, NY: Oceana Publications, Inc., 1974, pp. 66–68)

Birth control activists approached the League of Nations at the close of World War I, recommending that any discussion of future world peace include a serious discussion of birth control. Their efforts were in vain. However, within a half century the United Nations had embraced population control as one of its fundamental objectives. Though concerns of international security acted as an underlying element in the UN's address of population policy, public discussions of the international economy were far more common. In this resolution, adopted by the Second Population Conference at Tokyo, November 13, 1972, the prevailing sentiment linking births in the developing world to family economics and global economics is clear.

Having considered the necessity of formulating population policies and programmes as integral parts of the social and economic development process,

Recognizing the urgent necessity of succeeding in efforts for economic and social development for the benefit of the ECAFE [Economic Commission for Asia and the Far East] region,

Recognizing the human right of every couple to determine freely and responsibly the number and spacing of their children and the need to ensure their access to information, education and the means to do so, no matter what their financial or social condition,

Recognizing further the social and economic impact of individual family size on societies, and considering it appropriate for Governments to take social and economic measures, in addition to family planning programmes, that will make a smaller family more acceptable and beneficial to the individual couple,

Giving full recognition to national sovereignties and to the need for each country to consider the establishment of goals and programmes for an effective control of the growth of population in the light of individual national conditions and policies,

Reaffirming the importance of integrating population into the development strategy of the Second United Nations Development Decade,

Taking note of the Stockholm Declaration and stressing the impact that rapid population growth has on the human environment,

Having considered the fields of concern identified in the report of the present Conference,

Desirous of ensuring that the World Population Conference and the World Population Year contribute their utmost towards the universal resolution of the problems of population and development, bearing in mind the inherent differences in such problems from country to country, and

Emphasizing that the urgency of problems of population growth and distribution calls for intensive and dedicated work in various government sectors as well as innovative changes in many fields,

[the conference declares] that

1. While population has a direct effect on economic and social development and the human environment, conversely policies in the fields of education, health, housing, social security, employment and agriculture have an impact on population and, therefore, require integrated national planning and coordinating action at the highest government level.

2. It is important that the widespread benefits of economic growth should be ensured through policies and programmes to bring about a more equal distribution of opportunity and income, with particular attention being paid to health and nutrition programmes to reduce infant and maternal mortality, programmes to achieve full and productive employment, action to reduce excessive rates of migration to the larger cities, measures to improve the status of women and appropriate social security measures.

3. The priority of population and family planning fields should be recognized through the allocation of broad responsibilities in planning, evaluation and analysis of programmes in these fields to an appropriate organization within the governments.

4. Governments of the region which seek to fulfill the ideals of their people and their national goals through population policies and programmes should:

    (a) recognize the essential role of population and family planning programmes as a means of effectively achieving the aspirations of families and their societies and should provide information, education and services for all citizens as early as possible;

    (b) encourage small families in rural and urban areas through intensive efforts and information and education, with the help of all relevant institutions and resources and the enactment of appropriate social and economic measures;

    (c) include in population policy and programmes provisions to ensure that all pertinent information reaches the policy-makers, opinion leaders, and socio-economic planners;

    (d) encourage the development of new tools of communication and the utilization of existing ones so that knowledge may be shared at all levels of society;

    (e) consider establishing population commissions or any other bodies having multi-disciplinary and multi-departmental representation, to assess the current status and future needs in the fields of population and family planning;

    (f) ensure coordination among various agencies at the national, regional and local levels in order to expedite action and plans formulated in the light of integrated development policies;

    (g) provide essential training facilities with a view to improving planning skills, promoting comprehensive and innovative population policies and improving management skills in order to increase the administrative capabilities of population and family planning programmes.

5. The Economic Commission for Asia and the Far East (ESCAFE), with the cooperation of the United Nations Fund for Population Activities (UNFPA) and other United Nations bodies, should ensure that there are, within the region, facilities for training and research in the fields of population and development, to meet the countries' needs for people skilled in the various areas of policy formulation, planning, implementation and evaluation, and to promote the advancement of knowledge in these fields.

6. The problems encountered in dealing with rapid population growth are of vital concern to the entire world community, and the Second Asian Population Conference requests that the report of its deliberations be taken into consideration in the drafting of the World Population Plan of Action; it likewise calls upon the World Population Conference, in 1974, to consider the means which might be applied on a global level for the solution of these problems.

7. Leadership and assistance on the part of the United Nations and its associated agencies are of crucial importance to all countries in achieving population goals consistent with and fundamental to the purposes set forth in this Declaration.

3

—

Eugenics

For centuries, population experts seemed to have centered their discussions on numbers. However, many did not limit their reports and recommendations to quantity. Rather, there was a great deal of concern about quality. A continuous thread of concern about presumably inferior people having children tied the centuries together. There existed an overall theme that the lower class represented an inferior class, and that they generally had more children than they could afford, contributing to their own poverty. Some theorized that it was the poverty that made them inferior, while others contended that it was their inferiority that made them poor. In either case, there was an overall fear that they were having too many children.

By the late nineteenth century, discoveries in heredity had influenced new theories about what caused certain traits—both good and bad—in human beings, which would in turn influence new thoughts on population. According to the new science of genetics, mental and physical disabilities might be passed on to the next generation, as might a variety of illnesses—all of which proved costly to society. At the turn of the century, new notions of science, technology, and progress suggested that man might be capable of providing solutions to a variety of problems previously thought unsolvable, including the problem of the quality of population. Some experts believed that man had the capacity to engineer a better human race. The perhaps dubious science of eugenics was born.

Adolf Hitler became famous for his attempts at race manipulation, but before World War II, academics and elites throughout Great Britain and the United States had already embraced eugenics. Some recommended that the (implicitly white) race be improved through positive eugenics—that members of the better stock have more children. Others recommended that people of inferior stock be discouraged or prevented from having children. This was implemented in a variety of ways, from premarital testing for hereditary diseases to the sterilization of criminals and other so-called defectives. The following selections represent various perspectives on eugenics during the twentieth century.

DOCUMENT 3.1 Montague Crackanthorpe, *Population and Progress* (London: Chapman & Hall, Ltd., 1907, pp. 89–92)

This selection from English barrister and author Montague Crackanthorpe would be considered offensive in later decades, but it is representative of eugenics writings that appeared in the first decade of the twentieth century. At this point, eugenics was being applied in the United States primarily through marriage legislation, but Crackanthorpe suggests that stricter measures could benefit society as a whole.

For the present purpose I select from the common stock of humanity three classes, viz. (1) the luxurious rich, (2) the necessitous working poor, (3) the mentally and physically afflicted. I leave out of the account the class intermediate to (1) and (2), because this class has learnt to take care of itself. I also omit the tramps and the loafers, for these, when not being looked after by the Poor Law or the police, may be left to the care of the Salvation and Church Armies respectively.

I will begin with class (3), which includes all the "degenerates," since it offers less difficulty than either of the other two classes. And for this reason. In considering it, we are concerned mainly with biological facts on which science speaks with ever-increasing certainty. But in classes (1) and (2) we are confronted with problems both social and moral—problems as yet incapable of being expressed in scientific formulae.

I am aware that statistics are, as a rule, repulsive, yet a few must here be set down in order to make the position clear and show that a remedy is needed.

In 1859, there were in England and Wales 37,143 certified insane. In 1906, there were 121,802—an increase, in the space of less than half a century, of from 1 in 536 of the population to 1 in 285. In 1902, the rejections for the Army on the score of physical unfitness showed an increase of 26.77 per 1000 over the rejections of 1901. In 1903 the increase of such rejections was 14.61 per 1000 over that of 1902. On last census-day (1901), when the population of the United Kingdom was 41,458,072, every fifth person was disabled by illness. No less than thirteen million of pounds sterling are expended every year upon the maintenance of the mentally degenerate and the physically unfit—expenditure which, from a national point of view, is, of course, wholly unproductive.

Again, the number of cripples in the United Kingdom at the present time exceeds 124,000, and in the metropolis alone there are 7200 crippled children, without reckoning those in public institutions. Last Christmas Day, each of these 7200 received, as we are told, by the bounty of the Lord Mayor, "materials for a solid meal, and an ornamental box containing half a pound of tea." This is one instance (among many) of the efforts made by the charitably disposed on behalf of the "ineffectives"—many of whom are the result of parental neglect, either before or after birth.

It is far from my intention to imply that the money spent on supporting those who enter the race of life thus handicapped is not well laid out. It is better to expend thirteen millions a year than to relax the cords of human sympathy which bind us all together. No, the persons who, if they are consistent, should object to these subsidies are those who object to the "voluntary principle" on the ground that it is an "outrage on nature." For the effect of this particular kind of charity is to thwart the operation of the "law of natural selection," which, left to itself, makes short work of the unfit by a process of elimination. Still, whilst recognizing the duty of altruistic effort, we may, and we ought, to endeavour to get at the cause of the evil by using our common sense. If the doctors will not give us a lead by an authoritative deliverance on the misery caused by the marriage of "degenerates," the laymen—the ignorant laymen—must speak out. This they are at last beginning to do. Public opinion is being slowly formed.

DOCUMENT 3.2 C. V. Drysdale, *The Small Family System, Is it Injurious or Immoral?* (New York: B. W. Huebsch, 1914, pp. 107–108)

C. V. Drysdale voiced common concerns that existed in Europe and the United States that so-called defectives were a burden to society. Acknowledging that population theories throughout modern history addressed quantity, Drysdale urged modern policymakers to consider the importance of quality. As welfare programs were implemented more frequently at the national level, European and U.S. society became more easily persuaded that the restriction of births among those deemed inferior would be cost-effective.

Apart from questions of quantity, everyone knows that a most serious question to-day is the high birth-rate among the least desirable classes of the community—the indigent, the unemployable, the reckless, the drunken, and the mentally and physically deficient. On this account many Eugenists, especially in Germany, have been calling out for the educated and successful classes to redress the balance by having larger families, and thus to kill out the unfit by the struggle for existence. To this, however, there are two objections. One is that the educated classes have not responded, and will not respond to the call. They know too well the advantages they and their children gain by limitation. Indeed, the very people to call out for the larger families, whether in Germany, France, Hungary or England, are, as the Hungarian Medical Senate pointed out, the chief offenders against their own doctrine. The other objection is that, in these days of humanitarianism, society has an objection to the killing out process. The victims, strangely enough, have a habit of protesting. Anyhow, society does everything possible to maintain them (usually at a minimum of vitality) and to allow them to propagate to the fullest extent. Is it wonderful then that we have overcrowding, disease, and physical and mental deterioration? Mephistopheles himself could not have devised a better system for ruining the race than the one we have at present—the full licence to the unfit to breed at the expense of the fit, who limit their families more and more in order to maintain workhouses, hospitals and asylums for these poor creatures. There are only two alternatives for race improvement—either the fit must increase their own multiplication, and refuse all help to the unfit (with the spectre of the French Revolution to cheer them), or they must see to it that the unfit do not reproduce. The combined wisdom of the age can find no escape from this dilemma—unlimited reproduction and brutality, or humanitarianism with restricted reproduction of the unfit. The recent Mental Deficiency Bill is a first recognition of the latter principle. But why deal only with the extreme cases of mental deficiency? There are millions of poor physically and mentally unfit creatures who, if voluntary restriction were known to them, or they were not told it was unhealthy or immoral, would only be too glad to escape burdening themselves and the community with a numerous and weakly progeny. What is the use of deploring the increase of the unfit when the poor mothers among the working classes are only too anxious to avoid the misery of bearing child upon child in wretched surroundings, on miserably insufficient wages, and of seeing half of their children perish from semi-starvation before their eyes?

DOCUMENT 3.3 Charles H. Clark, M.D., "Prevention of Racial Deterioration and Degeneracy" (*Ohio State Institution Journal* 2, April 1920, pp. 5–11)

The following article by Dr. Charles H. Clark, superintendent of Lima State Hospital in Ohio, illustrates the role of the medical community in a society considering eugenics as a solution to many of its ills. Though there was no consensus on the subject of eugenics, physicians saw themselves as caretakers of those perceived as degenerates, many of whom resided in state institutions. In addition, physicians assumed the role of educator, passing on information from the scientific community to the public regarding disease and methods of prevention. They would be responsible for performing vasectomies and tubal ligations when eugenic sterilization was introduced, and often prescribed condoms in their promotion of social hygiene.

We are rapidly approaching the day of preventive medicine and physicians must take the initiative in disseminating knowledge on the subject of racial deterioration and degeneracy, otherwise they will be rightfully accused of moral cowardice.

Degeneracy is a relative term only, and it would be presumptuous on my part to attempt the definition of it. However, I would include under the classification of degeneracy certain forms of insanity, imbecility, feeblemindedness, idiocy, epilepsy, chronic inebriates, habitual criminals, congenital deaf and dumb, and the sexual perverts.

In every state there is relatively a large number of people who come under some one of the various headings. Many of them fortunately are segregated but many are outside of institutions, and even those who spend some time in institutional life have periods of liberty. A fairly large proportion of these are, or have been married. Many of them are the parents of children and a certain proportion of these innocent and helpless offspring inherit defective nervous systems, which result in the swelling of the defective and delinquent classes. . . .

The Causes of Deterioration and Degeneracy: When we contemplate this subject seriously, one of the first thoughts that occurs to us is, what is the origin of this dreadful burden of degeneracy which is imposed upon the state and the nation?

It is my opinion, after a careful study of racial deterioration and degeneracy, that there are two main sets of influences at work; first, those of environment, and second, those of heredity. I believe that it is true that environmental influences have received the most consideration, both by the medical profession and the laity.

It has been hoped by changing the circumstances and surroundings in which people live to better their state and lessen the liability of those, who, in the struggle of life, have a tendency to become insane, criminal, etc.

Our state has been very liberal with appropriations for her institutions and it has been hoped by the better care of its insane, epileptics, feebleminded, juvenile offenders, criminals, etc., that many of these persons might be reclaimed and restored to health and become efficient members of society.

A great deal has been accomplished in the past by improving our institutions, perfecting our methods of treatment and bettering the external conditions, but there remains still more to be done.

The interest in the movement against child labor, the improvement of factory and shop conditions, the campaign against the use and abuse of alcohol, the improvement in the condition of the poor, the education of the people regarding the dangers of infection, the instruction in personal and social hygiene, the better treatment of the insane and the criminal are accomplishing much and will do still more, but we must acknowledge that, with all these improvements to better the environmental condition of man, insanity, criminality, inebriety, feeblemindedness, epilepsy and prostitution have not diminished, but on the other hand, there has been a slow and gradual increase in all of these classes. . . .

To improve the conditions of society we must attack this problem at its very root. The fact is that members of this class to which I am referring are for the most part destined from birth to inefficiency or disease, because they are born with nervous systems which are abnormal. Too little attention is paid to the important matter of parenthood. Most people drift together into marriage without any thought of the supreme function of marriage, or of their fitness for participation in this function. Public opinion has not been properly informed as yet in this matter. Society must be brought to the point where it realizes that it is its duty to protect itself against the propagation of a degenerate stock.

DOCUMENT 3.4 Alexander Graham Bell, "Is Race Suicide Possible?" (*Journal of Heredity* 11, November 1920, p. 339)

Alexander Graham Bell is less known for his support of the eugenics movement than he is for his invention of the telephone. But inventors were welcomed into the community of scientists who promoted eugenics research and technology as fundamental to twentieth-century progress. Very importantly, Bell worked with the hearing impaired. It was common for those who studied disabilities to recommend eugenics measures as a preventive.

One of the most interesting of the questions of today relates to the powerful influence exerted upon populations by what we might almost call negative selection—a selection that produces the very opposite of that expected.

For example, no inheritable peculiarity associated with lack of offspring can be made to grow and flourish in a community. In spite of all efforts it will languish, and promote the growth of its very opposite. History is full of illustrations.

After the fall of the Roman Empire there was a great religious revival among the nations. The Middle Ages saw Europe filled with monasteries and nunneries, where enormous numbers of people took the vows of celibacy, and renounced all home and family ties. Even outside of the religious houses the celibate life was everywhere held up as the ideal one to be followed by the best and purest elements of the population.

Instead of helping the church this produced the very opposite effect, and actually paved the way for the Reformation! Large masses of the people who were most attached to the church led celibate lives, and left no descendents, whereas the independently minded who were not so devoted to the church were not limited in their reproduction.

As to the more general effects it may be safely said that the worship of celibacy during several hundreds of years in the past has not tended to the improvement of humanity but the very reverse; for, where the best and noblest led celibate lives, they left no descendents behind them to inherit their virtues, whereas the worst elements of the population continued to multiply without restriction.

It is now felt that the interests of the race demanded that the best should marry and have large families; and that any restrictions upon reproduction should apply to the worst rather than to the best.

DOCUMENT 3.5: Edward Byron Reuter, *Population Problems* (Philadelphia: J. B. Lippincott Co., 1923, pp. 303–305)

By the 1920s, the so-called science of eugenics had influenced various departments and disciplines in American universities. In his book entitled *Population Problems*, Edward Byron Reuter, member of the sociology faculty at the University of Iowa, described some of the problems that the "congenitally defective and inferior" posed to a society.

The problem of population, as a subdivision of sociology, relates exclusively to the number, distribution, and quality of the biological units included in society. It does not include the questions of education and character as psychic phenomena nor those of conduct. The present chapter has to do with those who, because of limited native endowment or the physical effects of social deprivation or misfortune, constitute a burden upon the group and a hindrance to its progress. The number of such individuals varies with the quality of the racial material and with the social practice of the society. The group may be composed of relatively low-grade human stock. Its social theory and practice may be such as to increase to the maximum or reduce to the minimum the number of the physically impaired. Within limits, every society has the number and the type of social derelicts its system deserves.

It should be remembered that the discussion runs in terms of persons and not of social classes. Human worth and mental and physical ability are individual characteristics. Persons with congenital defect or low native capacity are distributed through the population with nature's characteristic disregard for the artificial distinctions of wealth and social standing. The percentage of the incapable differs, sometimes differs widely, with different groups and social classes and so may affect the statistical average of the group capacity. But they do not form a class. Reference to the "inferior classes" may be a convenient means of designating the sum total of the discrete units, but it is a somewhat inaccurate one and open to the further objection that it frequently leads, as we have seen, to an unwarranted identification of the inferior and the economic lower classes of the social group. . . .

The problem of the inferior is the problem of their elimination or, where a complete elimination is not possible, the reduction of their number to the lowest point consistent with the moral customs of the group. It calls for the removal of existing inferiority where the causal conditions are remediable and thus a reduction, on the one hand, of the amount of needless suffering and misery and, on the other hand, of the social burden of dependency. It includes also means for preventing the reappearance of other inferior individuals and types to burden the society and retard its progress. On the physical side is the item of controlling to their ultimate extinction disease, defect, and deficiency so far as they are heritable conditions of the physical organism. On the social side is the matter of preventing potentially normal persons from becoming a burden upon the society because of remediable defects of social organization. The problem is one of the relative and possibly the absolute reduction of the number of defective and poorly endowed and so an advance in the average level of the group capacity.

There is little necessity to argue the desirability of lessening the number of the congenitally defective and inferior: as a general proposition that is perhaps universally admitted. Humanity should reproduce its numbers with intelligence and avoid waste of energy in struggling with needless misery. That it falls within the power of organized society, and is a proper function of the state, to exercise control over the population type is very generally accepted. Consequently the problem of the biologically inferior is chiefly one of determining the types to be eliminated and the methods of elimination to be employed.

DOCUMENT 3.6: Aldous Huxley, "What Is Happening to Our Population?" *Nash's Pall Mall Magazine,* April 1934, in *Aldous Huxley: Complete Essays, Volume III, 1930–1935,* ed. Robert S. Baker and James Sexton (Chicago: Ivan R. Dee, 2000, pp. 400–402)

Aldous Huxley is best known for the novel *Brave New World,* originally published in 1931, in which he seems to warn against a society that embraces eugenics. The following is excerpted from a popular magazine article written by Huxley at about the same time, and sheds light on his true sentiments regarding eugenics.

The way in which admirable reforms may produce evil as well as good is well illustrated by the recent history of mental deficiency. In 1929 the Mental Deficiency Committee estimated the number at 300,000. Twenty-five years ago there were between four and five halfwits to every thousand of population; today there are between eight and nine.

Some of this apparent increase is probably due to the fact that the later committee did its work more thoroughly than the Royal Commission of 1908. It looked harder and therefore found more. But when all the necessary discounts have been made, there is still good reason to believe that the number of defectives has increased, within a generation, to an alarming extent.

This increase is primarily due to a decline in infantile mortality—a decline which has affected every class of society, including that from which most defectives spring. This, in its turn, is due to improved sanitation and the wholesale establishment of Maternity and Child Welfare Centers. Mentally deficient children who, in the past, would have died in the cradle are now enabled to reach maturity. An environmental change for the better has resulted, among other things, in an hereditary change for the worse.

This is obviously a very serious matter. National survival depends on national efficiency. But a nation in which the number of halfwits is steadily growing is a nation whose potential efficiency is being steadily impaired. . . .

What is the remedy for the present deplorable state of affairs? It consists, obviously, in encouraging the normal and super-normal members of the population to have larger families and in preventing the subnormal from having any families at all.

DOCUMENT 3.7: Richard Lynn, *Eugenics: A Reassessment* (Westport, Conn.: Praeger, 2001, pp. 285–286)

The field of eugenics seemed to disappear in the post–World War II era, largely as a result of revulsion against Nazi Germany's implementation of a brutal race program. Though less prominent, the movement continued. In this excerpt from his book *Eugenics: A Reassessment*, University of Ulster (Northern Ireland) psychology professor Richard Lynn explains how advances in genetic technology can influence eugenics on an international scale. His research focuses primarily on the influence of gender and race on intelligence quotients, and on in vitro fertilization (IVF).

In the United States in the mid-1990s, it costs anywhere between $40,000 and $200,000 to have a successful IVF implantation. The additional cost of carrying out preimplantation genetic diagnosis of these embryos would not be great, nor would the culture of greater numbers of embryos; so the expense of embryo selection would not be appreciably greater than that of IVF. In Britain the cost of IVF is much lower, amounting to only around $3,000 to $4,000. . . .

Even if embryo selection remains fairly expensive, the desire to have successful children is strong, and it can be predicted that many couples will be willing to pay the costs to ensure that their children have a greater chance of a healthy and successful life than if they were conceived naturally. . . . Once it becomes understood that a child's chances of success are greatly enhanced by embryo selection for health, high intelligence, and sound personality qualities, couples will realize that it is more cost-effective to pay for an embryo-selected child than to pay for a quality education for a normally conceived child.

At the beginning of the twenty-first century, there is a fairly high level of public knowledge that genetic factors are important in the determination of a child's characteristics, and there is also a willingness to pay to ensure good genetic quality. This is illustrated by the growth of elite semen banks and by the growing practice in the United States of infertile women seeking eggs from high-quality donors by advertising in Ivy League college magazines and newspapers. In these ways and by these means, it can be anticipated that embryo selection will come to be used by increasing numbers of couples in the Western democracies, purely through private initiative and without any interventions from governments.

4

Race

Race made its way into population policy as experts categorized human beings by physical characteristics such as skin color, hair texture, and facial features. Historical encounters with people from distant places inspired written observations regarding physical differences. But from the beginning, comments on these physical differences paralleled those on social and cultural differences, suggesting that factors of culture were based on race. During the seventeenth century, observers commonly noted that certain races were more civilized than others; and during the nineteenth century, they noted that some races were more capable of progress than others.

Because such theories prevailed so widely, it became clear that they would shape population policy. Experts concerned about contemporary and future civilizations often considered race as an element worthy of study. Some pointed directly to numbers of people in different racial categories and directly sought to limit the size of certain races. Others simply warned of the destructive influence of so-called inferior races, regardless of their numbers.

DOCUMENT 4.1: H. G. Ward, *Mexico*, vol. 1 (London: Henry Colburn, 1829, pp. 21–27)

Race played a unique role in the history of population policy in Mexico. A caste system developed in the colonial period, with *peninsulares* (those born in Spain) holding the most prominent positions in politics and society. By the late eighteenth century, *criollos* (those of Spanish blood born in the New World) had gained in numbers and political strength, contributing to the independence movement. The large numbers of *mestizos* (those of mixed Spanish and Indian blood) and Indians concerned policymakers in the first years following Mexican independence in 1821. In this selection, Henry G. Ward, Britain's chargé d'affaires in Mexico from 1825 to 1827,

takes note of contemporary political concerns regarding the various seg-
ments of the population in this new nation in his report to the British crown.
His study was welcomed by British and Mexican leaders, who hoped to
establish good Anglo-Mexican political and economic relations.

Before the Revolution, [the] population was divided into seven distinct
Castes. 1. The old Spaniards, designated as Gauchupines, in the history of the
civil wars. 2. The Creoles, or Whites of pure European race, born in America,
and regarded by the old Spaniards as natives. 3. The Indians, or Indigenous
copper-coloured race. 4. The Mestizos, or mixed breed of Whites and Indians,
gradually merging into Creoles, as the cross with the Indian race became more
remote. 5. The Mulattoes, or descendants of Whites and Negroes. 6. The Zam-
bos, or Chinos, descendants of Negroes and Indians. And, 7. The African
Negroes, either manumitted, or slaves. . . .

It was the policy of Spain to promote a constant rivalry between the different
classes of inhabitants in her colonies, by creating little imaginary shades of
superiority amongst them, which prevented any two from having a common
interest. . . . Whiteness of the skin was the general criterion of nobility; hence
the expression so frequent in a quarrel, *"es possible que se crea V. mas blanco que
yo?"* (Is it possible that you think yourself *whiter* than I am?) But the King
reserved to himself the power of conferring the honours of whiteness upon any
individual, of any class, which was done by a decree of the Audiencia, com-
prised in the words, "let him be considered as white"; . . . For a long time they,
certainly, had the effect of keeping the different mixed breeds at variance with
each other: each was afraid of losing caste by an alliance with his inferior, while
the white Creole, proud of the purity of his own blood, was supposed to look
down upon the rest of his countrymen, with a contempt, very similar to that
which was entertained by the old Spaniard for himself. . . .

From the first breaking out of the Revolution, the Creoles were obliged to court
the alliance of the mixed classes, and in all their proclamations we find them representing their own cause, and that of the Aborigines, as the same. The distinctions
of Castes were all swallowed up in the great, vital distinction of *Americans,* and
Europeans; against whom, supported, as they were, by the whole force of Spain,
and holding, as they did, almost all the public employments in the country, nothing could have been done except by a general coalition of the natives. . . .

It is consoling to reflect, however, that this necessity of identifying themselves with the Aborigines, although absurd as argument, has led to good practical results. Castes can no longer be said to exist in Mexico, nor, I believe, in
any other part of Spanish America; many of the most distinguished characters
of the revolutionary war belonged to the mixed breeds; and, under the system
now established, all are equally entitled to the rights of citizenship, and equally
capable of holding the highest dignities of the state. . . .

I cannot conclude this sketch of the population of Mexico, without remarking
upon one great advantage which New Spain enjoys over her neighbours, both
to the North and South, in the almost total absence of a pure African population. The importation of slaves into Mexico was always inconsiderable, and
their numbers, in 1793, did not exceed six thousand. Of these, many have died,
many have been manumitted, and the rest quitted their masters in 1810, and
sought freedom in the ranks of the Independent army; so that I am, I believe,

justified in stating, that there is now hardly a single slave in the central portion of the republic.

DOCUMENT 4.2 Herbert Spencer, "A Theory of Population deduced from the General Law of Animal Fertility" (*Westminster Review* 57, 1852, pp. 468–501)

Herbert Spencer became well known by the late nineteenth century for his applications of Darwin's theory of natural selection to society as a whole. Social Darwinism, as this application was called, defended the political, social, and economic dominance of certain groups of people throughout the world. In the article from which the following passage is excerpted, published before Darwin's *On the Origin of the Species*, Spencer argues that "throughout the animal kingdom, fertility is inversely correlated with brain size, declining as the evolutionary scale is ascended, and that as the struggle for survival forces the latter to increase, the former will be lessened." This race theory, as it relates to population, contradicts the fears of others that lesser races tended to outbreed superior races. He argues, rather, that fertility rates are higher among the more civilized. He embraces Malthus's theory that population growth exceeds available resources, claiming that the competition that results from scarcity forces further evolutionary development. Because the lesser races of the world have not been forced to compete for resources, says Spencer, they have lagged behind in their development.

That an enlargement of the nervous centers is going on in mankind, is an ascertained fact. Not alone from a general survey of human progress—not alone from the greater power of self-preservation shown by civilized races, are we left to infer such enlargement; it is proved by actual measurement. The mean capacities of the crania in the leading divisions of the species have been found to be—

In the Australian . . . . .75 cubic inches.
    " African . . . . .82 "
    " Malayan . . . . . . .86 "
    " Englishmen . . . .96 "

showing an increase in the course of the advance from the savage state of our present phase of civilization, amounting to nearly 30 per cent on the original size. That this increase will be continuous, might be reasonably assumed; and to infer a future decrease of fertility would be tolerably safe, were no further evidence forthcoming. But it may be shown why a greater development of the nervous system *must* take place, and why, consequently, there *must* be a diminution of the present excess of fertility; and further, it may be shown that the sole agency needed to work out this change is—*the excess of fertility itself.* . . .

But this inevitable redundancy of numbers—this constant increase of people beyond the means of subsistence—involving as it does an increasing stimulus to better the modes of producing food and other necessaries—involves also an increasing demand for skill, intelligence, and self-control—involves, therefore, a constant exercise of these, that is—involves a gradual growth of them. Every improvement is at once the product of a higher form of humanity, and demands that higher form of humanity to carry it into practice. The application of science to the arts is simply the bringing to bear greater intelligence for satisfying our wants; and implies continued increase of that intelligence. To get more produce from the acre, the farmer must study chemistry—must adopt new mechanical appliances—and must, by the multiplication of tools and processes, cultivate both his own powers and the powers of his labourers. To meet the requirements of the market, the manufacturer is perpetually improving his old machines, and inventing new ones; and by the premium of high wages incites artisans to acquire greater skill. The daily-widening ramifications of commerce entail upon the merchant a need for more knowledge and more complex calculations; whilst the lessening profits of the ship-owner force him to employ greater science in building, to get captains of higher intelligence, and better crews. In all cases, increase of numbers is the efficient cause. Were it not for the competition this entails, more thought would not daily be brought to bear upon the business of life; greater activity of mind would not take place.

DOCUMENT 4.3 Charles Darwin, "The Races of Man," from *The Descent of Man, and the Selection in Relation to Sex* (1871) (New York: D. Appleton and Company, 1871, pp. 209–229)

> Inherent in Charles Darwin's theories of natural selection and survival of the fittest are explanations for the inferior position of certain races of people. In this excerpt, Darwin begins to categorize humans based on what he calls races of man, and these categories would be examined and refined by race theorists in subsequent decades. He gives some attention to fertility rates, noting in particular that so-called hybrids such as mulattoes are less vital as specimens and fail to perpetuate their kind due to lower fertility rates. In addition, he describes the characteristics and conditions of lesser tribes that contribute to their natural extinction. His opponents would blame the nature of colonial and imperialist policies for contributing to the destruction of certain cultures, while Social Darwinists would rationalize the existence of dominant and disappearing cultures as a consequence of natural selection.

We will first consider the arguments which may be advanced in favour of classing the races of man as distinct species, and then the arguments on the other side. If a naturalist, who had never before seen a Negro, Hottentot, Australian, or Mongolian, were to compare them, he would at once perceive that they differed in a multitude of characters, some of slight and some of considerable importance. On enquirey he would find that they were adapted to live under widely different climates, and that they differed somewhat in bodily constitution and mental disposition. If he were then told that hundreds of similar specimens could be brought from the same countries, he would assuredly declare that they were as good species as many to which he had been in the habit of affixing specific names. This conclusion would be greatly strengthened as soon as he had ascertained that these forms had all retained the same character for many centuries; and that Negroes, apparently identical with existing Negroes, had lived at least 4000 years ago. He would also hear, on the authority of an excellent observer, Dr. Lund, that the human skulls found in the caves of Brazil, entombed with many extinct mammals, belonged to the same type as that now prevailing throughout the American Continent. . . .

Our supposed naturalist having proceeded thus far in his investigation, would next enquire whether the races of men, when crossed, were in any degree sterile. He might consult the work of Professor Broca, a cautious and philosophical observer, and in this he would find good evidence that some races were quite fertile together, but evidence of an opposite nature in regard to other races. Thus it has been asserted that the native women of Australia and Tasmania rarely produce children to European men; the evidence, however, on this head has now been shewn to be almost valueless. The half-castes are killed by the pure blacks: and an account has lately been published of eleven half-caste youths murdered and burnt at the same time, whose remains were found by the police. Again, it has often been said that when mulattoes intermarry, they produce few children; on the other hand, Dr. Bachman, of Charleston, positively asserts that he has known mulatto families which have intermarried for several generations, and have continued on an average as fertile as either pure whites or pure blacks. Enquiries formerly made by Sir C. Lyell on this subject led him, as he informs me, to the same conclusion. In the United States the census for the year 1854 included, according to Dr. Bachman, 405,751 mulattoes; and this number, considering all the circumstances of the case, seems small; but it may partly be accounted for by the degraded and anomalous position of the class, and by the profligacy of the women. A certain amount of absorption of mulattoes into negroes must always be in progress; and this would lead to an apparent diminution of the former. The inferior vitality of mulattoes is spoken of in a trustworthy work as a well-known phenomenon; and this, although a different consideration from their lessened fertility, may perhaps be advanced as a proof of the specific distinctness of the parent races. No doubt both animal and vegetable hybrids, when produced from extremely distinct species, are liable to premature death; but the parents of mulattoes cannot be put under the category of extremely distinct species. The common Mule, so notorious for long life and vigour, and yet so sterile, shews how little necessary connection there is in hybrids between lessened fertility and vitality; other analogous cases could be added. . . .

Extinction follows chiefly from the competition of tribe with tribe, and race with race. Various checks are always in action, serving to keep down the numbers of each savage tribe,—such as periodical famines, nomadic habits and the consequent deaths of infants, prolonged suckling, wars, accidents, sickness, licentiousness, the stealing of women, infanticide, and especially lessened fertility. If any one of these checks increases in power, even slightly, the tribe thus affected tends to decrease; and when of the two adjoining tribes one becomes less numerous and less powerful than the other, the contest is soon settled by war, slaughter, cannibalism, slavery, and absorption. Even when a weaker tribe is not thus abruptly swept away, if it once begins to decrease, it generally goes on decreasing until it becomes extinct.

DOCUMENT 4.4: Francis Galton, *Inquiries into Human Faculty and Its Development* (1885) (London: Macmillan and Co., 1883, pp. 313–317)

Francis Galton is considered the father of eugenics and a pioneer in the study of intelligence. In this selection his arguments illustrate some of his understanding of race. Applying discoveries in heredity and genetics made by Gregor Mendel, Galton suggested that breeding practices among human beings could very much affect the quality of the race. But in addition to discussing the broad concept of improvement or degeneration of the human race, Galton described the characteristics and breeding practices of various races as having either a positive or negative effect on the human race as a whole. This selection also reflects growing concern about the mass migration of people from continent to continent, which he warned should be recognized as having a significant impact on the quality of any one nation for generations to come.

It must not be supposed that emigration on a large scale implies even a moderate degree of civilization among those who emigrate, because the process has been frequently traced among the more barbarous tribes, to say nothing of the evidence largely derived from ancient burial places. My own impression of the races in South Africa was one of a continual state of ferment and change, of the rapid development of some clan here and of the complete or almost complete suppression of another clan there. The well-known history of the rise of the Zulus and the destruction of their neighbours is a case in point. In the country with which I myself was familiar the changes had been numerous and rapid in the preceding few years, and there were undoubted signs of much more important substitutions of race in bygone times. The facts were briefly these: Damara Land was inhabited by pastoral tribes of the brown Bantu race who were in continual war with various alternations of fortune, and the several tribes had special characteristics that were readily appreciated by themselves. On the tops of the escarped hills lived a fugitive black people speaking a vile dialect of Hottentot, and families of yellow Bushmen were found in the lowlands wherever the country was unsuited for the pastoral Damaras. Lastly, the steadily encroaching Namaquas, a superior Hottentot race, lived on the edge of the district. They had very much more civilization than the Bushmen, and more than the Damaras, and they contained a large infusion of Dutch blood.

The interpretation of all this was obviously that the land had been tenanted a long time ago by Negroes, that an invasion of Bushmen drove the Negroes to the hills, and that the supremacy of these lasted so long that the Negroes lost their own language and acquired that of the Bushmen. The invasion of a tribe of Bantu race supplanted the Bushmen, and the Bantus, after endless struggles among themselves, were being pushed aside at the time I visited them by the incoming Namaquas, who themselves are a mixed race. This is merely a sample of Africa; everywhere there are evidences of changing races. . . .

In North America the change has been most striking, from a sparse Indian population of hunters into that of the present inhabitants of the United States and Canada; the former of these, with its total of fifty millions inhabitants, already contains more than forty-three millions of whites, chiefly of English origin; that is more of European blood than is to be found in any of the five great European kingdoms of England, France, Italy, Germany and Austria, and less than that of Russia alone. The remainder are chiefly black, the descendants of slaves imported from Africa. In the Dominion of Canada, with its much smaller population of four millions, there has been a less, but still a complete, swamping of the previous Indian element by incoming whites.

In South America, and thence upwards to Mexico inclusive, the population has been infiltrated in some parts and transformed in others, by Spanish blood and by that of the Negroes whom they introduced, so that not one half of its population can be reckoned as of pure Indian descent.

The West Indian Islands have had their population absolutely swept away since the time of the Spanish Conquest, except in a few rare instances, and African Negroes have been substituted for them.

Australia and New Zealand tell much the same tale as Canada. A native population has been almost extinguished in the former and is swamped in the latter, under the pressure of an immigrant population of Europeans, which is now twelve times as numerous as the Maories. The time during which this great change has been effected is less than that covered by three generations.

To this brief sketch of changes of population in very recent periods, I might add the wave of Arab admixture that has extended from Egypt and the northern provinces of Africa into the Soudan, and that of the yellow races of China, who have already made their industrial and social influence felt in many distant regions, and who bid fair hereafter, when certain of their peculiar religious fancies shall have fallen into decay, to become one of the most effective of the colonizing nations, and who may, as I trust, extrude hereafter the coarse and lazy Negro from at least the metaliferous regions of tropical Africa.

It is clear from what has been said, that men of former generations have exercised enormous influence over the human stock of the present day, and that the average humanity of the world now and in future years is and will be very different to what it would have been if the action of our forefathers had been different. The power in man of varying the future human stock vests a great responsibility in the hands of each fresh generation, which has not yet been recognized at its just importance, nor deliberately employed. It is foolish to fold the hands and to say that nothing can be done, inasmuch as social forces and self-interests are too strong to be resisted. They need not be resisted; they can be guided.

DOCUMENT 4.5: James Bonar, *Malthus and His Work* (London: Harper and Brothers, 1885, pp. 54–56)

In this selection, James Bonar of Balliol College at Oxford analyzes Malthus's theories on population among, as he terms them, the savages of the world. As global exploration and colonization continued, European observers made frequent attempts to explain variations in population density among the people they encountered. Generally convinced that population grew to the extent that resources were available, they tried to make sense of sparse populations in regions of abundant resources. Bonar's explanation is representative of many that credited behavior and lifestyle among those perceived as savage as contributing to their lower numbers. These arguments differed from those that categorized various races through blatant ranking based on perceptions of either quality or inferiority. However, Europeans' descriptions of different cultures reflected their common stereotyping of non-Europeans, whom they regarded as uncivilized. In this passage, Bonar attributes lower population density to violent battles, cannibalism, and infanticide.

[Malthus] says, that beyond a certain limit, hard fare and great want depress men below the very capacity of improvement; comfort must reach a certain height before the desires of civilized life can come into being at all. If the American tribes, he says, have remained hunters, it is not simply because they have not increased in numbers sufficiently to render the pastoral or agricultural state necessary to them. Reasons which Malthus does not pretend to particularize, and which he allows to be unconnected with mere increase or decrease of numbers, have prevented these tribes from ever trying to raise cattle or grow corn at all. "If hunger alone could have prompted the savage tribes of America to such a change in their habits, I do not conceive that there would have been a single nation of hunters and fishers remaining; but it is evident that some fortunate train of circumstances, in addition to this stimulus, is necessary for this purpose; and it is undoubtedly probable that these arts of obtaining food will be first invented and improved in those spots which are best suited to them, and where the natural fertility of the situation, by allowing a greater number of people to subsist together, would give the fairest chance to the inventive powers of the human mind." . . .

The account of the state of population among the South Sea Islanders, which comes next in order to the chapter on the American Indians, is an illustration of these remarks. These savages live in a fertile country and yet they make no progress. As this is not the only point illustrated, it is worth while to look at the chapter in detail.

Malthus begins by observing that population must not be thought more subject to checks on an island than on a continent. The Abbé Raynal, in his book on the Indies, had tried to explain a number of modern customs that retarded population by referring them to an insular origin. He thought that they were caused at first by the over-population of Britain and other islands, and were imported from there into the continents, to the perplexity of later ages. But as a matter of fact population on the mainlands is subject to the same laws as on the islands, though the limits are not so obvious to common observation, and the case is not put so neatly in a nutshell. A nation on the continent may be as completely surrounded by its enemies or its rivals, savage or civilized, as any islanders by the sea; and emigration may be as difficult in the one case as in the other. Both continent and island are peopled up to their actual produce. "There is probably no island yet known, the produce of which could not be further increased. This is all that can be said of the whole earth. Both are peopled up to their actual produce. And the whole earth is in this respect like an island. The earth is indeed more isolated than any island of the sea, for no emigration from it is possible. The question, therefore, to be asked about the whole earth as about any part of it, is, "By what means the inhabitants are reduced to such numbers as it can support?"

This was the question which forced itself on Captain Cook when he visited the islands of the Pacific and Indian Oceans. Some of his experiences there, especially in New Zealand, show that the native population was kept down in nearly the same way as the American. Their chief peculiarity is the extreme violence of their local feuds. The people of every village he visited petitioned him to destroy the people of the next, and "if I had listened to them I should have extirpated the whole race." A sense of human kinship is impossible at so low a level of being; and the internecine wars of the New Zealanders were the chief check to their numbers, which, from the distressing effects of occasional scarcities, would seem always at the best to have been close to the limits of the food.

DOCUMENT 4.6: Arthur Newsholme, M.D., *The Declining Birth-Rate: Its National and International Significance* (New York: Moffat, Yard & Co., 1911, pp. 54–56)

The first decades of the twentieth century brought a wealth of warnings that the decreasing birth rate among western Europeans—which had been on the decline for a century—would contribute to the demise of modern civilization if the trend were not checked and reversed. The warnings were particularly common among the British, but reflected concerns among Anglo-Americans, French, Germans, and, as prominent physician and author Arthur Newsholme describes here, the English-speaking races in Australia and South Africa. Concerned that other peoples would dominate the world's population—and his references to Asians reflects contemporary fears of the so-called yellow peril—Newsholme warned that people of western European descent had better procreate once again "to a normal extent." He and others were responding in particular to the increasing use of birth control methods to voluntarily limit family size.

It cannot be regarded as a matter of indifference whether the unfilled portions of the world shall be peopled by Eastern races (Chinese, Japanese, Hindoos, etc.), by negroes, by Sclavonic or other Eastern European peoples, by the Latin races, or by the races of Northern Europe. Experiments on a gigantic scale in the fusion and multiplication of races are going on in the United States, and more recently in Canada, in which all well-wishers of the best civilization must be intensely interested; and the problems of South Africa and Australia are only less important than those of the American continent. The conditions of the problem, especially in the view of the increasing refusal of western Europeans, Americans and Australians to multiply to a normal extent, are becoming artificially biased. In North America it may be a question not only of black and white, but also of Sclavonic races against Anglo-Saxons; in Australia, and possibly also in the American continent, it may become a question of Mongolian against European races. The problems suggested by current events do not appear likely, so far as can be seen, to be solved in the course of the next few generations by the adoption of the policy of the restricted family by the countries and races not at present adopting the practices leading to this result; though the current experience of Germany, which is now increasingly following the lead of France and England in this respect, makes the need for caution in forecasting obvious.

It is impossible to follow further the speculations suggested by such considerations as the above. Every Briton will wish that his race may have a prepon-
derant share in shaping the future destinies of mankind. Although it appears
certain that English-speaking races will exercise this predominating influence—the course of events in North America, in Australia and South Africa
points to this conclusion—these English-speaking countries unless the trend of
events is changed, will become occupied by Anglo-Saxons to a relatively diminishing extent. We must not, however, blind ourselves to the dangers of
prophecy.

DOCUMENT 4.7: Madison Grant, *The Passing of the Great Race: or, The Racial Basis of European History* (New York: Charles Scribner's Sons, 1918, pp. 4–8)

Madison Grant is considered by many the father of race theory. In his work
The Passing of the Great Race he describes the superiority and inferiority of
the various races of man and justifies the privileged position of those he
considers superior throughout history. He warns of the consequences of
allowing allegedly inferior people to influence society, preferring aristocracy to democracy.

As a result of certain religious and social doctrines, now happily becoming
obsolete, race consciousness has been greatly impaired among civilized
nations, but in the beginning all differences of class, of caste and of color
marked actual lines of race cleavage.

In many countries the existing classes represent races that were once distinct.
In the city of New York and elsewhere in the United States there is a native
American aristocracy resting upon layer after layer of immigrants of lower
races and these native Americans, while, of course, disclaiming the distinction
of a patrician class and lacking in class consciousness and class dignity, have,
nevertheless, up to this time supplied the leaders in thought and in the control
of capital as well as of education and of the religious ideals and altruistic bias of
the community.

In the democratic forms of government the operation of universal suffrage
tends toward the selection of the average man for public office rather than the
man qualified by birth, education and integrity. How this scheme of administration will ultimately work out remains to be seen, but from a racial point of
view it will inevitably increase the preponderance of the lower types and cause
a corresponding loss of efficiency in the community as a whole.

The tendency in a democracy is toward a standardization of type and a
diminution of the influence of genius. A majority must of necessity be inferior
to a picked minority and it always resents specializations in which it cannot
share. In the French Revolution the majority, calling itself "the people," deliberately endeavoured to destroy the higher type, and something of the same sort
was in a measure done after the American Revolution by the expulsion of the
Loyalists and the confiscation of their lands, with a resultant loss to the growing nation of good race strains, which were in the next century replaced by
immigrants of far lower type.

In America we have nearly succeeded in destroying the privilege of birth; that is, the intellectual and moral advantage a man of good stock brings into the world with him. We are now engaged in destroying the privilege of wealth; that is, the reward of successful intelligence and industry, and in some quarters there is developing a tendency to attack the privilege of intellect and to deprive a man of the advantage gained from an early and thorough classical education. Ignorance of English grammar or classic learning must not, forsooth, be held up as a reproach to the political or social aspirant.

Mankind emerged from savagery and barbarism under the leadership of selected individuals whose personal prowess, capacity or wisdom gave them the right to lead and the power to compel obedience. Such leaders have always been a minute fraction of the whole, but as long as the tradition of their predominance persisted they were able to use the brute strength of the unthinking herd as part of their own force and were able to direct at will the blind dynamic impulse of the slaves, peasants or lower classes. Such a despot had an enormous power at his disposal which, if he were benevolent or even intelligent, could be used and most frequently was used for the general uplift of the race. Even those rulers who most abused this power put down with merciless rigor the antisocial elements, such as pirates, brigands or anarchists, which impair the progress of a community, as disease or wounds cripple an individual.

True aristocracy of a true republic is government by the wisest and the best, always a small minority in any population. . . .

A true republic, the function of which is administration in the interests of the whole community—in contrast to a pure democracy, which in last analysis is the rule of the *demos* or a majority in its own interests—should be, and often is, the government of those best qualified by antecedents, character and education, in short, of experts.

DOCUMENT 4.8: Robert J. Sprague, "Constructive Aspect of Birth Control" (*Journal of Heredity* 8, February 1917, pp. 59–61)

In this paper, read at the thirteenth annual meeting of the American Genetic Association, December 27, 1916, in New York City, Robert J. Sprague describes the voluntary limitation of family size by the middle class as race suicide. As professor of economics and sociology at Massachusetts Agricultural College in Amherst, Sprague noted the devastating effects of small middle-class family size on the economy and society as a whole. The term *race suicide* was commonly used in these years to describe the practice of birth control by middle- and upper-class women. In 1916, birth control activists in the United States and Great Britain were calling for the legalization of contraceptives. As Sprague suggests, some people considered contraceptive practice among the lower classes desirable. But his arguments extend beyond economics and class, as he describes poverty and pauperism among various races and ethnic groups, whose numbers should be limited.

Birth control among the poor is needed for themselves but birth release among the upper classes is a greater necessity, both for their own welfare and the salvation of the nation. Excessive birth control by those well able to have families sufficient for the nation's growth weakens the nation at every point, necessitates the importation of indigestible foreign elements, good people in themselves but poorly adapted to American life, weakens patriotism and brings about a mixture of races which makes confusion of morals, dearth of art and literature and conflicts between classes.

Birth control among the poor is a problem, but race suicide among the middle classes is a racial menace which threatens by its influence to defeat the highest ideals of the nation.

There ought to be reasonable birth control by all classes based upon high ideals for the nation and family, responsibility for offspring, and refinement of soul and character of the parents. The free indulgence of sexual passions, coupled with the prevention of conception by mechanical contrivances, is possible better than no control whatever, but it deals with the matter on a low basis of animal appetite and gross physical force. It is not control of the highest and best kind; it throws all the burden and dangers upon the wife. But there is a control possible to people of high standards which is the result of forethought, character and mutual sincerity and which gives none of the dangers and secures the noblest end of spiritual union by means of physical function. . . .

Birth control must not stand by itself and be preached and judged as an unrelated thing: it is only one important factor in the great program of the nation's problem of population and race vitality. How is the population of America to increase in the future? The middle classes of the industrial regions are not maintaining their numbers by natural process. The birth control advocates would have the poor people restrict their families to the limits of their income and would show them how to do it. Where then shall we get the next hundred million which we are sure to have and which the nation needs and can easily provide for? Evidently from the poverty-stricken classes of the Russians, Italians, Syrians, Portuguese, Mexicans, Negroes, etc., because the western Europeans may have few emigrants to send us for years to come.

If the insufficient birth rate of the upper classes were to continue and we were obliged to get our increase in numbers either from the overflowing poverty-stricken families of foreign countries or from the poor classes of our own population, I should say, from the point of view of national welfare, let the increase come from our own people reared under our own flag, language and customs, even though in poverty. The adoption of birth control by poor families to the extent that it is practiced by the economically higher classes will condemn this continent forever to be, not only the mixing bowl of the world, but the scrap heap of the races. These people may be themselves as good as any of us, but forever mixed together from the ends of the world, they cannot make a nation. Nations composed of mixed races are weak in most of the things that make for national strength and progress. Lacking the unity of traditions, idealism and national spirit they are liable to have excessive individualism and turn to materialist goals.

DOCUMENT 4.9: Edward M. East, *Mankind at the Crossroads* (New York: Charles Scribner's Sons, 1923, pp. 116–118)

The following selection is representative of discussions of population that swept the most prestigious of the world's academic institutions in the 1920s.

It is unclear here whether Harvard University professor Edward M. East is attempting to provide a sort of optimistic encouragement to those who feared that the white races would lose the war for world dominance or giving in to warnings that the situation was hopeless. In any case, this document reflects characteristic population concerns among intellectuals of the Western world.

The white race is increasing rapidly. Why? Simply because it has political control of nine-tenths of the habitable globe, and because it has the ability to utilize the space it holds. The western hemisphere is completely within its grasp, and on the greater portion of it white populations can thrive. The tropics, represented by Central America and the interior of South America—roughly a territory one-third larger than the United States—are not congenial to it at present; but most of this country will be controlled by a white barrier at its outer limits. In the eastern hemisphere it holds all but eastern and southern Asia, the Malay Archipelago and Oceania, racially as well as politically. This statement may seem to be somewhat exaggerated; but practically it is not. The black zone simply does not count. The negroes, even with the help of white contact, cannot compete against white expansion. They will increase but slowly if at all during the next century, and within that time the white race will have colonized such parts of Africa as it finds possible to utilize. The white race, therefore, will be limited in the immediate future only by its efforts toward a superior culture that will hold away the results of overpopulation.

The various elements of the brown race may indeed throw off the white political yoke. Peacefully and gradually, or resentfully and suddenly, it may be expected that the brown men will finally shift for themselves. The white race will try to hold them in line as long as they are able to export food, but this cannot be for long. Nevertheless, a sweeping political change of this type will mean no united Malaysia crossing swords with the remainder of the world to seek to gain new lands. Individuals will wish to migrate, and will seek to break down by diplomatic representations the barrier to brown immigration set up in the undermanned tropics subject to white control. The effort will avail little. If Nordic labor will brook no competition from such sources now, it is not likely to give way when the economic stress reaches a higher peak. Clamourous propaganda will be the beginning and the end of the excitement. . . . Armed competition with the white man is unthinkable by a race living in a country where the sun burns the will-power out of every man, where time is long and life is cheap, and constructive thoughts are little moths that flutter briskly in the evening and die at sunrise.

There is good reason to suppose that realization of the aspirations of the malcontents of India and the Philippines is not going to be the broad road to progress they expect. Such ability as exists in India comes from the age-long current of white blood which has not been wholly subdued in all the veins. The dominant individuals of the Philippines are those with Spanish, Chinese, and Japanese names somewhere among the branches of the ancestral tree. The great voice of the common people will simply applaud automatically a change of governors when this millennium comes. And does any one, do even the Nationalist leaders, really believe the change will be an improvement? Our own political fortunes are hardly guarded as efficiently as those of the Filipinos.

Britain fumbles about with her home troubles more confusedly than with those of India. Will the natives of Malaysia teach us how to manage our own concerns by setting a bright and shining example? Such a thought is rather hard on one's imagination. One is more likely to find that there will be a decrease in efficiency and fall in agricultural production, and that population will early strike a dead level because of meeting the subsistence limit sooner than would have been the case had no political change devolved.

DOCUMENT 4.10: Marcus Garvey, "Shall the Negro Be Exterminated?" in *Philosophy and Opinions of Marcus Garvey on Africa for the Africans,* comp. Amy Jacques Garvey (London: Frank Cass & Co., Ltd., 1967, pp. 48–49)

Legislation was passed during the mid-1920s to restrict immigration from primarily southern and eastern European nations, pacifying Americans who feared that large numbers among those allegedly inferior ethnic groups would contribute to the degeneration of society. Consequently, fears turned toward the black population. Mass migration of blacks from the southern United States to northern urban areas added to fears, but demographers admitted that the black population was not increasing in numbers. In this selection, Marcus Garvey, founder of the Universal Negro Improvement Association, suggests that blacks develop a better awareness of historical plans for white racial dominance and fight to protect the black population.

We desire harmony and unity to-day more than ever, because it is only through the bringing together of the four hundred million Negroes into one mighty bond that we can successfully pilot our way through the avenues of opposition and the oceans of difficulties that seem to confront us. When it is considered that the great white race is making a Herculean struggle to become the only surviving race of the centuries, and when it is further considered that the great yellow race under the leadership of Japan is making a like struggle, then more than ever the seriousness of the situation can be realized as far as our race is concerned. If we sit supinely by and allow the great white race to lift itself in numbers and in power, it will mean that in another five hundred years this full grown race of white men will in turn exterminate the weaker race of black men for the purpose of finding enough room on this limited mundane sphere to accommodate that race which will have numerically multiplied itself into many billions. This is the danger point. What will become of the Negro in another five hundred years if he does not organize now to develop and to protect himself? The answer is that he will be exterminated for the purpose of making room for the other races that will be strong enough to hold their own against the opposition of all and sundry. . . .

The leadership of the Negro of to-day must be able to locate the race, and not only for to-day but for all times. It is in the desire to locate the Negro in a position of prosperity and happiness in the future that the Universal Negro Improvement Association is making this great fight for the race's emancipation everywhere and the founding of a great African government. Every sober-minded Negro will see immediately the reason why we should support a movement of this kind. If we will survive, then it must be done through our own effort, through our own energy. No race of weaklings can survive in the days of tomorrow, because they will be hard and strenuous days fraught with many difficulties.

DOCUMENT 4.11 J. C. Menham, "ATSIC's requirements for social statistics in the 1990s," in *A National Survey of Indigenous Australians: Options and Implications, Research Monograph No. 3*, ed. J. C. Altman (Canberra: Centre for Aboriginal Economic Policy Research, Australian National University, 1992, pp. 37–38)

In the latter half of the twentieth century, the field of sociology addressed race in ways that would respond to more complex and modern demands set by economic and social policymakers. Sociologists continued to study race as a determinant in the evolution and makeup of societies, but also recognized social needs as varying among different racial groups. There are few cases clearer than that of the aboriginal population in Australia. Marginalized to the extreme by the dominant Anglo culture, the aborigine of the late twentieth century required unique study, as Australia responded to civil rights struggles. Actual numbers would place the aboriginal population in the minority, but in modern society, the rights of the minority have been recognized. This report, published as part of a larger study by the Centre for Aboriginal Economic Policy Research, illustrates some of the consequences of centuries-long policies of discrimination against the minority population.

For ATSIC [the Aboriginal and Torres Strait Islander Commission], both planning and policy formulation begin, appropriately, with demography. In a fundamental sense, it is the Aboriginal and Torres Strait Islander populations (size, rate of growth, age distribution, location, fertility, and so on) that determine the broad parameters of ATSIC's charter. These populations and their characteristics provide the basis for assessment of fundamental issues of social justice, recognition of need, access and equity, and fair and equitable distribution of resources, as these affect Aboriginal and Torres Strait Islander people.

Planning is about people: as individuals, in relation to each other, in groups and in communities. It is about different groups of people such as the aged, the young, where they live, how they live, and how their situation compares with the population at large. For example, where and how Aboriginal and Torres Strait Islander people live, in what numbers, and how location patterns may be changing over time are all crucial influences in determining the kind of lives they are likely to lead. This dictates the nature of the social policy response. Age distribution is another key to planning and policy formulation. In broad figures, half of the Aboriginal and Torres Strait Islander populations are aged under 20 years, and 70 per cent are under 30 years. This remarkable demographic feature clearly has major consequences for planning priorities.

Demography is, however, only one aspect of the totality of data requirements. For effective planning and policy formulation, a whole range of information (on health, employment, housing, education, interaction with the legal system, etc.) is required to provide a picture of the overall quality of life. Policymakers and program managers need to know how things are changing over time and how programs are affecting the problems they are designed to address. . . .

DOCUMENT 4.12 Campbell Gibson and Kay Jung, "Historical Census Statistics on Population Totals by Race, 1790 to 1990, and by Hispanic Origin, 1970 to 1990, for the United States, Regions, Divisions, and States," Working Paper Series No. 56 (Washington, D.C.: Population Division, U.S. Census Bureau, September 2002, pp. 1–2)

Few directly refer to the modern census taken in the United States as racist, but the inclusion of race as a defining category suggests that the government has reasons for wanting to know how many people are represented in each racial category. This working paper, developed by the Population Division of the U.S. Census Bureau following Census 2000, notes that in recent years, race has come to be considered a *social* determinant rather than a biological one. The category of *Hispanic origin* drew much attention in conducting and interpreting the census.

Information on the race of the U.S. population has been collected in every decennial census beginning with the first census in 1790. The racial categories included on census questionnaires, as well as the wording of questions, have changed over time, reflecting changes in social attitudes and political considerations; however, in general, these categories have reflected social usage and not an attempt to define race biologically or genetically. . . .

The population of Hispanic origin (of any race) was first identified comprehensively in the decennial census in 1970. Previously, data on other topics, such as country of birth, country of birth parents, and mother tongue, were used to identify portions of the Hispanic population. Information on Hispanic origin was obtained again in 1980 and 1990; however, as with information on race, there were changes in question wording. . . .

Information on race was obtained primarily by enumerator observation through 1950, by a combination of direct interview and self-identification in 1960 and 1970, and by self-identification in 1980 and 1990. Information on Hispanic origin was obtained using various criteria in 1970, including self-identification (as discussed later), and was obtained using only self-identification in 1980 and 1990. With enumerator observation, a person of mixed White and other parentage was usually classified with the other race. A person of mixed race other than White was usually classified by the race of the person's father through 1970 and by the race of the person's mother in 1980 and 1990.

The major categories used to classify the population by race since 1790 in this report are those used in 1990 census reports: White; Black; American Indian, Eskimo, and Aleut; Asian and Pacific Islander; and Other race (U.S. Bureau of the Census, 1992, pp. B-7, B-8, and B-11 to B-13). In addition, data are shown for the White non-Hispanic (i.e., White, not of Hispanic origin) population in those years for which data are available on the Hispanic population. The terms White, Black, Hispanic origin, and White, not of Hispanic origin are used in time series tables for all census years for consistency of presentation, even though, as discussed in the sources cited earlier, there have been changes in terminology in census reports, including from Negro to Black between 1970 and 1980 and from Spanish origin to Hispanic origin between 1980 and 1990. The term American Indian is used prior to 1960, the first year in which data for Eskimo and Aleut were identified in tabulations (other than in Alaska prior to statehood). The term Asian is used prior to 1910 and for 1950 when no Pacific Islander categories were identified in tabulations (other than in Hawaii prior to statehood). . . .

The limitations to comparability of race data between 1990 and 2000 are substantial because for the first time in a decennial census, respondents in the 2000 census could report more than one race. As a result, data for 2000 are not included in this report, and a full comparison of 1990 and 2000 census data on race will require extensive research.

5

—

Colonialism and Imperialism

Population is related to colonialism and imperialism in a number of ways. First, early global exploration gave rise to new human encounters, which generated concerns regarding inhabitants of different continents. European settlers were concerned about their own numbers versus numbers of natives, though conquest and the introduction of disease devastated indigenous populations.

In some regions, Europeans were able to exploit the remaining native populations for their own political and economic gain. Others settled with large numbers of men, women, and children and developed significant European populations on other continents. In addition, colonial economies based on a plantation system initiated the transportation of Africans as slaves to places far from Africa. To some mother countries, colonies served as a release from population pressures at home.

In the transition from colonialism to imperialism, many of the same policies and attitudes remained. Ratios between native and imperial populations were of significant concern, and observations on numbers reflect that. Furthermore, critics of imperialism point to population programs of the twentieth century as an orchestrated method for wealthier nations to maintain control.

DOCUMENT 5.1: *The History of the Brasils, From the Original Discovery, in 1500, to the Emigration of the Royal Family of Portugal, in 1807: Comprising Every Interesting Fact Connected with the Geography, Extent, Boundaries, Population, Progressive Improvements, Religion, Singular Customs and Manners, Soil, Mineral and Other Produce, Political and Commercial Relations, Etc., Etc.* **(London: J. T. Ward and Co., 1808, pp. 37–43)**

This British description of Brazil is a noteworthy example of the early-nineteenth-century perspective on colonization and population. Its timing was significant, as Great Britain acknowledged that Brazilian independence was at hand, and it makes a detailed examination of Brazilian culture, geography, and population, etc., as desirable for establishing future trade relations. The author's analysis of population composition reflects general European notions of culture, behavior, society, and race, noting the ways in which the Portuguese colonized over the centuries. In addition, the descriptions of the Portuguese, particularly in their practice of Catholicism, suggest that the British saw even greater potential in extending their own influence—which they regarded as more civilized—in Brazil. In essence, relations that developed between Great Britain (and eventually other nations, including the United States) and various Latin American nations upon their independence can be described as neocolonial. Clearly, numbers of inhabitants were important to the observer, but an understanding of the population's composition was key to future development.

The ancient inhabitants of Brasil differed very little in stature or complexion from the Portuguese themselves; but much exceed them in strength and vigour. Some lived in villages, and others moved about according to their humours. These villages consisted of only three or four very large houses; in each of which a whole family or tribe lived together, under the authority of the eldest parent. They procured subsistence by fowling and fishing, and made up the rest of their diet with the fruits of the earth; but though they had no luxurious plenty, yet, in so fertile a country, they were in no great danger of want. They were, however, continually at war with each other; but for what cause is not easily determined, unless we should admit, what some old writers affirm, that they made these wars chiefly that they might kill and eat each other, esteeming human flesh the greatest dainty. . . .

The present inland Brasilians of both sexes still go entirely naked; but near the shore they put on different sorts of coverings, some wearing only shirts of linen or calico, and others dress after the European manner. The wives always follow their husbands to war; but while the man carries nothing but his arms, the woman supplies the place of sumpter horse, and loaded with such provisions as are thought necessary, with a child or children, and a hammock, which at night they hang on trees, or fasten to poles, making a defence from the rain with palm-tree leaves. These hammocks are the chief part of their furniture, and are made of cotton, and formed like network, six or seven feet long and four broad: but the Tapuyers make theirs twelve or fourteen feet long, so as to contain four and sometimes six persons; their cans, cups, or mugs, are made of calabashes, some of which hold thirty quarts. The poorer sort use knives of stone, while the others purchase theirs of the Europeans. When at home, the husband generally goes abroad in the morning with his bow and arrows, to kill birds or beasts, or goes to fish, while the wife either employs her time in working at a plantation, or attends the husband to bring home his game.

The inland Brasilians have some knowledge of a supreme Being, whom they call Tuba, which signifies somewhat most excellent; and the thunder they stile Tubakununga, which may be interpreted, a noise made by the Supreme Excellency. They have a confused knowledge of the general deluge, and believe that the whole race of mankind were extirpated by it, except one man and his sister; which latter was pregnant before it happened, and that these, by degrees, repeopled the world. With respect to a state of future existence, they believe that the soul does not die with the body; but is translated to some pleasant vales beyond the mountains, where they are to enjoy great pleasures, and spend their time in dancing and singing. These are those who have distinguished themselves by performing great actions in defence of their country, &c. but such as have been idle, are supposed to be tortured by evil spirits, whom they call by different names, and of whom they are excessively afraid; and though they pay them no religious worship, yet they sometimes endeavour to appease their wrath, by certain presents fastened to stakes, which they set in the ground. . . .

The European Settlers are in general gay and fond of pleasure, extremely observant of the ceremonies of religion, or rather of the etiquette of the Virgin Mary, who is stuck up in a glass case at every corner. The convents and monasteries are numerous, and the superstitious veneration of the Portuguese Settlers to the outward forms of the Romish Church, is here carried to the greatest excess. . . .

The population of this large portion of South America has not been accurately detailed, but it would seem that the Portuguese and their descendents do not exceed half a million, while the Natives may be three or four millions.

DOCUMENT 5.2: Alexis de Tocqueville, "Social Conditions in Ireland," in *Alexis de Tocqueville on Democracy, Revolution, and Society: Selected Writings*, ed. and trans. John Stone and Stephen Mennell (Chicago: University of Chicago Press, 1980, pp. 307–309)

This work was not a direct attack on imperialism by de Tocqueville, nor was the term *imperialism* used in this description of Ireland. But his observations on poverty and population gathered from a series of interviews during his travels in early-nineteenth-century Europe and America illustrate the conditions that often exist under oppressive colonial systems—in this case, the colony of Ireland under British rule. In this passage, de Tocqueville describes conditions in Ireland. In the selection that follows (Document 5.3), he interviews the Catholic bishop of Kilkenny, who blames poverty on overpopulation. The two selections together demonstrate both the severity of poverty and the rationalization that the poor were to blame (because they had more children than they could afford), rather than the economic injustice inherent in colonialism.

'[Y]ou have just seen men who ask for nothing but to work for their living, but cannot succeed in doing so; and when you think that in Ireland more than a million of our fellows are reduced to this extremity, do you not say, as I do, that such a state of things cannot be tolerated much longer?'

'I have heard,' said I in reply, 'that the Marquis of Sligo who, I believe owns large properties in this parish, has come to live in his castle. Do you think that, if he knew what was happening, he would not seek to lessen the extreme distress which at present prevails on his domain? . . .

'Sir, do you know what it is that prevents the poor from starving to death in Ireland? It is the poor. A farmer who has only thirty acres and who harvests only a hundred bushels of potatoes, puts aside a fifth of his harvest annual to distribute among those unfortunates who are the most terribly in need. In Ireland, Sir, it is the poor who provide for the needs of the poor.... The starving man presents himself at the door of the cottage without fear; he is sure to receive something to appease his present hunger. But at the doors of the mansions he will only meet liveried lackeys, or dogs better nourished than he, who will drive him roughly away.... Not only do they not help the poor in any way, but they profit from their needs to charge enormous rents which they spend in France or Italy. If for a short time one returns among us, it is only to evict a farmer who is behind with the rent and chase him from his home.'

DOCUMENT 5.3: Alexis de Tocqueville, "Conversation with Msgr. Kinseley," in *Alexis de Tocqueville's Journey in Ireland, July–August, 1835*, ed. and trans. Emmet Larkin (Washington, D.C.: Catholic University of America Press, 1990, pp. 63–64

Q. What is, in your opinion, the principle cause of the poverty of the country?

A. *A too-numerous population. It is certain that the land divided up, or rather not divided up, as it is in Ireland, cannot furnish a constant employment for our population. I believe that the consequences of absenteeism are exaggerated. It does harm but I regard it above all as a troublesome sign of the separation that exists between the different classes.*

Q. Do you think that a poor law is necessary?

A. *Yes, I believe so without hesitation.... [N]ot only is there a shortage of land, but many estates have been converted into grasslands; those where 150 laborers would be found, ten shepherds suffice. If there were a tax on estates, the owners of these grasslands would find that they gained little by disposing of the land in this way; for if the land thus yielded more, and the landlord were obliged by the poor law to give all or part of his surplus in order to feed those whom he prevents from subsisting, he would restore his grasslands to wheat, or at the very least, he would no longer put the wheat to grassland....*

Q. You have told me that morals were pure?

A. *Extremely pure. Twenty years in the confessional have made me aware that the misconduct of girls is very rare, and that of married women almost unknown. Public opinion, one might almost say, goes too far in this direction. A woman suspected is lost for life. I am sure that there are not twenty illegitimate children a year in the whole Catholic population of Kilkenny, which amounts to 26,000 souls....*

DOCUMENT 5.4: Edward Isaacson, *The New Morality: An Interpretation of Present Social and Economic Forces and Tendencies* (New York: Moffat, Yard and Co., 1913, pp. 194–197)

The turn of the twentieth century marked a shift toward imperialism on the part of the most powerful nations of the world, though western Europe still held on to many colonies in the more traditional sense. In this selection, Edward Isaacson refers to virtual partitions of the world as *spheres of influence*—a term whose use would continue through the century. Isaacson describes how European colonial/imperial powers linked internationalism to economics and warns of the international consequences of unchecked population growth and/or distribution in the underdeveloped regions of the world.

What can bring Western Europe to give up internal rivalries and organize into one social and economic group, not for warfare against other race groups, but for co-operation with them against the common danger of overpopulation?

The area of Western Europe is a very good unit of comparison for certain groups delimited by physiographical and racial conditions, which are sure to be the basis of large human relations in the future.

There are in the zones of progressive humanity three other such groups of about the same area; in China, South America and Australia, and one in the more passive zone to the south, India. The two other northern groups, North America and Russia, have each about four such units of area; and it is possible that China may develop within the territory controlled by the empire enough land to double its possibilities.

All these groups may within a hundred years or so reach the density of population of Western Europe. With people evenly distributed over this whole area, it will be impossible for Europe to live as it does now, by industrialism, on imported food; and wisdom certainly dictates careful consideration of measures looking toward the establishment of a racial static condition against that time.

One perplexing problem is the predatory attitude of Europe toward the tropical countries. The Europeans want the commodities of the tropics, but they are not willing to get them as they do what they get from the other northern nations. They go to the tropics, take possession of the resources, and force the native to work for them in their way, instead of letting him work for himself in his own way and exchange products on a fair commercial basis.

The ideal for the static condition must of course include the tropical peoples as well as the others; each group should develop according to its own natural resources, climate and surroundings. If the groups now populated up to the limit assume the static condition, with proper eugenics, they are sure to make great improvement in quality and so become still more the intellectual leaders; the other groups must look to them as examples in progress and education and send to them young men to bring back the knowledge of that progress for their own people to apply to their own conditions. This is the true programme for the advancement of the "inferior" peoples, rather than the attempt of missionaries to force upon the less advanced peoples the institutions of the more advanced, without regard to their fitness for the conditions. . . .

There is another possible programme, of wider scope, if we regard the whole world as one economic group with the fecund class in the temperate zone. In that case, some of the surplus of the cooler regions might be organized into an industrial army, and used as far as necessary in the tropics, somewhat as is done now in the management of the tropical dependencies. (An interesting thought here is a possible solution of the American Negro problem by sending the surplus of the "Afro-Americans" who have had the benefit of contact with the more advanced civilization, back to Africa as leaders of their race there.) There is a very strong tendency in the southern states of the Union to separate the races into territorial groups, which may be regarded as wholesome; for two races cannot live closely intermingled without friction, unless on terms of social equality. If we recognize and develop this tendency, give the Negroes every chance to make the best of themselves and send their surplus, instead of to the proletarian class in the American cities, to form new fecund groups in carefully selected localities (avoiding the mistake in the case of Liberia) on the native continent of the race, this would be a great gain for all parties.

In any case it will be a long time before the inhabitants of the tropics are brought up to a standard of intelligence and industry, of the kind adapted to their climate, which will make commercial relations between them and the people of the temperate zone satisfactory. Still, it seems that the results of commerce with the natives of the Amazon regions, where the question is one of trade with the natives for the product of their own native industries, are quite as good as those in Africa under "spheres of influence."

DOCUMENT 5.5: Leonard Woolf, *Empire and Commerce in Africa, A Study in Economic Imperialism* (New York: The Macmillan Company, 1919, pp. 27–28)

Following World War I, discussions of imperialism and colonialism changed significantly. In 1919, Leonard Woolf described a notion that was commonly held for centuries, that colonization served—at least in part—as a release for population pressures in the mother countries. But he notes in his comments on the current situations of France and Germany that such population pressure no longer exists. His observations reflect not only the shift in demographics in recent decades, but an overall condemnation of colonialism. The peace process following World War I called for decolonization and encouraged self-determination, forcing colonizing nations to reexamine traditional means of justifying their influence on different continents.

There was another kind of belief and desire which had more influence upon French than upon British Imperialism, and which at first sight appears to be unconnected with commerce. The French imperialist of the '80s believed that the acquisition of territory in Asia and Africa was a necessity for the French State in order to provide an outlet, not only for its goods, but for its "surplus population." Hence Frenchmen desired territory for the foundation of a "New France," just as Germans desired it for the foundation of a "New Germany," and French and German "colonial" writers and politicians drew a distinction between the "colonies d'exploitation," or "Handelskolnien," and the "colonie de peuplement," or "Bauernkolonien." The first were tropical lands in which the European could not live and multiply, but were desirable as "debouches a no produits," possessions to be exploited in the commercial interests of France or Germany; the second were places where the climate made it possible for the European to make a home and a settlement. There are two points which deserve remark in connection with this. In the first place, the reason why these beliefs and desires played a greater part in the colonial policies of France and Germany than in that of Britain was because by 1880 Britain already had in Australia and Canada sufficient inhabitable territory to absorb not only the surplus, but the whole population of the British Isles. It was impossible to raise in England a cry for land for emigration when Australia, New Zealand, and Canada were crying aloud for immigrants. But France, whose "colonies had only served to involve her in wars, and whose wars had only served to lose her colonies," and Germany, who had never had any colonies even to lose, were in a different situation; and many Frenchmen and Germans turned their eyes toward Asia and Africa as outlets for surplus populations.

It is true that this motive of French and German imperialism does not belong wholly to economic imperialism. There is a "natural" desire among Britons, Frenchmen, and Germans to increase the number of Britons, Frenchmen, and Germans respectively in the world, and perhaps to decrease the number of non-Britons, non-Frenchmen, and non-Germans respectively. This desire is partly sentimental, and partly founded upon the belief of all nations that their citizens are the salt and others the scum of the earth. The tendency to desire a high birth-rate and a low death-rate within one's own State, and a low birth-rate and high death-rate in other States, is also connected with the policy of power. For every living German is a potential soldier, and every unborn or dead French-man leaves a bland space in a French regiment. All these non-economic beliefs and desires had their share in forming the policy of Empire as an outlet for sur-plus population. And yet even behind this policy the economic motives show more strongly and persistently than the sentimental and the military. The argu-ments of those who urged it invariably in the end come back from nationalism and patriotism to trade and commerce. The "New France" and the "Greater Germany" which are at first seen in a vision as carrying, after the manner of the colonists of French and German culture, or, more prosaically, as providing a reservoir for the French and German armies, are always finally recommended as nationally desirable, just like the *colonie d'exploitation*, as "outlets for our goods." For a million Frenchmen in Africa, or a million Germans in the Pacific, would appear to provide better customers and a surer market for their mother-countries than a million naked savages.

DOCUMENT 5.6: Warren S. Thompson, *Danger Spots in World Population* (New York: Alfred A. Knopf, 1930, pp. 308–309)

In this piece, Warren S. Thompson argues that France should consider giving away some of its possessions in other regions of the world—based not on any political or moral objection to colonialism, but on France's ability to benefit in the long run. Thompson noted that France's population was not growing at a rate that warranted significant land holdings elsewhere, since colonization was historically encouraged by countries that needed a so-called safety valve for their population, or at least had a population strong enough to maintain colonies. Thompson argues that in 1930, neither condition was present in France. Interestingly, Thompson suggests that France cede unneeded territo-ries to Germany and Italy, which may be in greater need of a safety valve; and in turn, France could benefit diplomatically from such a goodwill gesture.

There is certainly no sound reason why France should permanently hold more than a small part of its present possessions. Its foreign holdings comprise almost five million square miles, and, as with Great Britain, a very large part of the territory in the colonies, protectorates, and mandates is held for future exploitation of its resources for the profit of a small group of adventurers and capitalists. It has been frequently said in what precedes that such tenuous possession does not give a valid title to any country to lands which are needed by other peoples who are hard pressed for resources. It rests on force alone and will be respected only as long as it can be defended. From the point of view of its own needs, there is no reason why France, along with Great Britain, could not contribute land to peoples less fortunately situated. This could be done both by the cession of some of its dependencies which are little developed and by permitting immigration from some of the crowded areas into certain of its possessions where population is scanty.

Permitting immigration from crowded areas into some of the French dependencies should prove a less difficult adjustment than in British dependencies. For the French have not the objection to intermarriage with other races and peoples that the British have. The assimilation of the Italians by the French in north Africa should not prove a very difficult matter. Indeed, it would appear that the working together of these two peoples in this area, even though it remained wholly under French sovereignty, might well lead to their closer cooperation in many other matters which would work to their mutual advantage.

DOCUMENT 5.7: Pierre Gourou, *The Tropical World, Its Social and Economic Conditions and Its Future Status* (New York: Longmans, Green and Co., 1953, pp. 113–115)

After decades of criticism, European nations—and increasingly the United States in the post–World War II era—still held their respective spheres of influence around the world. Twentieth-century modernization and improvements in medicine and health care spurred unprecedented population growth in undeveloped regions around the world. In this selection, Pierre Gourou, professor at the Collège de France and at the Free University of Brussels, credits colonization itself for this population growth. He warns of the consequences of such growth and suggests birth control as a solution.

European intervention has had immense consequences, especially in countries typical of the tropics—that is, those that are sparsely peopled and backward in civilization. In densely peopled areas European intervention has had less effect, for in such countries problems of development have not arisen, and the more civilized native communities have been less easily influenced.

The outcome of European activities has in many cases been disastrous to the natural wealth and the native peoples. Lack of understanding of environmental conditions affecting both Europeans and the natives has caused mistakes and failures; but the experience of these regrettable incidents should not be lost, and the lessons learnt from them should guide future European action in the tropics. . . .

Tropical diseases strictly limit the number, natural increase, and activities of Europeans as well as of the natives. They are especially dangerous for settlers if the country has natives to act as sources of virus. . . .

In hot, wet regions with a large population European influence has resulted in a rapid growth of this population by reducing the death-rate. Social ills have in fact been effectively combated. But this is a questionable benefit so long as the birth-rate is not lowered and the population increases too fast; for then it is difficult in countries like India to raise or even maintain the standard of living. Some people think that the Colonial system retarded the social development of India and in that way prevented native society from reacting by spontaneously lowering the birth-rate. The towns and industry would never have developed as they have done if India had been independent. Now, it is usually in towns that the first fall in the birth-rate takes place, and consequently it is in the towns that the beginning of a fall in the birth-rate might be hoped for.

DOCUMENT 5.8: Jordan Bishop, O.P., "Imperialism and the Pill: *Humanae vitae* in Latin America" (*Commonweal* 89, January 10, 1969, pp. 465–466)

> Following observations on the part of wealthier nations that developing regions were experiencing a so-called population explosion, funding was implemented for an international birth control program. Birth control activists of the early decades of the twentieth century saw the issue as international in scope and worked to extend their influence in places like India and China. But new and more comprehensive programs were implemented in the 1960s. The United States Assistance for International Development (USAID) agency introduced birth control initiatives into nations that received its aid, and organizations such as the International Planned Parenthood Federation and the Rockefeller and Ford Foundations heavily funded programs. Some critics saw this process as an extension of imperialism. In the following document, the Dominican priest Jordan Bishop outlines such an argument in relation to the 1967 papal encyclical *Populorum Progressio*.

Early last October, a peaceful demonstration of students from the Catholic University of La Paz was broken up by the police. Several students and a Jesuit priest were taken to police headquarters, but were soon released on the orders of the President of the republic. They were demonstrating against the alleged political use of birth control programs (read colonialist tool) and more specifically, against Robert McNamara's statement, reported in the local press, to the effect that World Bank loans should give preference to those underdeveloped nations which have implemented birth control programs. The following day President Rene Barrientos Ortuno declared that Bolivia's population problem is not a question of overcrowding. . . .

The encyclical gives the impression that population control would be desirable if it could be reconciled with the demands of a certain traditional natural law morality and with the tradition of the Magisterium. Since *Populorum Progressio* and even more recent papal declarations put the Pope in the camp of those who look for development rather than revolution, the breach between the opposition of the radical Left and the Pope regarding "developmentalist birth control programs" could hardly be greater. The fact that Mr. McNamara and many North American planners urge population control is most sufficient in itself to ensure the wrath of the Latin American Left, for whom birth control is seen not in the perspective of responsible parenthood, but rather as a political weapon aimed at limiting the revolutionary potential of a young and growing proletariat, assaulted on the one hand by consumer propaganda and on the other by the growing frustration of marginal economic and social conditions.

DOCUMENT 5.9: Bruce Fetter, "Demography in the Reconstruction of African Colonial History," in *Demography from Scanty Evidence: Central Africa in the Colonial Era*, ed. Bruce Fetter (London: Lynne Rienner Publishers, 1990, p. 7)

Here, historian Bruce Fetter describes more broadly how he considers international population control connected to imperialism. Issues of African demographics are uniquely complex. The continent of Africa was colonized by European nations relatively late—and remained colonized well into the twentieth century. Consequently, colonial and imperial forces were more clearly apparent. In addition, the race factor suggested that the dominant white cultures of the world worked to control the population of Africa out of racial fears. Very importantly, as Fetter suggests, data from censuses taken in Africa were questioned, demonstrating how political forces can influence demographic studies.

Analyses of the available data reflect the concerns of the governments of the time. The earliest studies were an extension of the colonial reconnaissance of newly conquered territories. They sought to ascertain the whereabouts of the indigenous populations to assess how they were faring under European rule. Although some studies were concerned with the question of whether or not the new rulers were killing off their charges, the major concern before World War II was to locate able-bodied men who could be taxed and thus forced to work for the government and for European entrepreneurs. During the 1930s the League of Nations began to amass data on colonial fertility, mortality, and migration without much effect on the policies of colonial powers.

The agenda of policymakers also included a set of demographic issues related to the allocation of public funds. In those days missions and private corporations played a relatively larger role in public health than at present, while governments spent most of their health budgets on campaigns to eradicate particular diseases. The demographic area on which colonial governments spent most time and effort was migration, encouraging men to seek work in distant mines and discouraging women and children from joining them at the work sites.

World War II brought greater concern for the welfare of the populations as a whole. German mastery of Europe imperiled the existing empires, detaching French and Belgian colonies from their metropoles and thrusting on British colonies a substantial role in the war effort. Systematic surveys of colonial censuses conducted after the war were part of a wider concern for assessing imperial assets and reorganizing colonial governments after the independence of most of the former colonies in Asia.

DOCUMENT 5.10: Amy Kaler, "A Threat to the Nation and a Threat to the Men: The Banning of Depo-Provera in Zimbabwe, 1981" (*Journal of Southern African Studies* 24, June 1998, pp. 352–375)

Analyses of the political nature of demographic studies and international birth control programs shaped future examinations of such connections to imperialism. In the 1994 United Nations International Conference on Population, held in Cairo, new voices were heard from women representing underdeveloped regions who claimed that international programs mistakenly sought solutions in population control rather than effective sustainable development. In addition, they claimed that contraceptive technology introduced into the developing world by wealthier nations threatened the well-being of women and traditional gender roles. In this article, Amy Kaler describes the effects of the Depo-Provera program in Zimbabwe.

Minister of Health Herbert Ushewokunze [in 1981 argued]: "Africa is certainly being used as a dumping ground for some of the most dangerous drugs in the world, drugs manufactured in the so-called developed countries, and Depo-Provera is one of these drugs. You will hear stories of people telling you that this drug is being used in 70 to 80 countries in the world. Look carefully at the 70 to 80 such countries, and you will find they are all in the Third World, not in the developed world. In Britain, our erstwhile colonial masters, [the drug is banned for birth control]. . . . Prohibited from selling the drug in the United States, the manufacturers Upjohn marketed it through their subsidiaries in Asia and Africa and in Third World countries . . . [In Rhodesia] this drug was being given predominantly to black women, and this is something I have noticed, only to black women. No prescription, but given willy-nilly to black women in the countryside. . . . Now who says the Zimbabwe women are going to be experimental animals? Who says they are going to use our women as guinea pigs?" . . .

The 1981 Depo-Provera decision [to ban] is located conceptually at the intersection of the "politics of reproduction" and the politics of national liberation. One of the best reasons to study this particular decision is that it illuminates the entanglement of gender issues and national political issues lying at this juncture. In Zimbabwe, the decision to ban Depo-Provera was justified on the grounds that it was in the best interests of both women and the state, as it both protected women's health and threw off some of the remaining vestiges of colonialism.

6

War

Some of the earliest human records demonstrate correlations between population and war. Essentially, people saw that there was strength in numbers. For example, Old Testament scripture refers to sons as arrows in a quiver, implying that the procreation of many children would ensure victory in future battles. Consequently, those lost through war would need to be replaced in order to rebuild a nation's strength.

The twentieth century intensified population concerns related to war. First, advances in military technology resulted in higher casualties, particularly among the civilian population. In addition, neo-Malthusians claimed that population pressures helped to contribute to the outbreak of war, even in this modern era. Progressives who sought a peaceful world responded to such claims, and supported international programs of population control. Cold war tensions readdressed population in light of nuclear proliferation and concerns for global security.

DOCUMENT 6.1: James Marchant, *Birth Rate and Empire* (London: Williams and Norgate, 1917, pp. 11–14)

As secretary of Great Britain's National Birth-Rate Commission and director of the National Council for the Promotion of Race Regeneration, James Marchant was one of the most outspoken critics of voluntary family limitation among the British. His arguments were many and varied, addressing all aspects of economics, politics, and society. In this selection, he notes the effects of the Great War on Britain's population. His deep concerns regarding the declining British influence in the world shaped many of his arguments, but war casualties intensified his fears. World War I marked a new age in military technology and its contribution to civilian deaths, but the concerns of replenishing the population outlined here are reminiscent of such concerns expressed throughout the ages.

. . . Our Empire covers over 18,000,000 square miles, or one-fourth of the land of the world, and our vessels freely traverse the seven seas. But our white population only amounts to sixty millions; forty-five millions constitute our home population, fifteen millions only remain to distribute over and to govern, develop, and defend our mighty daughter nations of Canada, Australia, and New Zealand, and immense vacant spaces in Africa and other lands. And these fifteen millions have been derived from the British Isles and are mainly replenished and reinforced from the same source of life. India, with her immense multifarious population numbering, in 1911, 161,338,935 males and 153,817,416 females, the births in 1915 (for British India alone) being 4,664,460 boys and 4,357,365 girls, must be left out of account in the present survey, and only those parts of the Empire considered which afford opportunities of prosperity to the white populations which are their mainstay. . . .

In the old world of Egypt, Greece, Rome, at the time of their decay, there may well have been those who not only marked the signs of degeneracy, but who also prophesied the coming of another age and another civilization, as we today are doing. And there were no doubt those who ridiculed them. But the old world died, and civilization found a new home in the West. After twenty centuries another catastrophe is upon us. Our civilization is on trial. What new order will emerge from this conflict? That it will be a better social order, that the world is to assume a new form and produce a nobler type of humanity to rule the earth, is our steadfast faith.

We have long enough tinkered with the ghastly effects we call poverty, crime, and prostitution, made more revolting by contrast with the lavish luxury on the every side. We must arrest our cut-throat competition, the break-up of family life, the deterioration of the moral and physical stamina of the people in sordid surroundings, evils which destroyed the Hellenic race and other ancient civilizations.

This war is designed, we cannot but believe, to bring all that to an end. It is, perhaps, the last deadly battle with the forces of evil for many centuries. After this we shall commence to reconstruct our own Empire upon the principles of true brotherhood, of the spirit of self-sacrifice, which is being so finely exhibited amongst us and which is so full of promise for the better day coming, when society will more and more check the brutal and sordid forms of the struggle for existence and give a chance to every life born to fulfill its highest purposes; then the will to live will be renewed.

After the war we must put both hands to the greatest task of reconstruction which has ever confronted our or any other country. The material loss is to a considerable extent measurable and may in time be made good; it is at any rate not the most serious aspect of the problem of renewal. The supreme task is to reconstruct our ideals, our ways of life, our religious beliefs; the whole religious, moral, and social fabric has to be placed upon better and stronger foundations. And at the centre of the problem is the question of refilling the vacant cradles at home, or fully caring for the children we have in our homes and schools that they may become healthy parents of a future generation, of adequately peopling our Colonies—in short, of renewing the race. Some of the work of race-renewal we men may be able to handle alone, although the advent of women into practically every part of the nation's operations will impose further limits upon the area of man's exclusive occupations. But in the problem of restoring the birth-rate to a healthier level, involving the establishment of a national system of education worthy of our land, in cleaning out our slums and building homes, in restoring religion to its rightful place in our lives, we shall need the whole-hearted co-operation of women. If we are to handle the birth-rate question with any real hope of solution, men and women must frankly unite in making the colossal effort.

This awful war itself, in which much of our false and wicked civilization, so called, is being burnt up, looks like a clear proof that we had missed the way of life and had gone far along the road of dissolution. But the truer view is that we may yet save the Empire and our souls as well. This holocaust of suffering, this letting loose of the powers of hell, may be at the bottom a work of mercy. The blood which is being spilt upon the earth, watered by the tears of millions of women and children, is the seed of a newer and better civilization for our Empire and the whole earth. The Eastern sky is already aglow with the flushes of the new-born day; is it the life-blood of the men who have been slain for its redemption that is crimsoning the horizon?

DOCUMENT 6.2: Dr. Anton Nystrom, "Over-Population of the Earth and Its Dangers," in *Report of the Fifth International Neo-Malthusian and Birth Control Conference*, ed. Raymond Pierpoint (London: William Heinemann, Ltd., 1922, pp. 175–179)

While Marchant expressed more traditional sentiment regarding war and declining population, a neo-Malthusian movement making significantly different claims was gaining strength in Europe and the United States. Embracing the teachings of Thomas Malthus, neo-Malthusians pointed to population pressures as a primary cause of strife in the world, and in this case, a primary cause of World War I. Stockholm physician Anton Nystrom spoke to the relationship between overpopulation and war at the Fifth International Neo-Malthusian and Birth Control Conference, held at Kingsway Hall in London, July 11–14, 1922.

History gives us many instructive lessons with regard to the dangers of over-population. It was their *great growth in numbers* and the consequent difficulty in obtaining food in their native country, *i.e., need*, that drove the *German barbarians to migrate* southwards, and overwhelm the Roman Empire, especially Italy's fruitful tracts; and this led to long and devastating wars. During the whole historic times, such migrations *from Asia* to Europe's farthest borders have taken place as a result of the *too great* increase of the population in proportion to the food supplies.

The *Colonial wars of later times* were caused by the necessity of colonization as a means against need, caused by *over-population*. The *United States of America* were originally colonies, but, at the present day, are so thickly populated that the authorities there endeavour to prevent the influx of fresh immigrants from Europe, China and Japan. In all colonies, the natives have been more or less ruthlessly treated by the usurping races. And the European nations have often carried on wars against each other for the possession of these colonies.

That over-population exists already in many countries cannot be denied, and even if there are immense territories on the face of the globe, such as in Africa, South America, Australia and Siberia, where millions may yet find a home, still it is none the less certain that *most civilized countries* are already so thickly populated that millions find a difficulty in obtaining subsistence, and that myriads of people live in a constant state of great want. It is clear, then, that the steady increase in the population of the earth *must soon become a factor of extreme danger*.

What has to be done now is to work everywhere for the spread of the *neo-Malthusian doctrines* by means of lectures, publications, the establishment of associations, etc., and not to allow ourselves to be dismayed by the external difficulties. Great aims create enthusiasm!

The people of every country must be thoroughly enlightened by means of books, pamphlets, newspaper articles, lectures, etc., as to the dangers of over-population. New-Malthusian associations should be established everywhere in the world, so as to organize a systematic propaganda. This work of enlightenment must be *universal*, so that no country, from ignorance and neglect, shall continue, or become, over-populated, thereby threatening the peace of other nations.

Writings by investigators and resolutions adopted by associations respecting the dangers of a too great birth rate and of over-population should be forwarded to the Governments in the different countries and to the League of Nations, which, in their turn, should do everything to promote the great reform. This idea may appear Utopian, and hardly in agreement with the old style of political appeals usually made to the representatives of the Powers. But this fact should not prevent its being carried out, so that it may bear fruit in one way or another.

It is to be deplored that in all the endless debates that have been carried on by statesmen, international commissions, the leading journals and political writers, etc., respecting the causes of the Great War and the ways and means of remedying the prevailing universal want and of reconstructing the world, the question of over-population and its decisive nature in these matters were never touched upon, not, at least, with the detail demanded by factors of such importance.

It seems as though there prevailed everywhere a *fear of touching on a subject* of such an intimate nature and which is in close connection with *sexual matters*—matters which few have cared to consider thoroughly, and which are considered *unsuitable for public discussion*, not *comme il faut*. The subject *must* be brought forward, however, for it deals with one of the most essential factors in human life.

DOCUMENT 6.3: Harold Wright, *Population* (London: Nisbet & Co., Ltd., 1923, pp. 131–134)

In his book *Population*, Harold Wright acknowledged claims that population pressures contributed to the outbreak of World War I, but he maintains that the causes of war are more complex. He noted the long-standing competition among European nations and the failure of diplomacy as significant factors. Wright asserted that Europeans competed for the greater exploitation of resources, raw materials and people, but not, he says, for subsistence. Still, according to Wright, this competition could lead to war, if not checked by diplomatic measures.

Wars . . . like all the events in which great masses of men are involved, are brought about by many and complex causes, among which conscious motives are often less important than hidden influences lying beneath the surface of things. To reveal these hidden influences is a necessary preliminary step to their control, and it is only by understanding the forces which are at work among us that we can hope to substitute human reason for blind impulse in the governance of the world. In this matter, therefore, . . . it is necessary to enquire whether the pressure of population may not have had an indirect influence of which the chief actors in the drama were scarcely conscious.

If provisions are scarce and employment difficult to obtain at home, it is natural that adventurous spirits should go abroad in search of better fortune. That was how the American colonies came into existence; and that is perhaps the main reason why the inhabitants of these small islands have spread themselves over the globe. If there had been ample room for an expanding population in the United Kingdom, it is very probable that the Empire would not have been invented. Then the colonial wars with France would not have taken place; a later generation would have had no reason to fear the power of Russia; the American and Boer wars would have been impossible, and the whole course of European history would have been different. Thus it may be seen at a glance how closely population questions are involved in the underlying cause of national and racial conflicts. But this, it must be admitted, is little more than saying that if human beings did not come into contact with one another they could not fight! The vital question is whether conflicts actually tend to arise through the competition of nations for the limited subsistence yielded by the earth to human efforts. Here, as we have seen, there are two opposing tendencies at work. On the one hand, there is the tendency for the total amount of human subsistence to be greatly increased by co-operation between man and man, by the division of labour and the application of science to nature. On the other hand, the Law of Diminishing Returns tends to develop a constantly increasing competition between nations for sources of food and raw materials and for markets in which to sell the manufactures which pay for the food. Unfortunately, the latter tendency exercises a greater influence on the conduct of diplomacy than the former. We have only to glance through the list of subjects which occupied statesmen during the ten years before the war—Morocco, Tripoli, the Baghdad Railway, the Congo, Mexico, China—to see that this is true. The scramble for first place in the exploitation of backward races and undeveloped territories, for markets and for sources of raw materials, is one of the most potent causes of international friction. Are we not then forced to the conclusion that the fundamental problem of human life—the pressure of population on the means of subsistence—plays a considerable part in creating the atmosphere in which wars arise? The fact that the real nature of these issues is little recognized, and still less discussed, by diplomats is itself a source of danger. In many cases a solution tolerable to all parties to the dispute could be found: free access to raw materials or markets—the Open Door in Morocco, for instance—would be a small price to pay for co-operation instead of conflict; but the underlying issue is seldom brought to light, and some artificial cause of quarrel, like the dispatch of a gunboat to an obscure harbour, proves more dangerous than the tangible interests would be if they were squarely faced. Not, indeed, that there is any way by which the nations can go on multiplying without creating a scarcity in the products of the soil. It is not suggested that an easy solution of the subsistence problem awaits the statesman who is clear-sighted enough to face it. It is a hard nut to crack. But it is not made any easier by war; on the contrary, it is rendered more difficult. If war had been avoided in 1914, the inhabitants of Europe would have been living today on a relatively high standard and receiving generous supplies of food and raw materials from every quarter of the globe. It is the war itself which has made the population problem a burning question.

DOCUMENT 6.4: Rosika Schwimmer, "Birth Control or War," in *Problems of Overpopulation*, ed. Margaret Sanger (New York: American Birth Control League, Inc., 1926, pp. 133–136)

Rosika Schwimmer's discussion of "Birth Control or War" at the Sixth International Neo-Malthusian and Birth Control Conference, held in New York City in 1925, illustrates the genderization of birth control arguments. Here Schwimmer, a Hungarian-born feminist and pacifist, speaks as a woman, suggesting that the voices of mothers can temper barbaric militarist claims that women have a duty to bear children to ensure the strength of future armies. Modern military technology brought unprecedented destruction, and pacifists and progressives alleged that the traditional soldier was being reduced to being so-called cannon fodder. The emerging right of a woman to be heard in the political sphere coincided here with an emerging female perspective on birth control and war.

A few months ago in America there took place . . . a very important international meeting, where an American general figured out that this country having today a certain population, will within one hundred years even under the most restricted immigration laws be so overpopulated that it will be obliged to attack other countries to provide for its over-population. I do hope that there are many here who will remember that statement.

Well, while the object lesson of the war has taught millions of people the seriousness of the necessity of spreading Birth Control knowledge and practice to avoid over-population, the militarists also have been aroused to the danger of over-population. There is being conducted at this moment, not far from here, a militarist meeting at which they are talking about the same thing that we are discussing here, but from the opposite point of view. Militarists too have been aroused to the danger of our having learned a lesson, and in all countries you will find that militarists are pressing for more strict legislation against Birth Control in theory and in practice.

As people who have no arguments always do, they call their adversaries names, and I have found that the militarists are more violent than they ever were before in calling us names. And the chief means by which they frighten away respectable women—especially respectable women—is by telling them that we are a horribly immoral lot. They dare to call us immoral, they who have coined a slogan which was more degrading for womanhood than anything that was said before. "Breed before you die," they told the men before they started for the trenches. That was the most obscene and most brutal thing that ever has been offered to women with regard to motherhood.

Which of you, busy in Birth Control work or in other social work, has not encountered heart-rendering examples of the consequences of this command to women to breed before the men die?

I read the other day an extract from a lecture which was given in a school of journalism—a very famous school of journalism—in America. That lecture recorded a meeting recently held in Washington and the record says "the pupils are a hundred women, the representatives of a million more who have bred men for war or are the descendants of women who did."

To breed men for war, as you breed cattle for stockyards—is there anything more brutal? Is there anything more cruel and disgusting in human relationship? I think that when women say, as it was quoted, "We are glad to give our sons to war"—we are facing a spectacle that is so extraordinary that we must say, "There is no more unnatural phenomenon in all creation than the mother who says, 'I give my son gladly to war.'" . . .

The danger of the present world situation to me seems to be this: the defeated countries have lost territory and millions of population. In these countries, the women, "doped" as they are, do strongly believe that they have to take back territory and to get back population, and that it can be done only through war, through conquering wars. In these countries we have lost our ground for Birth Control with most of the women. All the other reasons we have for Birth Control—because besides the question of avoiding war, we have so many reasons for checking the birth rate—are eliminated in the defeated countries, and people will not listen to them, because they have been told, and taught through all history that only through wars can wrong be adjusted, and of course, everybody considers himself wronged by the loss of the transferred territory and population.

In these countries we have lost ground with Birth Control, because they say, "How shall we be if we are facing the necessity of reconquering in warfare what has been taken away from us?" They don't realize that they lost it by their own insanity in going into the game of war.

DOCUMENT 6.5: Harold Cox, "A League of Low Birth Rate Nations," in *Problems of Overpopulation*, ed. Margaret Sanger (New York: American Birth Control League, 1926, pp. 150–152)

Harold Cox, eugenicist and editor of the *Edinburgh Review*, was one of the first outspoken proponents of birth control. As a participant in the Sixth International Neo-Malthusian and Birth Control Conference, he outlined a proposal made to the League of Nations recommending that it consider an international birth control program as fundamental in its efforts to ensure future world peace. Employing neo-Malthusian arguments linking population pressure to war, Cox described how the belligerent participants in World War I were already encouraging higher birth rates. He warned that

future peace depended on international population control. Though the
League of Nations ignored the proposal, fears that uncontrolled population
growth could threaten international security influenced population programs of later decades.

Each nation, as it increases its numbers to guard against the dangers of the
next war, will find itself in need of more territory for its expanded population.
It will therefore, as the Germans did before 1914, deliberately plan war for the
purpose of conquest. Presently another war with all the latest scientific horrors
added will burst upon the world. While the war lasts there will be a set-back to
civilization and an incalculable addition to human suffering. When the war
ends a good many hundreds of thousands, perhaps millions, of men will be
missing on both sides, and a good many women too. But enough will be left to
carry on the same policy—the policy of breeding people to kill other people. To
that policy there can be no end. It means, as I have just said, an interminable
succession of devastating wars.

I submit therefore that the problem of war must be approached from exactly
the opposite point of view. Instead of each nation arguing that it wants more men
to win the next war, all nations ought to argue that with an adequate check to
over-population the next war could be indefinitely postponed. To persuade the
nations of the world to adopt this point of view is not likely to be an easy matter.
But it will at any rate be easier to win acceptance for this view than to secure the
adoption of schemes put forward by the League of Nations at Geneva.

That body, in the vain hope of preventing war under existing conditions, has
issued a Protocol in which it is proposed that the different nations composing
the League should all agree, when any war breaks out, to entrust their military
forces to the Council of the League for use against the country which the Council judges to be the aggressor. The countries that constitute the League of
Nations will doubtless discuss this proposal with much politeness, but there is
not the remotest chance of any great nation seriously accepting it. Nations
require their military forces for purposes of their own—aggression or defence
as the case may be—and no nation is going to hand over to any external body
the control of a force that it regards as essential to its national life.

The League of Nations makes the fatal error of concentrating its attention on
machinery for settling national disputes when they have arisen. What the
world wants is a League which will set to work to remove the main cause
which brings national disputes into being. That main cause is the overgrowth
of population. If all the nations of the world had plenty of elbow room, there
would be little cause left for quarreling.

I therefore urge the members of this Conference to consider whether it may
not be possible to establish an international movement for the restriction of
population as a necessary step to the avoidance of warfare. Those nations
whose inhabitants are intelligent enough to grasp this necessity might begin by
forming among themselves a League of Low Birth [Rate] Nations. The purpose
of that League would be not to preach the abstract beauties of peace, but to
press upon every nation the practical importance of limiting the number of its
people so as to avoid the risk of conflict with other peoples. When the ultimate
necessity for this policy of limitations composing the Low Birth Rate League
might take the definite step of guaranteeing one another against attack by any

nation that was continuing to expand its population so rapidly as to threaten the security of its neighbours. As soon as that step had been reached the favourite militaristic argument for a high birth rate would at once lose even the plausible value it now possesses. For the collective strength of the low birth rate countries would be sufficient to outweigh any possible advantages that the high birth rate nation could derive from the policy of big battalions.

DOCUMENT 6.6: Bertrand Russell, *Marriage and Morals* (New York: Horace Liveright, 1929, pp. 249–251)

English logician, philosopher, and pacifist Bertrand Russell embraced neo-Malthusian arguments that population pressures could contribute to the out-break of war, but he also warned of too sharp a population decrease among the more civilized nations. Recognizing the increased use of artificial con-traceptives, he warned that a declining birth rate among the better classes of people could have a devastating effect on the world. Russell recommended maintenance of numerically stable populations, which he suggested might demand state intervention in the affairs of other nations.

We have every reason to rejoice that the knowledge of birth-control methods is causing the population of civilized countries to become stationary.

The matter would, however, be quite otherwise if the population were actually to diminish, for a diminution, if it continues unchecked, means ultimate extinction, and we cannot desire to see the most civilized races of the world disappear. The use of contraceptives, therefore, is only to be welcomed if steps can be taken to confine it within such limits as will preserve the population at about its present level. I do not think there is any difficulty in this. . . . Any such measure, however, in the present nationalistic world, would be very dangerous, since it would be used as a method of securing military preponderance. One can imagine all the leading military nations adding to the race of armaments a race of propagation, under the slogan: "The cannon[s] must have their fodder." Here, again, we are faced with the absolute necessity of an international government if civilization is to survive. Such a government, if it is to be effective in preserving the peace of the world, must pass decrees limiting the rate at which any military nation may increase its population. . . . But it cannot be expected that the most powerful military nations will sit still while other nations reverse the balance of power by the mere process of breeding. Any international authority which is to do its work properly will therefore be obliged to take the population question into consideration, and to insist upon birth-control propaganda in any recalci-trant nation. Unless this is done the peace of the world cannot be secured.

DOCUMENT 6.7: Irving Fisher, "War and Eugenics, Symposium" (*Eugenics: A Journal of Race Betterment* 3, November 1930, p. 424)

The November 1930 issue of *Eugenics* devoted notable attention to the sub-ject of war. The interwar years marked an escalation in the eugenics move-ment in the United States and Europe. Germany's race doctrine gained the most attention, but the so-called science of eugenics influenced philosophy and policy throughout the Western world. Lingering concerns over World War I and the fractured state of the world in 1930 triggered new discussions of the relationship between war and eugenics. In the selection presented here, Irving Fisher of Yale University claims that war is "dysgenic" rather than eugenic, as it tends to take the lives of the best specimens of the race.

Time was when war was probably eugenic. When practically all of the males in a tribe fought and fighting was hand to hand, the fittest would survive and become ancestors of the future generations. But little by little the effects of war have changed. . . .

Today not all males fight nor do they fight in single combat. Instead the weaklings are kept at home and carefully protected from destruction, whereas the strongest, bravest and those most fit to become ancestors of posterity, are sent off to war. The separation between the fit who are thus to be sacrificed and the unfit who are to be preserved is performed by careful medical selection. To that extent at least war has become dysgenic. It is still true that under some war systems the officers are protected more than the buck privates and to that extent the dysgenic effect is mitigated; but this practice is not universal nor is it clear that it would entirely overcome the dysgenic tendency first mentioned.

A recent study by Professor Harrison Hunt in his book, *Some Biological Aspects of War*, shows the dysgenic effects of the World War upon the Graduates of Harvard College. Professor E. L. Bogart has likewise condemned war on eugenic grounds. As long as war would have been dysgenic, but today, the reverse being presumably the case, the more we can safeguard ourselves against war the better for the human race. In short, the League of Nations, Locarno Pact, Kellogg Pact, World Court, and London Disarmament Agreement are steps forward eugenically.

DOCUMENT 6.8: Guy Irving Burch and Elmer Pendell, *Population Roads to Peace or War* (Washington, D.C.: Population Reference Bureau, 1945, pp. 46–48)

World War II strengthened previously expressed arguments by policymakers that serious action must be taken to bring peace and stability to the world. Those who saw population control as a solution restated their case, with new intensity. The postwar period set the stage for the United States to take the lead in developing new demographic studies and implementing programs that would guarantee a stable global population. In *Population Roads to Peace or War*, Guy Burch, director of the Population Reference Bureau, which published the study, and Elmer Pendell, editor of *Society Under Analysis*, add recent historical developments to their lines of reasoning. Widespread expansionist policies by totalitarian dictators were used as evidence of links between population and international confrontation.

It will be interesting to observe how an innocent-looking problem of population slowly and unnoticeably grows into the monster problem of war. . . .

A nation begins to increase rapidly in population when everything looks bright. Perhaps rapid strides in industrialization have enabled a nation to support more people at a somewhat higher standard of living. This appears to have been the case in Germany and Japan, and to a minor extent in Italy. Perhaps a nation has won a war which brought it new territory and resources which permitted a high birth rate. This appears to have been the case in Germany after the Franco-Prussian war in 1870, and in Japan after her victories over China and Russia. Or perhaps a nation exports surplus population to other countries, often resulting in higher natural increase rates than would have been if that country had been required to support the numbers she sent abroad. This appears to have been the case in many European countries, and particularly Italy, which since 1880 has sent more emigrants abroad than any other country in Europe. (The one instance in which emigration decreased numbers is Ireland, where emigration in conjunction with delayed marriages and bachelorhood decreased her population and greatly improved her standard of living.)

First there is an increase in the child population due to a high birth rate or to a lower infant mortality rate, or both. As time goes by the children grow into young men and young women. When this begins to happen there is an increasingly larger proportion of the population in the productive, military, and reproductive ages. Because of the many people at these ages, production per capita increases; more young men are ready for the army each year; and a higher proportion of the population reaches the peak reproductive ages. This has a tendency to stimulate the birth rate. So far so good. The nation assumes a superiority complex and imagines that it is headed for Utopia unlimited.

Unfortunately, this is only part of the story. In due time the young people produced by the upsurge of population begin to grow old and dependent, and, if the birth rate is not kept high to produce a bumper crop of oncoming youth, in time the nation not only decreases its potential cannon fodder but also has an abnormally large proportion of oldsters to take care of. On the other hand, if the birth rate is kept high the total population eventually reaches the "must expand or explode" stage. (Incidentally, a high birth rate for each thousand of the population now produces many more births than in former years because the population is much larger.)

When this act in the tragedy is reached, the nation is trapped. It might be said that the nation is caught between the "devil" (an attempt at war for conquest of more territory and resources) and the "deep blue sea" (the eventual disorganization of political and economic conditions such as the unfortunate peoples of China and India are experiencing).

The way is now prepared for the despot. When a nation reaches this explosive population stage it is ripe for the dictator as would-be conqueror. The nation is so crowded that there is good excuse for regimentation to keep law and order. As population pressure becomes more intense, the people work harder and longer and try every means known to them to escape their predicament, yet they cannot free themselves from sinking deeper into the quicksand of overpopulation. Not only is this the case, but any would-be dictator who can read population statistics can assure the people that their condition is likely to become worse and worse for at least a half century.

In such a state of affairs the masses of the people become desperate and fanatic, and grasp at any straw or theory that has any hope of relieving their plight. The dictator's solution to all their problems is very clear-cut and simple. It is a war for conquest of more territory, natural resources, and wealth—just what the people need!

To assure his hold on the people and to recruit cannon fodder for future conquests, the would-be conqueror calls for a higher birth rate. We hear much about the "survival of the nation," the "right to have children," the "law of nature," etc. Sex regulations often are relaxed. If argument is not enough, laws are enacted to serve the same purposes.

In the meantime the would-be conqueror flatters his people by calling them a "vigorous, prolific, and young" nation destined for grandeur. On the other hand, he constantly refers to the lower-birth-rate nations as "has been" powers. In due time, he adds the claim that his people are a race of "supermen" blessed by the Almighty with exceptional heredity. Having "established" these "truths" in the minds of his regimented and fanatical followers he reasons that such a "superior" people should inherit the earth. This is pleasing to the ears of his overcrowded people, and finally the stage is all set for the saber-rattling despot to put on his uniform and lead his "long suffering" nation into a "holy" war for the "just" distribution of the world's resources.

This has been the program followed by Hitler, Mussolini, and the military party in Japan in launching the most destructive of all wars. But they could never have done this had not the population situation, which began to develop before Hitler, Mussolini, and Tojo were born, reached a critical stage. The Kaiser and his group used much the same methods from 1901 to the outbreak of World War I in 1914, as is shown by a pamphlet issued at Washington in 1918 by the Committee on Public Information with the title "Conquest and Kultur: Aims of the Germans in their Own Words."

DOCUMENT 6.9: "Editorial: The Only Real Defense" (*Bulletin of the Atomic Scientists* 3, September 1951, pp. 242–243)

While population theorists continued to argue that overpopulation and population pressures contributed to the outbreak of war, the presence of nuclear weapons confronted modern thinking. The atomic bomb, and the subsequent development of the more powerful hydrogen bomb, threatened entire populations of the world's major cities. World War II air raids had devastated Europe's urban centers, and the dropping of the atomic bomb had catastrophically reduced the populations of Hiroshima and Nagasaki. Sociologists and demographers argued that the encouragement of larger families might act as some protection against potential casualties on an unprecedented scale in the case of nuclear attack, but governments of the self-proclaimed free world resisted implementing pronatalist programs reminiscent of those developed under Hitler and Stalin. The United States embraced a new culture of family resulting in a so-called baby boom. However, policymakers warned that increased family size could never serve to replace the hundreds of thousands of lives that might be lost in an atomic war. The solution lay in dispersal of the population, and a program designed to facilitate suburban development began. This 1951 editorial in the *Bulletin of the Atomic Scientists* outlines prevailing concerns.

In addition to costs, powerful political and psychological obstacles stand in the path of a determined dispersal policy. Dispersal not only threatens innumerable vested interests, but also tends to disrupt forcibly the accustomed ways of living. It violates the desire of most Americans to shape their lives without official advice and interference. . . . It is unlikely that the American urban population will be willing to maintain, throughout the years to come, a sufficiently large and permanently alerted civil defense—except under a compulsive civil defense service law.

The most exhaustive preparations for first aid, fire fighting, and relief after an atomic attack, while they can promise a considerable reduction in the number of casualties, could do little to protect the productive facilities of an attacked city—facilities whose incapacitation is likely to be the prime aim of the attack. Radical alterations of many existing buildings, creation of broad fire lanes and wide new radial and circular thoroughfares, obviating the danger of "fire storms," and permitting rapid access of fire fighting equipment to any part of the stricken city, may save some plants; but peacetime dispersal of critically important facilities into satellite communities may be not much more expensive—and a great deal more effective.

City planners were quick to point out the advantages to health and happiness of the population and to the efficiency of the national production and transportation plant which could be brought about by judicious dispersal. By reducing the fear of an atomic attack, both in new, dispersed communities and in old urban centers deprived of their present concentration of attractive targets, dispersal may permit the government to dispense with the many restrictions of freedoms and civil rights which will become unavoidable if present industrial citadels are permitted to survive and grow.

DOCUMENT 6.10: David Cushman Coyle, "Japan's Population: Past Achievements and New Problems" (*Population Bulletin* 15, November 1959, 122–129)

The case of population policy in Japan during the mid-twentieth century attracted the world's attention for a number of reasons. First, concerns of a proverbial yellow peril lingered, and the memory of Japan's imperialist policies of expansion in recent decades sustained considerable concern. Modernization and Western influence suggested that birth control practices might be embraced in Japanese culture by midcentury. But implementation of a structured program under U.S. occupation would suggest unsolicited control, even genocide, in light of attacks on Hiroshima and Nagasaki. Still, Japan was the subject of numerous studies and population reports, such as the following by economist David Cushman Coyle.

The American Occupation was not in a position to take a positive attitude on Japanese population policy. American tradition in this field is conservative, resting mainly on the prohibition of abortion and restriction of birth-control facilities, with some light gestures toward subsidizing children. Even though Japanese imperialism had been recognized as an effect of population pressure, the Americans, with their background, could hardly be expected to prescribe a treatment to reduce the rate of population growth.

But the Americans could not avoid studying the economic problems of the country which they had undertaken to govern. The Economic and Scientific Section of SCAP (Supreme Commander Allied Powers) made estimates of the future population, and the National Resources Section analyzed future requirements in the light of the population projections. In its report, the National Resources Section came to the natural conclusion that the discrepancies between population and resources could hardly be met in any "humane" way except by a reduction of the birth rate. . . .

The Japanese got the point that Americans in general favored birth control as a means of economic protection for the family. They did not fail to observe that personally most Americans were evidently limiting their families, and under far less economic pressure than was felt by the Japanese. . . .

The effects of the American Occupation were generally favorable to family limitation. The land redistribution, by relieving rural distress, might have made room for the production of more children, other things being equal—which they were not. The abolition of primogeniture, equal rights for women, wider education, and in particular the contacts with Americans and their movies and other productions, tended to encourage birth control.

DOCUMENT 6.11: *Population Control and National Security: A Review of U.S. National Security Policy on Population Issues, 1970–1988,* **IPFA Paper #1 (Washington, D.C.: http://panindigan.tripod.com/pcns1.html)**

> During the 1960s and 1970s, the United States became a major donor to international population programs. Public discussions of this trend centered primarily on topics of economic development and the right of women to reproductive choice. However, security concerns motivated much of the funding. This paper, distributed on the Internet by the Information Project for Africa, Inc. (IPFA), examines U.S. concerns and policy during the Nixon administration. The paper is introduced as saying: "Population assistance has been a major part of the United States' foreign aid program since 1965. This document, the first in a series of working papers on U.S. foreign policy toward Africa, is based on memoranda from the National Security Council which have been declassified since mid-1989 and on reports by the General Accounting Office and private publishers. Its purpose is to provide background on objectives which form the basis for U.S. population intervention in the developing world."

On April 24, 1974, Henry A. Kissinger sent to the Secretary of Defense, the Secretary of Agriculture, the Director of Central Intelligence, the Deputy Secretary of State and the Administrator of the Agency for International Development, with a copy to the Chairman of the Joint Chiefs of Staff, a memorandum titled "Implications of Worldwide Population Growth for U.S. Security and Overseas Interests" (National Security Study Memorandum 200).

That memo stated: "The President has directed a study of the impact of world population growth on U.S. Security and overseas interests. The study should look forward at least until the year 2000, and use several alternative reasonable projections of population growth."

The memorandum requested that those agencies address such issues as "trade problems the U.S. may face arising from competition for resources" and the "likelihood that population growth or imbalances will produce disruptive foreign policies and international instability."

It requested opinions on "new initiatives" that might be used to "focus international attention on the population problem" and ways in which the U.S. might "improve its assistance in the population field." . . .

The document advises "that the President and the Secretary of State treat the subject of population growth control as a matter of paramount importance. . . . " Moreover, executive endorsement of the recommendations—contained in the study—included "a global target of replacement fertility levels by the year 2000." . . .

A central theme of the study is the need for greater expenditures to combat population growth in the developing world. While it concedes that "bilateral assistance to some of these countries may not be acceptable," . . . it nonetheless proposes an increased USAID population control budget as well as a larger donation for population assistance to multilateral agencies. Three areas of special emphasis are suggested: making population a part of host-country development plans; ensuring wide access to contraceptive technology, and the implementation of those foreign assistance projects "offering the greatest promise of increased motivation for smaller family size." . . .

Because of "the major foreign policy implications of the recommended population strategy" and the "wide agency interests in this topic," . . . the study recommended that responsibility for policymaking and executive review of population activities be vested in the Under Secretaries Committee of the National Security Council.

7

Nation and Migration

The idea that there was power in numbers intensified during periods of nationalism. The world's leaders declared that a nation's strength lay in its people. But not only were numbers important; leaders emphasized national characteristics and identity. As nations expanded through technological advances and economic development, population growth was viewed as a sign of progress. Industrialization usually brought a lower birth rate, but longer life expectancy and immigration helped to increase population.

The migration of people challenged the concept of nationhood. First, nations were defined by their borders, and migrating people often crossed borders. Nations were also defined by the character, ethnicity, language, and heritage of their people. When people of other cultures entered a new nation, their effect was to challenge traditional beliefs, politics, and ways of life.

Very importantly, migration is often a consequence of population growth. As sociologists point out, real population numbers are affected by three factors: birth, death, and migration. In the twentieth century, population in the developing world grew considerably due to lower death rates and continued high birth rates, contributing to significant migration. Receiving nations worked to develop international policies that would stabilize economies elsewhere, with the hope of stabilizing migration.

DOCUMENT 7.1: Benjamin Franklin, *The Interest of Great Britain Considered, With Regard to her Colonies, And the Acquisitions of Canada and Guadaloupe. To which are added, Observations concerning the Increase of Mankind, Peopling of Countries, Etc.* **(London: T. Becket, 1760, pp. 55–56)**

By 1751, when Benjamin Franklin wrote this essay on population, it had been long understood that the strength of a nation lay in its people. Numbers were important, as was quality, but Franklin takes the notion a step further in portraying the American colonies as unique. He demonstrates an awareness of the connection between population, development, and economy but maintains that conventional principles of demographics and subsistence cannot be applied to America—he sees the British colonies as being tremendously capable of sustaining population growth. He adds that high birth rates might well reflect the industriousness of a people, suggesting that America was developing a special character that was reflected in the strength of its people.

19. The great increase of offspring in particular families, is not always owing to greater fecundity of nature, but sometimes to examples of industry in the heads, and industrious education; by which the children are enabled to prove better for themselves, and their marrying early is encouraged from the prospect of good subsistence.

20. If there be a sect therefore, in our nation, that regard frugality and industry as religious duties, and educate their children therein, more than others commonly do; such sect must consequently increase more by natural generation, than any other sect in *Britain*.—

21. The importation of foreigners into a country that has as many inhabitants as the present employments and provisions of subsistence will bear, will be in the end no increase of people, unless the new-comers have more industry and frugality than the natives, and then they will provide more subsistence and increase in the country; but they will gradually eat the natives out.—Nor is it necessary to bring in foreigners to fill up any occasional vacancy in a country; for such vacancy (if the laws are good) will soon be filled by natural generation. Who can now find the vacancy made in *Sweden, France,* or other warlike nations, by the plague of heroism 40 years ago; in *France,* by the expulsion of the protestants; in *England,* by the settlement of her colonies; or in *Guinea,* by 100 years exportation of slaves that has blackened half *America?*——The thinness of the inhabitants in *Spain,* is owing to national pride and idleness, and other causes, rather than to the expulsion of the *Moors,* or to the making of new settlements.

22. There is in short no bound to the prolific nature of plants or animals, but what is made by their crowding and interfering with each other's means of subsistence. Was the face of the earth vacant of other plants, it might be gradually sowed and overspread with one kind only; as for instance, with Fennel; and were it empty of other inhabitants, it might in a few ages be replenished from one nation only; as for instance, with *Englishmen.* Thus there are supposed to be now upwards of one Million *English* souls in *North-America,* (tho' 'tis thought scarce 80,000 have been brought over sea) and yet perhaps there is not one the fewer in *Britain,* but rather many more, on account of the employment the colonies afford to manufacturers at home. This million doubling, suppose but once in 25 years, will in another century be more than the people of *England,* and the greatest number of *Englishmen* will be on this side the water. What an accession of power to the *British* empire by sea as well as land! What increase of trade and navigation! What numbers of ships and seamen! We have been here but little more than 100 years, and yet the force of our privateers in the late war, united, was greater, both in men and guns, than that of the whole

British navy in queen *Elizabeth*'s time.——How important an affair then to *Britain,* is the present treaty (1751) for settling the bounds between her colonies and the *French,* and how careful should she be to secure room enough, since on the room depends so much the Increase of her people?

23. In fine, a nation well regulated is like a polypus; take away a limb, its place is soon supply'd; cut it in two, and each deficient part shall speedily grow out of the part remaining. Thus if you have room and subsistence enough, as you may by dividing, make ten polypuses out of one, you may of one make ten nations, equally populous and powerful; or rather, increase a nation ten fold in numbers and strength.

DOCUMENT 7.2: T. R. Edmonds, *An Enquiry into the Principles of Population, Exhibiting a System of Regulations for the Poor; Designed Immediately to Lessen, and Finally to Remove, the Evils Which Have Hitherto Pressed Upon the Labouring Classes of Society* **(London: James Duncan, 1832, pp. 276–278)**

Economist Thomas Rowe Edmonds recommends emigration as one way of getting rid of the existing "redundancy of population" in the United Kingdom. By this time, Britain had lost 13 of its American colonies, and was shifting its attention elsewhere. Edmonds suggested that emigration through further colonizing efforts could alleviate population pressures in the mother country while strengthening Britain's position in the world and its economy. Though emigration might have weakened a nation in the past, the populating of colonies could make an empire stronger.

It need hardly be observed, that by the term redundancy of population is meant a supply of labourers exceeding the demand for their services: now, an adjustment can be brought about in two ways: either by diminishing the supply, or by increasing the demand. The supply is at once diminished by emigration; but it is important to consider, that by judicious colonization the demand for labour at home may be increased at the same time. On referring to the state of things in an improving colony, the contrast with an old country, in respect to the remuneration of labour, is so striking, as to create a feeling of surprise that objections should arise in any quarter to bring about a mutual adjustment. The colony is in great want of the very same thing which is redundant in the mother country. . . . Though oceans roll between the two classes of people, it forms no obstacle to a commercial and maritime nation. The necessity imposed for extensive naval communication may do more than compensate for the inconveniences of distance. There is no reason, therefore, why such possessions should not be viewed as synonymous with the domestic territory, in respect to commercial capabilities or advantages. Through their instrumentality unproductive paupers at home are converted into productive labourers abroad, relieving rate payers of an oppressive tax. If for example, 300,000 paupers emigrated, the industrious part of the community may be relieved of payments to the extent of three millions sterling annually; and there would, consequently, be this sum at their disposal for other purposes of expenditure. Employment at home must be increased owing to this fund, which previously went to the support of paupers in idleness, being directed to a productive channel. Many paupers who still remain in the mother country will thus be elevated to the condition of labourers, further relieving the rate payers. But this is not the entire of the advantage. These 300,000 emigrants, settling in a prosperous colony, create a demand for the manufactures of Great Britain to an extent much greater than labourers at home could hope to effect. Settling in an agricultural territory, they will confine their attention to that species of industry which is most productive, and thus, avoiding manufactures for a very long period, they take, as has been truly observed, every made up article from a needle to an anchor from the mother country. In conducting the interchange, moreover, ships are required, with all the collateral trades, rope-makers, sail-makers, and the like, dependent on navigation; so that it is not extravagant to assert that 300,000 paupers, converted into prosperous colonists, would lessen the redundancy to the extent of 2,000,000; that is, by the conjoint operation of diminishing the supply of labourers, and increasing the demand for their services, it produces benefit in geometrical extension.

DOCUMENT 7.3: John Ilderton Burn, *Familiar Letters on Population, Emigration, Home Colonization, &c. &c.* (London: Hatchard & Son, 1832, pp. 12–15)

In the following report, John Ilderton Burn provides an elaborate list of recommendations to Robert Lord Henley regarding the poor "to alleviate their distress, and at the same time, and by the same means, benefit those who employ them." Philanthropic in intent, Burn's analysis was critical of theorists who warned of numbers but provided no solutions. He connected poverty to lack of available work, not to any personal character flaw or inherent failure of one who happened to be unemployed, and feared the impact of industrialization on the need of laborers. He recognized continued dependence on agriculture for subsistence and the trend toward market production, which encouraged emigration to regions with better land. However, he concluded that such emigration would hurt, rather than help, a nation.

The strength of a nation is in its people. The greater their numbers the more powerful the state. All calculations are thus founded on the relative empires of the world.

The love of native country is indelibly impressed upon the human mind. It is a fertile source of every virtue—a perfect protection against foreign invaders. But the more excellent the country—the more esteemed—the more renowned—the higher the character, and the greater the blessings showed on all—the stronger, in consequence, is this love of native land. This needs only to be called to our recollection, not any argument to prove it: well then, the obvious conclusion is, that in no respect should its sacred ties be unloosed, or the valuable feeling be obliterated or destroyed. When Nelson hoisted the memorable flag, that "England expected every man to do his duty," it was on the thorough knowledge that the call was made to men fully resolved from the *love of their country* to subdue all opposition, to keep her honour and glory untarnished. The invitation to Canadian or American colonists could not have been answered with the same kindred feeling—the same force of moral obligation. Surely then to preserve this feeling and the people who are governed by it must be a vital object to any government. Emigration of such men destroys in a great measure the force of it, and their offspring in a foreign country have their earliest associations blended with interests and feelings vastly below the standard alluded to. England cannot expect of them the same hearty support in her need as from her native population. Thus far then it is a loss to the country every way. But to compensate this, we are told that they will cultivate better soils, which will yield greater abundance and better pay an interest on the capital to be embarked in their outfit. Let us calmly examine into the truth hereof, and for the purpose of trying the argument in the fairest way, make admissions that in many respects may be questioned. Admit then that the soil is richer than the waste land in Britain; that the expense of cultivation is less and the produce more; in short, a surplus beyond the maintenance of the cultivators, to be sold, in order to realize the profits or interest on the capital. This surplus produce must be sold somewhere. It must be taken to another market, that in Canada being already supplied; it must, in short, be brought to England, and thus employ our shipping interest. Well, the surplus is brought here, and sold here, and the produce of the sales is assumed to be so far beneficial that a reasonable interest is paid on the capital thus embarked. But mark the consequences; as inevitably as closely adhering to the course assumed, and as detrimental and disastrous to the general interest of the country as can well be imagined. Will not every bushel of this imported corn tend to displace an equal quantity now produced here on soils inferior to the Canadian? Will not this as inevitably tend to increase the evils of a redundant population, by pushing the agriculturalists here on such poorer lands out of their employment? Thus, although A and B may benefit partially by this emigration experiment, do not all the other members of the community suffer injury? Can there be a doubt here that men thus displaced from a state of partial production, are not, *ipso facto*, an additional burden on society, and must be provided for by, perhaps, a portion of this very imported corn, which occasions the mischief? The evil is not only corrected by this mode of sending labourers out of the country, but appears fairly to be increased by it; and so it must be, the longer it is persevered in, till the disastrous consequences shall become without cure or remedy. Emigration then, on this ground, appears fully as exceptionable as on the former. The emigrants are not only in a great measure lost to their country, but their exertions are, in truth, injurious to its best interests.

Document 7.4: "Marcus," *The Book of Murder! A Vade-mecum for the Commissioners and Guardians of the New Poor Law Throughout Great Britain and Ireland, Being an Exact Reprint of The Infamous Essay on the Possibility of Limiting Populousness* **(London: William Dugdale, 1839, pp. 12–13)**

Originally published in 1838, this pseudonymous attack on Malthus chastised population theory that categorized human beings, and warned essentially of excess population among the lower classes. In later passages, it offers a variety of remedies for excess population. Here, it emphasizes the concept of country and its relationship to population.

1. We may pass with brevity some current phrases such as this:—The strength of a country is the people. And need not stop long to shew, that they are but reasons ostensible, never meant to be scrutinized. For let us but examine more closely the phrase above, and we shall find, that for it to be true, it is a requisite condition, that of the people in question every individual have his *place;* whence the corrected proposition comes to be. The strength of a country consists in the number of those places; that is to say, in the multitude of the country; a truism or a tautology:—that for the purpose of abundance in the choice of persons, and of wholesome competition, is wanted a reserve, a supplementary number, it is true; but not a crowd or a confusion:—that as for the greatness of the state, it is itself desirable only as a means of happiness; and that to obtain it by the sacrifice of that very happiness will hardly be a gratification even to vanity and pride. Not to say, that degradation and misery in the interior will not really contribute to political grandeur even indirectly or by any means or sacrifice whatever. These considerations will not be disputed.

2. But of far greater importance are those pre-occupying ideas, which have really intercepted men's clear view of the great question. I will here give of them only one instance:—the Servile State: which among the ancients formed an essential and component part of their civilization.

It is singular that the great ulcer of modern nations, a proletarian populousness, should have superseded exactly the grand evil of antiquity, personal slavery: the disappearing of the one being the immediate cause of the appearing of the other. As if there were some necessary principle of Evil, commutable in shape, but eternal and constant in essence. It is not so however. Slavery has, we hardly know by what means, by what gradations, or at what epoch, disappeared. The supervened luxuriance of population, with its catalogue of miseries, will, as we have a lively hope, disappear, it too, in its turn.

The slaves of antiquity were cattle. Without much difficulty the sexes might be kept effectually separated. Or if, by some relaxation of this rigour, the offspring came to be more than was wanted, it was destroyed, as a matter of course.

Now the slaves formed the larger part of the whole body: so that the Great Evil, existing only for the other or the smaller part, would already be the less visible, and would the less loudly call for a remedy.

But further still. The practice of infanticide, rendered familiar by its frequency among the slaves, was nowise shocking when applied to the other part of the population—to the favoured slaves, to the freed men in dependence, and to the citizens themselves. Only being optional and not enforced, it did not reach the point we have in view, *the presenting of the existing of persons for whom there were no places.* Still this partial relief broke the force and importunity of the complaint. It is then no wonder that ARISTOTLE, or his coevals, thought other matters more pressingly important, and more worthy their attention than this of over-populousness. And if that great man ever carried his imagination so far as to the emancipation of labourers (that is to say, a state of exemption and security from pain that might be inflicted at the will of another), still he never dreamt that that emancipation would be granted without any condition, and that the greatest of all disorders, procreation without rule or limit, would pass unprohibited and unheeded. The truth is, this great change came about surreptitiously. It never was deliberated or accorded by any lawgiver or lawgiving body. Up to this day then the omission has never been rectified: the condition in the bargains of liberty remains still to be imposed and enforced: the means of enforcing it are to be invented: and the delicate task of introducing a new practice is yet to be performed.

DOCUMENT 7.5: Edward Alsworth Ross, *The Principles of Sociology* (The Century Social Science Series) (New York: The Century Co., 1920, pp. 32–37)

The work of Edward Alsworth Ross, professor of sociology at the University of Wisconsin, reflected early-twentieth-century concerns of high fertility among undesirable immigrants arriving on America's shores. In his *Principles of Sociology*, Ross draws connections between the population theories of Malthus and Darwin, suggesting that they are fundamental in understanding the United States' immigration problem. In this and other works, Ross calls for immigration restriction, which was legislated in 1924 and 1925 by the U.S. Congress. By the twentieth century, race theory had introduced new ideas of nation and ethnicity into the population debate.

The specific fecundity of mankind became established hundreds of centuries ago and insured it the power of expanding even under the hard conditions of primitive life. In the most advanced stage of civilization this capacity is about *four times* what man needs in order to maintain his numbers and *three times* that which will cause population to grow about as fast as the food supply can be augmented. Hence, for man to shut his eyes and propagate without taking thought for the morrow is to act as if he were living in olden times, when a twentieth of the population died in a year instead of to-day when not over an eightieth dies in a year. For him to let himself go in respect to the instincts centering about reproduction is almost as disastrous in its effects as for him to give free rein to his pugnacious instinct, his destructive instinct, or his acquisitive instinct.

. . . It is possible . . . for public opinion to discourage immoderate fecundity. When each trudges the road by himself, it is loosely his own affair how many bundles he loads himself with. But when we go by train, it is everybody's concern how many bundles a passenger brings aboard. The more one brings, the fewer others can bring and the greater the general discomfort. Hence, an opinion grows up as to what is a reasonable amount of luggage for a passenger to travel with.

In the same way, once it is realized that only by a certain self-control in propagation is it possible for a people to enjoy health, comfort, and length of life, an idea forms as to what is reasonable family size, and disapproval is shown those who without warrant exceed this. No doubt the exceptionally endowed who offer society a "full quiver" of children will find favor; but the subcommon—who are the most reckless in multiplication—will be made to feel community resentment when they propagate as if the world could not have too many of their ilk. The man of poor stock who begets a family of ten or fifteen will be looked upon as a fool or an egoist.

. . . But what of forethoughted parentage by the advanced peoples while there are peoples and races which multiply blindly and threaten to flood their neighbors with their surplus population? Now that cheap travel stirs the social deeps and beckoning opportunity fills the steerages, immigration becomes ever more serious to the people, which hopes to rid itself utterly of slums, "submerged tenth" and "poverty" classes. Wherefore should it practice family prudence if hungry strangers may crowd in and occupy at the table places it had reserved for its children? Shall it in order to relieve the teeming lands of their unemployed abide in the pit of wolfish competition and give up the prospect of a betterment of the lot of the masses?

There is no doubt that barriers to immigration will be reared which will give notice to the backward peoples that enlightened humanity is not willing to cramp itself in order that these people may continue to indulge in thoughtless reproduction. Let a people make itself miserable by multiplying like an animal not endowed with foresight and reason, but why should this people expect other peoples to allow themselves to be made miserable in order to accommodate its overflow?

Unless family restriction becomes general over the world, it is vain, therefore, to expect acknowledgment of the right of any well-behaved and self-supporting human being to settle where he will. From the standpoint of the brotherhood of man such an acknowledgment would be most desirable. But there is no blinking the fact that it would handicap the advanced peoples and in time cause the world's population to consist more of unthinking races and less of thinking, aspiring races.

DOCUMENT 7.6: Adolf Hitler, *Mein Kampf* (New York: Reynal & Hitchcock, 1939, pp. 297–598)

In his address on "The State" in *Mein Kampf* (1924), Adolf Hitler used contemporary race theory to rationalize Germany's economic and social problems. Here, he outlines his nationalist philosophy based on race and ethnicity.

Unfortunately, our German nationality is no longer based on a racially uniform nucleus. Also, the process of the blending of the various primal constituents has not yet progressed so far as to permit speaking of a newly formed race. On the contrary: the blood-poisoning which affected our national body, especially since the Thirty Years' War, led not only to a decomposition of our blood but also of our soul. The open frontiers of our fatherland, the dependence upon un-Germanic alien bodies along this frontier district, but above all the strong current influx of foreign blood into the interior of the Reich proper, in consequence of its continued renewal does not leave time for an absolute melting. It is not a new race that results from the fusion, but the racial stocks remain side by side, with the result that especially in critical moments when in other cases a herd would assemble, the German people run in all directions of the winds. The racial elements are situated differently, not only territorially but also in individual cases within the same territory. . . . In this side by side placement of our basic racial elements, which remained unblended, is rooted what with us one calls by the word *super-individualism*. In peaceful times it may sometimes render good services, but taken all in all it has deprived us of world domination. If, in its historical development, the German people had possessed this group unity as it was enjoyed by other peoples, then the German Reich would today probably be the mistress of this globe.

DOCUMENT 7.7: Adolf Hitler, *My New Order*, ed. Raoul de Roussy de Sales (New York: Reynal & Hitchcock, 1941, pp. 635–637)

In this speech given to the Reichstag in Berlin on April 28, 1939, Hitler justifies his expansion into surrounding territories. He condemns the division of Germany mandated by the Treaty of Versailles following World War I and claims that Austria and part of Czechoslovakia are bound to Germany historically, politically, and culturally because of the German people living in those regions.

Not only was the German Reich destroyed and Austria split up into its component parts by the criminals of Versailles, but Germans also were forbidden to acknowledge that community which they had confessed for more than a thousand years. I have always regarded elimination of this state of affairs as the highest and most holy task of my life. I have never failed to proclaim this determination. And I have always been resolved to realize these ideas which haunted me day and night. . . .

When in the course of the migrations of peoples, the Germanic tribes began, for reasons inexplicable to us, to migrate out of the territory which is today Bohemia and Moravia, a foreign Slav people made its way into this territory and made a place for itself between the remaining Germans. Since that time the living space of this Slav people has been enclosed in the form of a horseshoe by Germans.

From an economic point of view independent existence is, in the long run, impossible for these countries except on a basis of relationship with the German nation and German economy. . . . The policy of national annihilation which set in, particularly after the Treaty of Versailles under pressure of the Czech majority, combined, too, with economic conditions and a rising tide of distress, led to emigration of these German elements so that Germans left in the territory were reduced to approximately 3,700,000.

The population on the fringe of territory is uniformly German, but there are also large German linguistic enclaves in the interior. The Czech nation is, in its origins, foreign to us, but in the thousand years in which the two peoples have lived side by side, a Czech culture has, in the main, been formed and molded by German influences.

DOCUMENT 7.8: Lawrence de Besault, *President Trujillo: His Work and the Dominican Republic* (Washington, D.C.: Washington Publishing Co., 1936, pp. 340–341)

Nationalist sentiment continued to emphasize numbers as a demonstration of strength in various regions of the world. Such was the case with Rafael Trujillo, dictator of the Dominican Republic from 1930 until his assassination in 1961. Trujillo was criticized for inflating numbers, but he used every means possible to portray a powerful Dominican Republic. Lawrence de Besault, in his glowing biography of the Dominican dictator, described the census project undertaken in the 1930s.

President Trujillo appreciated the urgent necessity of an adequate census as a basis for proper governmental operation, and with the dynamic energy which characterizes him, he worked out a plan for it, and then put it into execution, which combined rapidity, economy and accuracy. . . .

Four enumerations were made: homes, population, farms and livestock, and forests and mines. For the first three (the fourth required technical men) more than 30,000 people were mobilized to cover the entire nation in a single day. This civilian army had been perfectly trained for its work, and took a census equal in accuracy to the best of its kind anywhere in the world, at the incredibly low cost of $70,000.

There is little doubt that a task of this nature would be difficult to duplicate in any other civilized nation. That it was possible in the Dominican Republic is due to the zeal with which Dominicans comply with the wishes of their leader, the love they have for him, and their faith that the Government is bringing them rich rewards. . . .

President Trujillo announced the basic figures in an eloquent proclamation on August 16th, 1935. His proclamation says:

"On this day, the anniversary of the restoration of our independence, I salute the nation, and pay homage to the memory of our national heroes, and I take the opportunity to offer my fellow-citizens the exact figures of our population census. This census is one of the accomplishments of which I am most proud, in the first year of my second term, because it was compiled by the Dominican Party, the fruit of my arduous efforts, and the crystallization of my highest ideals."

DOCUMENT 7.9: Gunnar Myrdal, *Population: A Problem for Democracy* (Cambridge, Mass.: Harvard University Press, 1940, pp. 189–191)

Swedish sociologist Gunnar Myrdal was one of the first to outline a need for developing a population policy at the national level. Sweden was among the most progressive of Western nations in implementing social welfare programs designed to protect the interests of children and the family. At mid-century, Myrdal described how democracy could be strengthened by a rational population policy. Sweden's open discussions of sexuality and birth control shocked foreign observers, but similar discussions soon took place in other European nations and the United States. Here he ties population policy to democracy.

In a democratic society we must definitely direct our attention to the abolition of both poverty and ignorance, that is to say, the very factors which for a long time have stimulated a high birth rate; we must do so even though the abundance of children produced by these factors is the only thing at present which prevents the population situation from being even more catastrophic

than it is. In a democratic society we must continue to disseminate and officially sanction, through the schools and adult education, demands for cultural
and hygienic standards of living which, for the broad masses of the people with
current real incomes, are quite incompatible with a normal family size—that is,
with a four-child system—and which therefore directly create motives for
increased birth control. On these principles we can accept no compromises. We
cannot think of raising the number of children by holding back the advance of
civilization. Moreover, it would be impossible even if we wished to do so. A rise
and leveling off of the *standards* of living—what people are taught to *want*—
always precedes, with us, the rise and equalization of the *level* of living—what
people actually *have*.

This is the deepest dilemma in the population policy in a democratic nation.

This first principle for a positive population policy in a democratic country,
that undesirable births shall be prevented, is closely associated with the second
principle, that the birth rate shall not be maintained by the *undesired* births.
Birth control must be openly and officially declared to be good in itself, and the
self-evident superiority of the most effective means of birth control must then
also be recognized to have a positive value.

DOCUMENT 7.10: *Proceedings of the World Population Conference,*
Rome, 31 August–10 September 1954, Summary Report **(New York:**
United Nations Department of Economic and Social Affairs, 1955, p. 58)

Meeting 10 of the World Population Conference held in Rome in 1954 was
devoted to discussion of international migration and the impact it had made
on demographic and economic trends in countries of emigration. This summary report gives findings of participants who based their discussion on
documents prepared by the United Nations, the International Labour Office,
the Office of the United Nations High Commissioner for Refugees, and the
Intergovernmental Committee for European Migration.

The effects of emigration on the growth and structure of total population and
of the economically active population of a country may also have an economic
effect on the levels of living of the population of the country. The considerations
discussed above are therefore important in evaluating the effects of a flow of
migration on the economic situation of a country.

As a number of scientific papers show, real *per capita* income has risen in certain cases (Puerto Rico); in others the most obvious effects are the inflow of capital in the form of remittances of savings by emigrants (Puerto Rico, India,
where, however, this flow is tending to decrease and disappear as a result of
restrictions imposed by the countries of immigration on the export of capital or
the weakening of ties between emigrants and their countries of origin). The
effects of emigration on the economic situation of the country of origin have
also been deduced from the extent to which emigration helps to reduce population pressure. In a paper on overseas migration in relation to population pressure in Europe, it was noted that emigration to overseas countries has
contributed to European economic recovery, although emigration can only be
considered a safety valve for the population pressure of certain countries and

cannot serve as a total substitute for other factors such as capital investment, increased trade and a better internal distribution of population within Europe. In the countries of southern Europe in particular (with the exception of Greece), overseas emigration since the war has continued to be an important outlet for surplus man-power. In Italy, overseas emigration since the war has absorbed one-fifth of the natural increase of population; it has been an important, although not a decisive, factor in reducing population pressure. Italy has also been helped by emigration to other European countries. In Portugal overseas emigration has absorbed one-quarter of the natural increase, whereas in Spain it has absorbed only one-tenth of the population increase. In Greece, overseas emigration has not been a decisive factor in solving the problems of agricultural underemployment or the increase in the labour force. In the United Kingdom emigration has been at a higher level (30 per cent of the natural increase of the population), but its effects on the national economy have been counterbalanced by immigration from other European countries. In the Netherlands, emigration to overseas countries has compensated for the effects of large-scale repatriation of Netherlands citizens from Indonesia. In the case of the Federal Republic of Germany, overseas emigration has helped to solve the problem of the non-German refugees, but the inflow of refugees and expellees has been much greater than the number of persons leaving the country. This phenomenon has, moreover, been accompanied by a steady increase in per capita income. The demographic disequilibrium in some eastern European countries has been reduced since the war by the territorial changes resulting from the war, industrialization and mass transfers of population.

DOCUMENT 7.11: Katherine Organski and A.F.K. Organski, *Population and World Power* (New York: Alfred A. Knopf, 1961, pp. 125–126)

University of Michigan political science professor Abramo Fimo Kenneth Organski and his wife Katherine wrote extensively on population trends in the mid-twentieth century, as dramatic increases in populations of the developing world created fears of mass immigration in the developed world. In this selection from *Population and World Powers*, the Organskis provide a rational discussion of historical migration patterns.

[Modern demographers] note that the great migration of the nineteenth century left hardly a dent behind it in growing Europe. Only Ireland, a small country in dire straits, appears to have been much reduced in size by emigration. Her population shrank from more than eight million in 1841 to less than three million today. Even here, however, starvation and disease cut away part of the total, and a general practice of late marriage has helped to keep the population down.

Among the nations developing today, Puerto Rico has unquestionably benefited from a steady exit of willing migrants. Her total population has remained almost constant for the past ten years, despite the fact that Puerto Ricans are born in far greater numbers than they die.

Emigration, however, is not a very promising solution to the population problems of larger countries. For a giant nation such as India, it would require the departure of some seven million people every year just to offset natural increase—for China, perhaps 17 million each year. Despite the fears of Westerners that crowded Asian land may someday flood the West with migrants, such a likelihood is slight. It is certain that Asian governments deeply resent the immigration policies of Western nations such as the United States, Australia, and the Union of South Africa; for these policies are clearly based upon an assumption that non-Europeans are inferior and therefore undesirable. The resentment, however, stems more from insult and outrage than from any real desire to send out hordes of migrants. The overpopulated nations of today place their hopes in economic development and birth control. They do not look to solve their problems by exporting such a valuable commodity as population.

DOCUMENT 7.12: T. Lynne Smith, "The Population of Latin America," in *Population: The Vital Revolution*, ed. Ronald Freedman (Garden City, NY: Doubleday & Co., 1964, pp. 182–183)

In this essay, T. Lynne Smith details mid-twentieth-century population trends in Latin America. Historically sparsely populated, Latin America experienced notable population growth by the 1960s. This caused a great deal of concern in the United States, which would receive increasing numbers of Latin American immigrants. However, more serious problems developed within Latin American nations, where internal migration overwhelmed sprawling urban areas, as Smith describes.

Rivaling in importance the spectacular rates at which the populations of the Latin American countries are growing are the drastic changes now underway in their spatial distribution. The South American continent contains, of course, a major portion of the unused and underutilized land on earth. This land is sufficiently favored by climatic, soil, and other features to permit it, in our present stage of cultural development, to maintain large numbers of human beings. There are also extensive areas still awaiting the fructifying effects of man's efforts in Mexico and the Central American countries. Extensive portions of such countries as Brazil, Venezuela, Colombia, Peru, Bolivia, and Paraguay are almost devoid of inhabitants, and other large areas in the same countries are very sparsely populated. In many other parts of Latin America there are also other immense tracts of land fully capable of supporting large populations and still awaiting man's efforts to conquer the tropics. However, the push of settlement into virgin territory is involved only to a limited extent in the drastic changes in the distribution of population now underway in the Latin American countries. Rather, the tendency of overwhelming importance (and that which for better or worse is affecting economic and social development in all twenty of the countries under consideration) is the extreme concentration of population growth in the already densely populated areas of the various countries. Most of the population increase is accounted for by the mushrooming of existing cities and by the rapidly mounting numbers of people in extensive suburbs, or "bands of misery," which surround all of the principal urban centers.

DOCUMENT 7.13: Rasha Faris, "Population in Israel," in *Essays on the Israeli Economy*, ed. Yusuf Shibl (Beirut: Palestine Research Center, 1968, pp. 16–20)

Nowhere is the connection between population and nation more clear than in the case of Israel. For decades, Zionist writings reacted to anti-Semitic policies that attacked Jewish populations in Europe and elsewhere. The successful creation of the state of Israel in 1948 would depend on the migration and settlement of Jews from around the world. The 1967 Israeli-Palestinian conflict shifted borders, prompting population studies such as the following, which would justify either Israeli or Palestinian claims to the territory in dispute.

The Jewish population in 1948 was 765,000 . . . , making up 83% of the population, and 150,000 Arabs, or 17% of the population. This means that the Jewish population had trebled since the establishment of the state. The Arab population, on the other hand, has only doubled. It is interesting to note that the non-Jewish population has doubled only due to a high rate of natural growth, while no less than two-thirds of the increase of the Jewish population was due to the influx of immigrants. . . .

Between 1932 and 1938, following the rise of Nazi power, an economic depression in the West, and also pressure in the Middle East on Jews, due to economic hardships, 217,000 immigrants moved into Palestine. . . .

Arabs were beginning to get agitated due to this mass infiltration of Jews, and so, they revolted in the mid-thirties. The British government had to issue the white paper in 1939, limiting the number of Jewish immigrants allowed into Palestine to 15,000 per year, for the next 5 years. This policy was continued throughout World War II. . . .

The years after WW II were years of terror and fighting among Arabs, Britishers and Jews. This tense situation went on until the United Nations took its final decision of dividing up Palestine into two portions; one went to the Arabs, the other to the Jews. Hundreds of thousands of Arabs, estimated at 3/4 of a million, left the Jewish part of Palestine—especially after acts of terror in such villages as Deir Yassin, undertaken to scare the Arabs away. The flight of the Arabs was to the advantage of the Jews, who made good use of the empty homes.

8

Religion

Religions of the world have both influenced and responded to population theories for millennia. Contemporary policymakers understand the power of religious opinion, particularly in debates over birth control. While some would prefer to eliminate religion from the process, religious leaders view any consideration of matters of life and death—in this case the creation of life—as lying clearly within their boundaries.

Some of the religious discussions have limited themselves to doctrine, speaking only to followers of particular denominations. Others, however, have become quite political. Some denominational doctrine allows for, or even encourages, lobbying efforts in the political sphere, at the local, national, or international level. And where politics is concerned, numbers are important. As a result, denominations that encouraged large family size among themselves were viewed by others as gaining inordinate political strength in population politics. The following selections illustrate a few of the many religious perspectives on population.

DOCUMENT 8.1: William Falconer, M.D.F.R.S., *Remarks on the Influence of Climate, Situation, Nature of Country, Population, Nature of Food, and Way of Life, on the Disposition and Temper, Manners and Behaviour, Intellects, Laws and Customs, Form of Government, and Religion, of Mankind* **(London: C. Dilly, 1781, pp. 212–220)**

This treatise from physician and scholar William Falconer is one of many from the period to examine cultures around the globe. The gathering of such knowledge was common during the Enlightenment in the creation of comparative studies. Such studies often included rather academic discussions of religions. This was the case with Falconer, who drew connections between religion and health in his other works. In this selection, Falconer notes a relationship between population and religion, not only commenting on the beliefs of a particular group, but also on the influence religious beliefs had on attitudes toward childbearing and family.

I am inclined to believe, that a great population is apt to make the laws more severe in some instances. Thus in China idleness is a crime; and in India . . . that it was capital to lame an artificer in the hand, or to put out or blind him of an eye; which was not so penal if done to any other person. These laws originated from the necessity of universal industry in such countries. A great degree of population naturally produces a rigid and exact police. The danger of sudden disturbances and insurrections, in a populous country, both to individuals and to the state, point out the necessity of repressing them as quickly as possible. . . .

I am inclined to believe, also, that a great degree of population tends to multiply capital punishments. As the importance of each individual to the state is diminished—which is the case in a numerous society—the legislators have become more careless of their preservation, and less scrupulous in inflicting the punishment of death. Thus, in Japan, where the population is immense, several crimes are capital, which in other countries are scarcely animadverted by the laws. The increase of population also, in our own country, has probably been the principal cause of the increased severity of our penal laws, which was remarked so many years ago.—China and the East Indies are, however, exceptions to this observation; but this I take to be owing to particular circumstances. The necessity that there is in China for regularity or police, and for the insuring to every man the fruits of his labour, prevent very rigourous executions of justice; and in India, the nature of the food, of which I shall speak hereafter, inspires a disposition that is adverse to sanguinary punishments. A great degree of population has also a considerable effect upon the customs, several of which are connected with what has been before mentioned as the object of government. . . .

An excessive population, in some respects influences the religion of a country, and supersedes the disposition naturally inspired by the climate. When the numbers are increased to such a degree as in China, it becomes necessary, in order to their maintenance, to promote industry by religious, as well as political or moral precepts. There were formerly in China, as well as in the other eastern kingdoms, great numbers of monasteries of Bonzes, an idle kind of religious devotees, who contributed nothing to the public by their industry. But when the population of the country increased, it became necessary to change the genius of the religion, from one that favoured indolence, to one that encouraged activity. It was then adopted as a religious, as well as a political maxim, that if there was a man who did not work, or a woman that was idle, somebody must suffer cold and hunger in the empire. And upon this principle, a vast number of monasteries of Bonzes were destroyed.

From an attention to the maintenance of the inhabitants of a highly-populous country, religion has been even made to publish dictates inconsistent with nature and humanity. Thus the religion of the Isle of Formosa does not suffer the women to bring children into the world before they are thirty-five years old. If they are pregnant before that time, the priestess, by bruising the belly, procures abortion. . . .

A very small degree of population produces an opposite effect in most respects. I am apt to believe, that a people under such circumstances would be inclined to an indolent disposition.

DOCUMENT 8.2: George Ensor, *An Inquiry Concerning The Population of Nations: Containing A Refutation of Mr. Malthus's Essay on Population* (London: Efingham Wilson, 1818, pp. 195–196)

Public discussion of religion and sexuality has been a constant throughout the ages. Many of the examinations originate within a particular denomination, in an effort to clarify doctrine. But a good number of treatises reflect the ongoing politics of religion. Conflict between Catholics and Protestants on issues of sexuality and procreation began with the Reformation. Both religious groups expressed concern over numbers, as they vied for political strength in Europe and the rest of the world. In addition, doctrinal debate analyzed differing sexual mores. This essay by Irish political writer George Ensor exemplifies common concerns regarding the practice of celibacy.

Whatever caused the institutions of this ecclesiastical country, it is probable that celibacy enjoined by the Catholic church had no regard to restricting the numbers of the people. As polygamists, through jealousy, employ eunuchs in their harams [*sic*], and as Asiatic tyrants have used the same contemptible and envious wretches as their ministers of state,—so the papacy separated, by celibacy, its agents from all civil and kindred affections; the priests were not permitted to marry, that they might be *papists;* and monasteries, or spiritual barracks, were built and encouraged, to dissociate the spiritual soldiery from all lay intercourse. As men were subtracted from society, women were removed also, just as in India, when a husband died, a wife was burned. All these practices, though for a different purpose, checked population; and whether it will surprise Mr. Malthus or not, it increased the poor, for it increased the idle. The celibacy of any description of persons could not retard population; for society might be divided into breeders and workers, and population advance:—celibacy must be excessive; to withdraw so many as to leave insufficient breeders to support the stock. When Lorenzo de Medici, one art envoy from Cairo asking him how so few madmen were at Florence, pointed to a monastery, saying, "We shut them up in such houses," his jocularity was beneath the evil; for such houses and establishments are a bounty on the worst infatuation, which not only withdraws so many from contributing to society, but withdraws so much and so many from the state, as those monkeries and nunneries require to maintain them. Thus, if we should say that Spain had ten millions of people, of which 200,000 were of the sacred order, we should, in speaking of effectives, deduct with the 200,000 all those who contributed to their support; so that the effective force of the country, instead of ten would now be nine millions; whereas, if these 200,000 monks were citizens under a tolerable government, instead of being a reduction of power and numbers, they, on the contrary, would effectually multiply both. This sort of celibacy is pernicious to population, as it wastes produce, and makes no return. Similar, or connected with monkeries as affecting population, is the custom in Catholic countries, particularly where the law of primogeniture triumphs in its iniquity, of sending the younger females to nunneries, that they may not impair the family fortune by requiring a dowry, nor *disgrace* their family by a plebeian marriage. This is a sample of the connection of church and state. These sad sisterhoods and holy fraternities, the eulogy of Mr. Burke, have been restored by the twice restored Louis the Eighteenth:—the revolution swept away the nuisances, Louis labours to re-establish them. Yet Louis the Fifteenth passed an ordonnance directing that no religious community should receive a novice under the age of twenty-four; he should have doubled the age and thus approached the permissive years of an officiating Pythoness. I should observe that celibacy and libertinism are frequently companions; the husband of none is often the paramour of many.

DOCUMENT 8.3: G.W.F. Hegel, "Address on the Tercentenary of the Submission of the Augsburg Confession (25 June 1830)," in *Political Writings*, ed. Laurence Dickey and ed./trans. H. B. Nisbet (New York: Cambridge University Press, 1999, pp. 192–193)

In this work, Georg Wilhelm Friedrich Hegel further discusses differing views among Protestants and Catholics regarding celibacy. One of the most influential nineteenth-century German philosophers, Hegel attacks the "older Church" (the Catholic church), criticizing its attitudes toward family, civil society, and the state and defending Protestant glorification of marriage and the family.

May I . . . invite my esteemed audience to recall what the duties of human life are, and how they were attacked and indeed corrupted by the doctrine of the older Church. The duties in question are familiar to everyone: firstly, there are those which relate to the family, such as conjugal love and mutual love of parents and children, then justice, equity, and benevolence towards others, diligence and honesty in administering property, and finally the love of one's country and its rulers, which even requires us to lay down our lives in their defence. . . .

[W]e maintain and believe that those duties which relate to the family, to the commerce between human beings, and to one's country and its ruler are indeed based on the will of God, and the corresponding virtues are certainly confirmed by Christian piety . . . and should in no way be looked down on, despised or dismissed by it. But these duties and virtues are weakened and destroyed by those which the Roman Church set up as rules of sanctity and imposed on its members; and in case these should appear vague and empty words, we shall now describe the rules in question specifically.

The [Roman] Church accordingly claimed that *the unmarried state and childlessness are holier in terms of love and piety* than matrimony . . . itself. We are indeed impelled to this [matrimonial] union by nature, whereas it is characteristic of human beings to transform this impulse into a bond of love and piety. . . . We need not mention what moral abuses this rule of celibacy gave rise to, for it is well enough known that most of those clerics who were committed to sanctity of this kind, including those of the highest rank and authority, were the most licentious and openly dissolute of men.

DOCUMENT 8.4: Archibald Alison, *The Principles of Population, and Their Connection with Human Happiness* (Edinburgh: William Blackwood & Sons, 1840, vol. 1, pp. 366–368)

In this work, Archibald Alison (attorney and author of *History of Europe During the French Revolution*) attempted to explain Hindu attitudes toward childbearing and their impact on population. By this time, the British had become acutely aware of the differences between India's population and its own. Protestants of the Western world were generally having fewer children, which they sometimes explained as a character of their industriousness. India's Hindus, Alison argues, lacked industriousness and the motivation of self-sacrifice because of the caste system.

. . . The second great cause of the redundant population of India is to be found in the influence of the established religion, and the habits which superstition has formed.

All classes in India, with the exception of a few among the Bra[h]mins, are involved in the *deepest ignorance*. The obscurity in which the people are involved is not the result of negligence: it is the effect of a deliberate and deep laid scheme, on which the priests everywhere act, to keep the great body of mankind in a state of mental darkness. Their canonical books are regarded as a bequest too sacred to be committed to vulgar hands: to the greater part of the people, they are strictly forbidden, and doomed to remain in the most emphatic sense a dead letter. Few individuals are taught to read and write; and those who are can derive no useful information from their knowledge: for science has never been addressed, or adapted to the wants of mankind, and the extravagant price of manuscripts confines the information which they contain to a limited number of the higher orders.

Akin to this principle of the priesthood to keep the people in darkness for the sake of their own power, is the doctrine of passive obedience, which they inculcate as a duty of religion, and have succeeded in almost engrafting on the human mind in these unhappy regions. The Hindoo has no conception of any dignity, or importance, or respectability being attached to his situation. A consciousness of inferiority continually haunts him; and he obeys any superior authority with a promptitude which is so astonishing, as to appear rather the dictate of nature, than the result of habit. It is to this cause that the frequent and easy conquest of Hindostan is to be imputed; and to its gradual influence is to be ascribed the humble, submissive character by which they are now distinguished. In every European state, the lower classes imitate the manners, dress, and style of living of their superiors, and the desire of rising in society forms the most powerful restraint upon the principle of increase. In Hindostan this is never done: the attachment of a Hindoo to his station is equal to that to his religion itself. The desire of rising in the world; the dread of falling in society; the pride of superior condition; the consciousness of political power, which are intended to be so many restraints on the principle of increase, are prevented from developing themselves, by the slavish submission which the priests have interwoven with the Hindoo character.

The superstition of the country encourages the disposition to early marriage. Sterility is esteemed a severe misfortune, or rather a curse of the offended Deity.

All ranks are extremely solicitous to have children to perform the funeral service over them, for they conceive that this mitigates their punishment in a future state. Parents are enjoined by the precepts of religion to marry their children at their eleventh year; and if no children result from the first marriage, polygamy is allowed; and such is the anxiety for an offspring, that, if all these methods fail, it is usual to adopt a son.

DOCUMENT 8.5: Leitch Ritchie, *A History of the Oriental Nations, Chiefly Possessions of Great Britain, Comprising India, China, Australia, South Africa, and Her Other Dependencies or Connexions in the Eastern and Southern Seas, A Complete Account of Their History, Religion, Laws, Manners and Customs, Commercial Resources, &c.,* vol. 2 (London: W. H. Allen & Co., 1848, pp. 403–417)

In this selection, Scottish novelist and essayist Leitch Ritchie highlights the differences between traditional religious beliefs in the islands of the Pacific and Christianity in the nineteenth century. The piece reflects the ongoing work of missionaries in the conversion of natives around the world, and the various attitudes toward sexuality. In the case of the Sandwich Islands, Ritchie explained that Taboo created an inferior role for women, which he contended was improved through contact with Europeans. An underlying theme in Ritchie's essay is the politics of conversion. The islands serve as an example of how religious denominations competed for a majority of the population.

The appearance of human beings, growing like animals and plants on groups of islands that are often many hundred miles apart from each other, and several thousand miles from any continent, is perplexing to the imagination. The question as to whether the insular population of the Pacific came from Asia or America has excited much discussion; but the opinion which appears to be best supported by argument is, that both the latter continent and the intermediate islands were peopled from the former. . . . The people were divided into classes: first, the aristocracy or large proprietors; second, the smaller proprietors or middle classes; and third, the common people including the retainers, servants, and slaves of the others. Women were eligible to the throne, and in one respect enjoyed great liberty. Among a simple people, enjoying a heavenly climate, and a soil that yielded almost spontaneously, not only the necessaries but many of the luxuries of life, there were few questions of property to embitter the intercourse of the sexes. Polygamy to any convenient extent was permitted; and the husbands were only offended by what in another state of society would be called the profligacy of their wives when it was practiced without their sanction. . . .

The people [of the Sandwich Islands] . . . were kept in by the chain of the Taboo. One end of this chain was held by the gods, while the other was fastened round the affections, memories, hopes, fears, and habits of men. The taboo was not their religion, but the foundation of their religion; it was not their human law, but the principle which made human law divine. The taboo was the quality of *sacredness* to which the deities owed their place in heaven; the departed great their canonization; the kings and priests their infallibility; the princes and nobles their privileges; the male sex its superiority over the female. The taboo, though divine, was pliable and elastic: it had its particular and temporary, as well as its general and unchanging application. . . . The penalty of any breach of the taboo was death.

It was a great thought to cast down this taboo, to which the temples, altars, and idols were only physical accessories; but the thought grew in the brain of the great Kamehameha, and the deed was accomplished by his son. The thralldom of the taboo had weighed more especially upon the women, who were not allowed even to eat of the same meat as their masters; and, in all probability, the fair sex rose in value as the intercourse with Europeans went on, and the injustice of their treatment came to be more obvious. However this may be, it was through them that the decisive blow at the taboo was struck. . . .

The Protestant missionary rule was perhaps not well adapted to the gentle, light-hearted savages of Tahiti; and its stringency increasing with its power gave rise, it may be suspected, to much open profligacy on the one hand, and more hypocrisy on the other. The ministers are said to have interfered even with the innocent usages of society, to have usurped many of the functions of government, and to have taken advantage of their position to obtain an undue share of trade. . . .

The elements of disorder, however, were set in motion by political occurrences. The French, or rather their officers in the Pacific, were jealous of the power of Protestantism, and at length contrived to force the helpless Queen to accept of the *protection* of their flag. Their next step was to take possession of Tahiti for the crown of France . . .

The other islands, though occasionally visited by European ships, are not as yet of sufficient commercial importance—with one remarkable exception—to warrant their introduction into these pages. The Marquesas, we believe, still continue to resist the efforts of the missionaries, whether Protestant or Catholic, their wild inhabitants continuing idolators and cannibals to this day; while in the Friendly, Navigation, Hervey's, and various other groups a fair proportion of the inhabitants are already Christians.

DOCUMENT 8.6: R. Heber Newton, *Womanhood, Lectures on Woman's Work in the World* (New York: G. P. Putnam's Sons, 1881, pp. 120–121)

The women's movement that took hold in England and the United States in the mid-nineteenth century inspired a wealth of literature reminding women of their true nature. Clergy were responsible for many of the treatises, as new notions regarding gender roles and sexuality seemed to warrant religious commentary. Some of the pronouncements appeared in a presumably more official manner from the church hierarchy, but many came from the average pulpit. The following lecture by R. Heber Newton, rector of the Anthon Memorial Church in New York, is one example that uses Mary as the model for "ideal motherhood."

The ideal motherhood lifts for the world's adoration the perfect child through whom the new heavens are opening above the new earth. Eighteen centuries' retrospect of thankful, worshipful love are in the hushed look we raise to that sacred symbol. Our religion's faith reaches back to root in the story signed therein, as we worship Him who was 'born of the Virgin Mary.' Our religion's onward-looking hope springs joyously therefrom, as we see there a vision of that which is coming upon the Earth; when out of that historic motherhood in the Nazarite home, rooting through it in God, fed by its forces and patterned after its example, there shall issue upon the race, far on in the future, the ideal motherliness in actual women, and the divine humanity born therefrom in common men. The canvas glows not only with the sacred reflection of that which has been once *for* all, but, with the blessed prophecy of that which is to be *in* all—the Christ-child held in the arms, not alone of Jewish mother, but of Human Motherhood the wide world over, when every house shall be a Holy Family. The pilgrims from afar have the same story to tell as they of old, how 'when they were come into the house they saw the young child with Mary his mother,' the blessed among women, living once that she might give the holy child to the world, receiving now the honor of all who through her Son have become partakers of the divine nature, and saying silently to her sisters everywhere—Womanhood's highest vocation is to realize the holy motherhood which shall bequeath to earth the heavenly child, the Son of man who can rise to be the Son of God; womanhood's deepest homage is from those who, feeling the power of the great man in thought and action, as a salvation out of error and death, shall turn back to see the young child with his mother, and lay before her who fashioned the earth-Saviour the thankful reverence of the saved; womanhood's truest fame, the fit crown of the self-immersing love which liveth in another's being, is to be known as still is she who through the ages has been to the missions blessed through her, "the mother of Jesus."

DOCUMENT 8.7: Rev. William R. Inge, D.D., "Some Moral Aspects of Eugenics" (*Eugenics Review* 1, April 1909, pp. 26–36)

The Reverend William R. Inge, professor of divinity at Cambridge and later dean of St. Paul's Cathedral, offered some of the first public clerical support for birth control. His writings and lectures were eventually quite influential in initiating a doctrinal shift in the Lambeth Conference of Anglican Bishops (1930) toward the acceptance of contraceptive use. In this article, Inge demonstrates how eugenics appealed to some modern church spokesmen.

Since the object of all social morality is the good of the human race, and since eugenics also has no other end in view except the improvement of the human race, it is plain that social morality and eugenics are indissolubly connected. The moralist and the biologist may have a somewhat different standard of values, but they want the same thing—to make them better. They further agree in one very important principle, which distinguishes them from the advocates of some other causes and movements. The moralist and the biologist both maintain that the test of the well-being of a country is not the amount of its exports and imports, nor the diffusion of its wealth, nor its military and naval strength, nor its educational efficiency, nor its political freedom, but the kind of men and women that it turns out. Progress, for the moralist and for the biologist alike, means improvement in the people themselves, and not in their conditions. Both agree with Herbert Spencer that you cannot get golden conduct out of leaden instincts. In more homely language you cannot make a silk purse out of a sow's ear. No political machinery can prevent an aggregate of degenerate citizens form being a degenerate nation. . . .

So far, social morality and eugenics seem to be perfectly harmonious in their aims. The opportunity for discussion, and probably disagreement, first appears when we ask what types of humanity we wish to encourage, and what means we wish to employ to produce them. . . .

One general principle which I believe to be incontestable is, that if natural selection is inhibited, if nature is not allowed to take her own way of eliminating her failures, rational selection must take its place. Otherwise nothing can prevent the race from reverting to an inferior type. Humanitarian legislation, or practice, requires to be supplemented, and its inevitable evil effects counteracted, by eugenic practice, and ultimately by eugenic legislation. The need is more urgent when, as in our own country, the constitution of society favours the multiplication of the unfit and the elimination of the higher types. Among the successful classes, prudential limitation of the family, by late marriages or by other means, is the rule. . . .

The aim of Christian ethics is, quite definitely, the production of "the perfect man." (The word translated *perfect* means full-grown, complete and entire. The perfect man is the man who has realized in himself the ideal of what a man should be.) . . .

[T]he Churches must recognize that increasing knowledge has revolutionized our methods of dealing with evil. Instinct and superstition have been useful to the race in many ways; but in the higher states of culture they must give way to a far finer instrument, namely, reason. It is not Christian, it is only barbarous and mediaeval, to say that cure is right, and prevention is wrong. Be patient, my scientific friends, with us clergy, for we are the natural custodians of various race-traditions which are by no means so absurd as they often appear in our homilies; but be quite firm with us in insisting that our common enemy must be met with modern weapons, and not with the cross-bows and battle-axes for which most of us have such a sentimental affection.

DOCUMENT 8.8: John A. Ryan, *Family Limitation* (New York: Paulist Press, 1916, pp. 4–13)

While some Protestant leaders were beginning to support birth control publicly, Catholics were forced to take a stand against it. Birth control activists attacked the Catholic church as grounding its anticontraception stance in antiquated doctrine, though virtually all religious denominations officially opposed it. Monsignor John A. Ryan, director of the National Catholic Welfare Conference, was one of the first Catholic spokesmen to attack birth control publicly. But his argument addressed economics more than it did doctrine. Ryan argued that people of the working class—at whom birth control literature was directed—should not be blamed for their poverty. Ryan maintained that a fair wage would benefit working-class families more than would birth control.

Non-Catholics sometimes assume that the Church forbids family limitation by any means whatever. They seem to think that the main object of the Church in her legislation on this subject is the greatest possible increase in population. Apparently they are unaware that it is not the deliberate control of births, but the positive and unnatural means to this end that falls under the Church's condemnation. Against parents who keep their families small by chaste abstention from marital intercourse the Church has not a word to say.

That all positive methods of birth prevention (abortion and all the so-called contraceptives) are condemned by the Church as grievous sins, is evident from the long list of official declarations on the subject during the nineteenth century by the Roman Congregations. These merely reaffirm and make more precise the traditional discipline as proclaimed in Holy Scripture, and in patristic and theological literature.

What is the rational ground of this condemnation? The fact that all these devices constitute the immoral perversion of a human faculty. According to natural reason, the primary and fundamental criterion of good and bad is human nature adequately considered. Actions which are in harmony with nature are good; those which are not in harmony with nature are bad. Now, to exercise a faculty in such a way as to prevent it from attaining its natural end or object is to act contrary to nature.

The application of this principle to the subject of contraceptives is obvious. The generative faculty has as its specific and essential end the procreation of offspring. That is the object which explains and rationalizes this particular faculty. When the faculty is so used that the very use of it renders the fulfillment of its very purpose impossible, it is perverted, used unnaturally, and therefore sinfully. Such perversion of the generative faculty is on exactly the same moral level, and is wrong for precisely the same reason as the practice of the solitary vice. In either case the immorality consists in the fact that a function is performed in such a way as to frustrate its natural end. . . .

Are the great masses of underpaid laborers to be forbidden to raise their remuneration through the simple device of lowering their birth rate? Emphatically, yes. The end does not justify the intrinsically immoral means, the practice of contraception. The condition of the poorer classes would not be genuinely improved through the adoption of devices and ideals which make inevitably for egotism and materialism.

Moreover, it is not at all certain that the immediate aim, the diminution of the unskilled section of the population, would be as effective as its advocates assume. The laboring masses of France, who quite generally restrict their numbers artificially, are not so well paid as those of Germany. The excessive size of the group of unskilled laborers could be reduced to normal proportions by industrial education—to say nothing of immigration restriction—by improving their earning power instead of forbidding them to live normal family lives.

In general, the proper remedy is a better distribution of our industrial opportunities and products.

DOCUMENT 8.9: John M. Cooper, *Birth Control* (Washington, D.C.: National Catholic Welfare Council, 1923, pp. 5–7)

Following the initial writings of Ryan, John M. Cooper, professor of sociology at Catholic University of America in Washington, D.C., outlined Catholic teaching on birth control in more detail. Here, Cooper responds to a growing shift in attitudes toward marriage. Some denominations in the United States and Europe were embracing new models presented by sociologists and psychologists, who held that companionship and conjugal love should play a more prominent role than procreation. This de-emphasis of procreation allowed mainline Protestant denominations to condone contraception in marriage by the 1930s. Cooper reinforced the significance of procreation in Catholic teaching.

Marriage has a threefold purpose. First and primarily, its purpose is the begetting and rearing of children. Secondly, it fosters conjugal love and mutual helpfulness between man and wife. Thirdly, it allays the dangers of incontinence.

Promiscuous or free love relations might conceivably maintain the existence or being of the race; but its wellbeing would, under such a regime, suffer beyond description. Marriage makes for the maximum wellbeing of the race by providing maximum and permanent care by both parents in the upbringing of children; it ensures the maximum protection of the mother by the father; it pins down responsibility on the father by determining clearly who the true father is.

Marriage and parenthood are sacred. Parents are not in a figurative sense but literally the agents and representatives of God in rearing children to be worthwhile citizens of the commonwealth of man and the commonwealth of God. Their task is to train up souls for this life and for the next. Their mission is a trusteeship than which none is more exalted and sublime. The vocation of a father and of a mother is a sacrosanct and holy one, so sacred that Christ saw fit to re-consecrate marriage by raising it to the dignity of a sacrament. The Catholic Church extols virginity as holy, for those who can take it. She likewise honors parenthood as holy and sacred. And she holds aloft both ideals in her reverence for and devotion to Mary, Virgin and Mother.

Time and again, in the history of Christianity, heretical groups have maintained that marriage is unlawful, and that the exercise of marital relations and the begetting of children thereby is sinful. The Church has consistently condemned in the strongest terms this suicidal position. Sexual intercourse within the marriage union is the means divinely established for the propagation of the race. But such intercourse outside the marriage union strikes a deadly blow at all three values that marriage protects and that promiscuous mating would utterly blast. For extra-marital intercourse tends to bring children into the world without definite determination of paternity and paternal responsibility.

Within, however, the marital union, intercourse is not only lawful. It is divinely planned and sanctioned. The vague feeling sometimes met with that even within the marriage union such relations are indecent, or little short of sinful, or only reluctantly tolerated by morality, is an outgrowth of various causes. This feeling is in no sense an outgrowth of Catholic teaching, and it can find no shadow of support therein. . . .

The Catholic position on the limitation of offspring is frequently misinterpreted by non-Catholics and sometimes misunderstood by Catholics themselves. It does not hold that married couples are under obligation to bring into the world the maximum number of children, to exercise no foresight or prudence, to bear offspring up to the limit of physiological fertility, to labor for the maximum increase of the population, to bring on "an avalanche of babies"—all regardless alike of circumstances and consequences. It holds no brief for imprudence or intemperance. It does emphatically stand for marital chastity against artificial prevention of conception.

DOCUMENT 8.10: M. K. Gandhi, "Birth Control" (*Young India: A Weekly Journal 7*, March 12, 1925, pp. 88–89)

India drew a great deal of attention from birth control activists, who saw overpopulation as an international problem. The introduction of birth control literature invoked a response from Indian nationalist Mohandas Karamchand Gandhi. In the following column published in his magazine *Young India*, Gandhi opposed artificial means of birth control. He instead recommended the traditional Hindu practice of self-control.

There can be no two opinions about the necessity of birth control. But the only method handed down from ages past is self-control, or *Brahmacharya*. It is an infallible sovereign remedy doing good to those who practice it. And medical men will earn the gratitude of mankind, if instead of devising artificial means of birth control they will find out the means of self-control. The union is meant not for pleasure but for bringing forth progeny. And union is a crime when the desire for progeny is absent.

Artificial methods are like putting a premium upon vice. They make man and woman reckless. And respectability that is being given to the methods must hasten the dissolution of the restraints that public opinion puts upon one. Adoption of artificial methods must result in imbecility and nervous prostration. The remedy will be found to be worse than the disease. It is wrong and immoral to seek to escape the consequences of one's acts. It is good for a person who overeats to have an ache and a fast. It is bad for him to indulge his appetite and then escape the consequences by taking tonics or other medicine. It is still worse for a person to indulge in his animal passions and escape the consequences of his acts. Nature is relentless and will have full revenge for any such violation of her laws. Moral results can only be produced by moral restraints. All other restraints defeat the very purpose for which they are intended. The reasoning underlying the use of artificial methods is that indulgence is a necessity of life. Nothing can be more fallacious. Let those who are eager to see the births regulated explore the lawful means devised by the ancients and try to find out how they can be revived. An enormous amount of spade-work lies in front of them. Early marriages are a fruitful source of adding to the population. The present mode of life has also a great deal to do with the evil of unchecked procreation. If these causes are investigated and dealt with, society will be morally elevated. If they are ignored by impatient zealots and if artificial methods become the order of the day, nothing but moral degradation can be the result. A society that has already become enervated through a variety of causes will become still further enervated by the adoption of artificial methods. Those men therefore who are light-heartedly advocating artificial methods cannot do better than study the subject afresh, stay their injurious activity and popularize *Brahmacharya* both for the married and the unmarried. That is the only noble and straight method of birth control.

Document 8.11: M. K. Gandhi, "Some Arguments Considered" (*Young India: A Weekly Journal* 7, April 2, 1925, p. 118)

Gandhi received numerous responses to his column, particularly from those who supported artificial means. In a subsequent issue of his journal, he answered his critics.

If it is contended that birth control is necessary for the nation because of over-population, I dispute the proposition. It has never been proved. In my opinion, by a proper land system, better agriculture and a supplementary industry this country is capable of supporting twice as many people as there are in it today. But I have joined hands with the advocates of birth control in India from the standpoint of the present political condition of the country.

I do suggest that men must cease to indulge their animal passions after the need for progeny has ceased. The remedy of self-control can be made popular and effective. It has never had a trial with the educated class. That class has not yet, thanks to the joint family system, felt the pressure. Those that have, have not given a thought to the moral issues involved in the question. Save for stray lectures on *Brahmacharya* no systematic propaganda has been carried for advocating self-control for the definite purpose of limiting progeny. On the contrary the superstition of a larger family being an auspicious thing and therefore desirable still persists. Religious teachers do not generally teach that restriction of progeny in given circumstances is as much a religious obligation as procreation may be under certain other circumstances.

I am afraid that advocates of birth control take it for granted that indulgence in animal passion is a necessity of life and in itself a desirable thing. The solicitude shown for the fair sex is most pathetic. In my opinion it is an insult to the fair sex to put up her case in support of birth control by artificial methods. As it is, man has sufficiently degraded her for his lust, and artificial methods, no matter how well meaning the advocates may be, will still further degrade her. I know that there are modern women who advocate these methods. But I have little doubt that the vast majority of women will reject them as inconsistent with their dignity. If man means well by her, let him exercise control over himself. It is not she who tempts. In reality man being the aggressor is the real culprit and the tempter.

I urge the advocates of artificial methods to consider the consequences. Any large use of the methods is likely to result in the dissolution of the marriage bond and in free love. If a man may indulge in animal passion for the sake of it, what is he to do whilst he is, say, away from his home for any length of time or when he is engaged as a soldier in a protracted war or when he is widowed or when his wife is too ill to permit him the indulgence without injury to her health notwithstanding the use of artificial methods?

DOCUMENT 8.12: Stephen Wise, "The Synagogue and Birth Control," in *Religious and Ethical Aspects of Birth Control*, ed. Margaret Sanger (New York: American Birth Control League, Inc., 1926, pp. 33–35)

Reform rabbi and leader of the Zionist movement Stephen Wise offered early Jewish support for artificial contraception and lectured often at birth control conferences. In this presentation, given at the Sixth International Neo-Malthusian and Birth Control Conference in New York City in 1925, Wise, though not an official spokesman for Judaism, notes the differences in birth control positions among Jews. By the 1930s, Reform rabbis had condoned contraceptive use—in opposition to their Conservative and Orthodox counterparts.

You know that there is a great deal of misunderstanding, even by teachers of religion, with regard to the things that are commended or condemned by the Bible. For example, there will never be a time when the Chambers of Minneapolis and Salt Lake City will not insist that poverty can never be abolished from the world; because Jesus said, "The poor ye have with you always." Well, there are two things to be said about that, either that Jesus was vastly and tragically mistaken, or (and this is my own hypothesis) that Jesus was stating a lamentable fact, rather than indulging in a glorious prophecy. Jesus was too great and perfect a humanitarian to assent to the notion that poverty was inextinguishable, that it was indestructible. He looked around him and he saw that poverty was—that poverty is—"The poor ye have with you always." Had Jesus been asked, "Must this always be so? Will the poor always be suffered to perish from the earth?" if I understand the mind of Jesus, he would have said, he must have said, something such as this: "No, the day will come when in obedience to the will of God, you will find a way of ending the sin of poverty in the world."

In our Jewish faith, or rather among the members of the household of Israel, I think it is true from one point of view that there has been a less critical and urgent need for the acceptance of the teaching of Birth Control than among some other groups. I am not prepared to say that a child born a Jew is more viable, more nearly viable, than a child born to non-Jews: but it is true that Jewish mothers, and only mothers (the only parents children have) did what they could, perhaps in some more effective way than any other group of mothers that I know, to insure the advantage of that viability which is the endowment of a child. Of course you know what the figures are with respect to the death rate among children in two squares in the East End of London. The death rate among the children of the poor, the Jewish poor in London, is distinctly and quite indubitably lower than the death rate among non-Jewish children, very largely because, whether Jewish mothers are members of Birth Control societies or not, they have some understanding of the significance, of the supreme significance of it; and again because I think that Jewish parents, among the poor and only the poor, perhaps the lower middle class, as some of you English folks say, give themselves utterly to the physical, mental and spiritual well-being of their children.

The one thing that I mean to say this afternoon, I can say in just one word. I believe in the teachings and I believe in the practice of Birth Control. I am not a fanatical believer—that the Messianic reign will dawn when Birth Control is universally accepted. I ought to make that reservation (I am saying, of course, the things that I believe, not that you believe), because, frankly, I think of Birth Control as an item, an important item, but just an item in the eugenic program. I think it is supremely important as an item in the eugenic program, and the eugenic program is not Messianic. It again is an item, a very important item in a still larger program, and that larger program for me means this: The translation of the ideals of human justice and human decency and human brotherliness in the life of the world. That is all. But without a eugenic program we shall not have the beginning, let alone the end of the realization of the social programs of which we are dreaming, and Birth Control, I repeat, is the fundamental, primary element or item in the eugenic program. . . .

DOCUMENT 8.13: John Rock, M.D., *The Time Has Come: A Catholic Doctor's Proposals to End the Battle over Birth Control* (New York: Alfred A. Knopf, 1963, pp. 168–170)

Catholic physician John Rock confronted Church teaching on birth control during the 1960s. The sexual revolution was presenting the Church with new challenges, and the reforms initiated by the Second Vatican Council suggested that the Church might be open to change on the topic of contraception. In addition, the introduction of the birth control pill called into question the nature of the Church's position. In its condemnation of contraception in previous decades, the Church had drawn the line at so-called artificial barriers. Oral contraceptives, Rock argued, did not act as an artificial barrier.

The steroid compounds are the first *physiologic* means of contraception; that is, they prevent reproduction by modifying the time sequences in the body's own functions, rather than by use of an extraneous device or by a wholly artificial chemical action. In the decade during which I have been associated with the development of these compounds, it has been my consistent feeling that, when properly used for conception control, they merely serve as adjuncts to nature, but the Catholic moralists who thus far expressed themselves publicly on the subject certainly do not share my belief. . . .

[T]he rhythm method, which is sanctioned by the Church, depends precisely on the secretion of progesterone from the ovaries, which action these compounds merely duplicate. It is the progesterone, in the healthy woman, that prevents ovulation and establishes the pre- and post-menstrual "safe period." The physiology underlying the spontaneous "safe period" is identical to that initiated by the steroid compounds and is equally harmless to the individual. Indeed, the use of the compounds for fertility control may be characterized as a "pill-established safe period" and would seem to carry the same moral implications. . . .

They merely offer to the human intellect the means to regulate ovulation harmlessly. . . . Indeed, the serious consideration of medical, eugenic, economic, and social indications for family limitation which Pius XII stipulated in his allocution to midwives can be undertaken only by the intellect. It is difficult not to believe that God gave man his intellect to safeguard him whenever his inner biology is inadequate. One might even tend to think it immoral for husband and wife, aware of the indications Pius XII listed, to reject their God-given intellect and trust only to the automatic action of female sex glands or to their ability to suppress the powerful love urge which their Creator fused with their sex instinct.

DOCUMENT 8.14: Pope Paul VI, *Humanae Vitae (On the Regulation of Birth)*, encyclical letter, July 25, 1968 (Washington, D.C.: United States Catholic Conference Publishing Services, 1968, pp. 7–9)

> The death of the considerably liberal Pope John XXIII brought to an end any hopes of relaxation of Church teaching on birth control. The conservative Pope Paul VI reinforced the Church's opposition to contraception in his 1968 encyclical *Humanae Vitae*. The encyclical has come to be considered the consummate statement of official Catholic birth control doctrine. Section 14 prohibits abortion, sterilization, and the use of artificial barriers and the pill.

God has wisely disposed natural laws and rhythms of fecundity which, of themselves, cause a separation in the succession of births. Nonetheless the Church, calling men back to the observance of the norms of the natural law, as interpreted by their constant doctrine, teaches that each and every marriage act (*quilibet matrimonii usus*) must remain open to the transmission of life.

12. That teaching, often set forth by the magisterium, is founded upon the inseparable connection, willed by God and unable to be broken by man on his own initiative, between the two meanings of the conjugal act: the unitive meaning and the procreative meaning. Indeed, by its intimate structure, the conjugal act, while most closely uniting husband and wife, capacitates them for the generation of new lives, according to laws inscribed in the very being of man and of woman. By safeguarding both these essential aspects, the unitive and the procreative, the conjugal act preserves in its fullness the sense of true mutual love and its ordination towards man's most high calling to parenthood. We believe that the men of our day are particularly capable of seizing the deeply reasonable and human character of this fundamental principle.

13. It is in fact justly observed that a conjugal act imposed upon one's partner without regard for his or her condition and lawful desires is not a true act of love, and therefore denies an exigency of right moral order in the relationships between husband and wife. Likewise, if they consider the matter, they must admit that an act of mutual love which is detrimental to the faculty of propagating life, which God the Creator of all has implanted in it according to special laws, is in contradiction to both the divine plan, according to whose norm matrimony has been instituted, and the will of the Author of human life. To use this divine gift destroying, even if only partially, its meaning and its purpose is to contradict the nature both of man and of woman and of their most intimate relationship, and therefore it is to contradict also the plan of God and His will. On the other hand, to make use of the gift of conjugal love while respecting the laws of the generative process means to acknowledge oneself not to be the arbiter of the sources of human life, but rather the minister of the design established by the Creator. In fact, just as man does not have unlimited dominion over his body in

general, so also, with particular reason, he has no such dominion over his generative faculties as such, because of their intrinsic ordination towards raising up life, of which God is the principle. "Human life is sacred," Pope John XXIII recalled; "from its very inception it reveals the creating hand of God."

14. In conformity with these landmarks in the human and Christian vision of marriage, we must once again declare that the direct interruption of the generative process already begun and, above all, directly willed and procured abortion, even if for therapeutic reasons, are to be absolutely excluded as licit means of regulating birth.

Equally to be excluded, as the teaching authority of the Church has frequently declared, is direct sterilization, whether perpetual or temporary, whether of the man or of the woman. Similarly excluded is every action which, either in anticipation of the conjugal act, or in its accomplishment, or in the development of its natural consequences, proposes, whether as an end or as a means, to render procreation impossible.

DOCUMENT 8.15: Nigel M. de S. Cameron, "Cairo's Wake-up Call" (*Christianity Today* 38, October 24, 1994, pp. 20–21)

Throughout the twentieth century, the Catholic church was perceived as the enemy of birth control, and many assumed it acted as the only religious opposition. However, various denominations continued to prohibit contraceptive use. Here, Nigel M. de S. Cameron, associate dean for academic doctoral programs at Trinity Evangelical Divinity School in Deerfield, Illinois, and editor of *Ethics and Medicine*, highlights some elements of the evangelical Protestant stand in an article published in *Christianity Today*. He is responding to the outcome of the United Nations Population Conference held in Cairo in 1994. That conference marked a historical turning away from unchecked international funding of family planning programs that served the interests of wealthier nations.

[T]he global question [is]: Is population growth a problem? . . . We were told that Thomas Malthus, the doomsday demographer of two centuries ago, was basically right: population growth would outstrip our ability to feed ourselves. . . .

In fact, food production has grown faster than population. Human ingenuity has not run out of steam. . . .

Second, we have the micro questions for us and our families—the Bible questions: Does "go forth and multiply" give us any alternative? To what extent is contraception a Christian option? The point has often been made that the Genesis command is to fill, not overfill, the earth. But since the first argument is focused on the capacity of the earth, that does not really help. . . .

The third set of questions run broader. The social and sexual ethics of Cairo is that of the liberal Western elite, for whom "satisfying" sex lives (meaning, "what I find satisfying") have become a human right, for whom "couples" have replaced marriages, and above all, for whom the only norm of family life is that there is none. . . . The continuing dominance of the West gives inordinate opportunity to its cultural elite to shape the values of the world in its own post-

Christian image. These secular missionaries, despite all their talk of pluralism and respect for aboriginal cultures, are hell-bent on spreading such blessings as adolescent sexual liberation and, of course, abortion packaged with other "reproductive rights."

Which, finally, raises the question of evangelical involvement in public policy. The amazing growth and culture-defying survival of postwar evangelicalism has borne little fruit in the public life of our nation. It was the Vatican, with Islamic support, [that] went toe-to-toe with the U.N.-U.S. at Cairo, and praise God they did.

DOCUMENT 8.16: Rita M. Gross, "Buddhist Resources for Issues of Population, Consumption, and the Environment," in *Population, Consumption, and the Environment: Religious and Secular Responses*, ed. Harold Coward (Albany: State University of New York Press, 1995, p. 167)

> Comparatively little literature exists that explores religious teachings on birth control outside of Western culture. This does not suggest that non-Western religions are not interested in matters of birth control. Rather, the absence of literature mirrors the absence of these religions from the public debate. The following selection provides some rare insight into Buddhist teachings on procreation.

[F]or reproduction to be a valid Buddhist choice and alternative lifestyle, it must be motivated by Buddhist principles of egolessness, detachment, compassion, and *bodhisattva* practice, not by social and religious demands, conventional norms and habits, compulsive desires, biological clocks, or an ego-based desire to perpetuate oneself. I also believe that such detached and compassionate motivations for parenthood are fully possible, though not anywhere nearly as common as is parenthood. In my own work as a Buddhist feminist theologian, I have also consistently stressed the need to limit both biological reproduction and economic production, as well as to share those burdens and responsibilities equitably between men and women so that meaningful lay Buddhist practice can occur.

The lifestyle that promotes the attainment of detachment, the Middle Way, wisdom, compassion, and the development of *bodhicitta* is encouraged and valued by Buddhists. Therefore, in many Buddhist countries, celibate monasticism is preferred over reproductive lifestyles. Though the Buddhist record is far from perfect, in many, but not all Buddhist societies, this option is also available to women, who are no more regarded as fulfilled through childbearing than men are regarded as fulfilled through impregnating. In much of the contemporary Buddhist world, lifelong monasticism is less popular and less viable, but the movement toward serious lay Buddhist meditation practice is growing dramatically, not only among Western Buddhists, but also in Asia, not only among laymen, but also among laywomen. Serious Buddhist meditation practice is difficult and time-consuming. When lay people become engaged in such practices, they must limit both their economic and their reproductive activities appropriately. Thus, both excessive consumption and overpopulation, the twin destructive agents rampant in the world, can be curbed at the same time by coming to value the human potential for enlightened wisdom and compassion and striving to realize them.

9

Children and Family

Notions of children and family are unequivocally linked to population. In societies where children were valued and large family size was a sign of status, populations thrived. Where population growth was desired, social mores encouraging procreation flourished.

Though the direct correlations still remain unexplained, industrialization generally has resulted in smaller family size. Agricultural economies for the most part depended on larger families, as children's labor proved valuable. In turn, a man's prosperity was evident in the number of acres of land and cattle he owned and in the number of children he had. Industrialization made children less valuable, especially after passage of legislation that prevented child labor in the factories. However, industrial societies eventually placed a different emphasis on children, as focus shifted from childbearing to child rearing.

Where infant mortality rates decreased, parents could assume that a greater percentage of their offspring would survive into adulthood, and the concept of procreation changed. In turn, the concept of marriage changed, as couples were urged to expect satisfaction from love and companionship in addition to parenthood. Outside western Europe and the United States, ideas of children and family remained more traditional, well into the twentieth century. In the developing world, a culture of family continued to promote childbearing, confronting notions of modernity accepted among population policymakers.

DOCUMENT 9.1: John Cowan, M.D., *The Science of a New Life* **(New York: J. S. Ogilvie & Co., 1869, pp. 131–133)**

In the following selection, physician John Cowan responds to the growing trend of limiting family size. Social scientists proclaimed the benefits of having fewer children, placing greater importance on child rearing. For economic and other reasons, couples were choosing to have fewer children.

Cowan's essay condemns birth control by proclaiming the glories of parent-hood. He advocated voluntary abstinence for married couples, except for the purpose of procreation.

It is absolutely essential to the perfect union of a man and woman that they be endowed with large parental love—the desire for and love of children; for if they possess not this requisite, it is next to needless for them to marry. The command to "increase and multiply" should be obeyed only in a pure and loving spirit. The originating of children in God's own image should be an intensely active, loving desire on the part of both man and wife. The non-observance of this requirement is the underlying cause of the dislike for offspring—a dislike that is observable among the higher and especially the wealthier classes. It is the underlying cause for the so-called trouble in rearing children; for when they are not propagated under right conditions, how can any sane parent imagine they can be reared under right conditions? Children can as easily be brought into the world with happy, sunny, laughing natures, as with cross, fretful, irri-table natures.

It is a practice to be greatly deplored, this aversion on the part of intelligent, educated and wealthy people to having large families; for they could, if their thoughts and actions were rightly directed, do much toward peopling the earth with a better and nobler class of beings. As it is, what a pitiable sight! A hus-band and wife, educated and surrounded with all that wealth can command, with one or two pale, sickly children, the result of perhaps a ten or twenty years' union. And this dislike for rearing children is infecting the middle and lower classes, and the effects can be distinctly observed in many localities on this broad continent. . . .

A married life without children is an unlovable and unsatisfactory life. It is incomplete. It lacks the bands that make perfect the love-union between man and wife—the new birth, that makes the twain as one in flesh and spirit. But this incompleteness continues, is widened and confirmed, when the new birth is undesired by either party.

Men and women do not reach their true status in this world—do not fulfill their mission to populate—do not attain the full royalty of their natures, until they originate and rear a child; and in proportion to the number of children they rear is the royalty of their souls perfected . . .

DOCUMENT 9.2: Emmet Densmore, M.D., *Sex Equality: A Solution of the Woman Problem,* 2nd ed. (London: Swan Sonnenschein & Co., Ltd., 1907, pp. 365–368)

Emmet Densmore, author of *The Natural Food of Man, How Nature Cures,* and *Consumption and Chronic Diseases,* takes a considerably modern approach to gender roles and parenthood in the following selection. While nineteenth-century industrial society had placed the lives of men and women into separate spheres, the modern woman sought to participate in areas denied to her. To Densmore, this was an admirable goal, but one which would be more easily attained through limiting family size.

How can the woman of the future become the fit and equal partner of the future man if she is doomed to a life by which her brain must retain qualities of immaturity? If exclusion from industrial and intellectual activities necessarily causes immaturity and deterioration of power; if the penalties for disuse of brain and muscle are stagnation and misery; and if the woman of the future is to be man's equal partner, have we not a sure promise that any custom which interferes with woman's industrial and intellectual activities is destined to be done away with?

. . . Even under the restricted conditions which have prevailed in civilization, large numbers of women who have borne and successfully reared children have at the same time become eminent in intellectual and artistic pursuits. It is the teaching of science that the natural life of an animal is six times the period necessary for its growth, and by this computation the normal life of man is from one hundred to one hundred and twenty years. When the earth has become fully peopled and man has learned to live in obedience to physiological law, approximately all the children that one woman will need to produce are the two necessary to replace their parents. Thus, there would be eighty to one hundred years of adult life to each individual, and it is clear that two children, or even three, would be no appreciable handicap to the women who are moved to engage in intellectual and industrial pursuits.

If human matehood and companionship be the highest expression of life, and not the "dream of an enthusiast," there is no reason why the enlightened father should not take an active and effective interest in the uprearing of the children; and when he does this, there will be all the more time for the woman to companion the man in life's various activities.

DOCUMENT 9.3: William J. Robinson, M.D., *Eugenics, Marriage and Birth Control* (New York: The Critic and Guide Co., 1917, pp. 18–20)

Dr. William J. Robinson prefaced his work by stating, "No book has a right to exist that has not for its purpose the betterment of mankind, by affording either useful introduction or healthful recreation." A noted supporter of eugenics, Robinson was among the first to write openly in support of birth control. He published a number of books on sexuality and the prevention of conception before producing the work from which this passage is drawn, *Eugenics, Marriage and Birth Control*, in which he considers the responsibility of parents in producing quality children.

. . . [H]ere is a summary of my reasons why I so persistently advocate teaching the people the use of means of prevention, and why I consider this knowledge of such vital importance. My reasons are:

1. Because I know of thousands of families who would be perfectly happy if they only knew the proper method of regulating the number of their offspring.
2. Because I know thousands of young men who would be glad and happy to get married, but are restrained from doing so by the fear of *too many* children.

3. Because I know of thousands of young men who, restrained from marrying by fear of too many children, have in consequence contracted venereal disease or have become addicted to dangerous sexual irregularities.

4. Because I know of thousands of women who have become chronically invalided by too frequent childbearing and lactation.

5. Because I know of thousands of women who have become incurable invalids by *improper* attempts at prevention.

6. Because I know of thousands of men who are pitiable sexual neurasthenics from coitus interruptus, which they practice thru ignorance of better methods of prevention.

7. Because I know of thousands of women who have actually killed themselves, have been driven into early graves by abortions or attempts at abortions.

8. Because I know of thousands of children whose education has been neglected, who have been improperly brought up on account of the mother's inability to attend to too many.

9. Because I know of thousands of children who, born by their mothers unwillingly, in anguish and in anger, were born mentally and physically below par, only to be a burden to themselves and to others.

10. Because I know of thousands of children, born of epileptic, syphilitic or tuberculous parents, who should not have been born at all, because they came into life handicapped, had to fight against severe odds, lived a poor life and died an early death.

11. Because I know of many other things which on account of our prudery cannot be spoken of, but which cause boundless misery to men, women and children; and this unnecessary misery will disappear only when the people have learned the proper method of regulating the number of their offspring.

12. Because human beings are not animals, and they should have a right to say how many children they will have, how frequently they will have them and when they will have them.

DOCUMENT 9.4: Theodore Roosevelt, *The Foes of Our Own Household* (New York: George H. Doran Co., 1917, pp. 250–264)

Theodore Roosevelt was well known for the bold domestic and foreign policies that he carried out as president of the United States. But he also took stands on issues of the family. Presenting his positions as part of his Progressive philosophy, Roosevelt portrayed responsible parenthood as fundamental to a strong society and a strong nation. He especially criticized the practice of birth control, which he feared would contribute to so-called race suicide among those valued as good stock. He reported that, by comparison, the lesser stock might increase disproportionately, and recommended that women of the middle and upper classes have more children. He was the father of six children.

Reforms are excellent, but if there is nobody to reform, their value becomes somewhat problematical. In order to make a man into a better citizen, we must first have the man. In order that there shall be a "fuller and better expressed life for the average woman," that average woman must be in actual existence. And the first necessity in "bringing up the child aright" is to produce the child.

Stated in the abstract, these propositions are of bromidic triteness. But an astonishingly large number of persons, including a lamentably large number who call themselves social reformers, either are, or act as if they were, utterly blind to them when they try to deal with life in the concrete. This is true of every group of persons who treat Bernard Shaw seriously as a social reformer. It is true of every group of reformers who discuss the home and the school, but regard it as indelicate to lay stress on the fact that neither is worth discussing unless there are children in sufficient numbers to make the home and the school worth perpetuating. It is true of all blatant sham reformers who, in the name of a new morality, preach the old, old vice and self-indulgence which rotted out first the moral fiber and then even the external greatness of Greece and Rome. It is true of the possibly well-meaning but certainly silly persons who fail to see that we merely enunciate a perfectly plain mathematical truth when we say that the race will die out unless the average family contains at least three children, and therefore that less than this number always means that, whether because of their fault or their misfortune, the parents are bearing less than their share of the common burdens, and are rendering less than their due proportion of patriotic service to the nation. . . .

Under any circumstances an average of one or two children means rapid race suicide, and therefore profound moral delinquency in those willfully responsible for it. But this is not all! At present whoever has only three children must be understood to represent a slight drag on the forward movement of the nation, a slight falling below the average necessary standard in the performance of the indispensable duty without which there will in the end be no nation; the duty, failure to perform which means that all talk of eugenics and social reform and moral uplift and self-development represents mere empty threshing of the air, as pointless as similar talk by a suicide. . . .

We are dealing with rules, not with exceptions. We are discussing the birthrate in any given community, just as we discuss the ability of a community in time of war to provide soldiers for the nation's safety. In any small group of men it may happen that, for good and sufficient reasons, it is impossible for any of the members to go to war: two or three may be physically unfit, two or three may be too old or too young, and the remaining two or three may be performing civil duties of such vital consequence to the commonwealth that it would be wrong to send them to the Front. In such case no blame attaches to any individual, and high praise may attach to all. But if in a group of a thousand men more than a small minority are unwilling and unfit to go to war in the hour of the nation's need, then there is something radically wrong with them, spiritually or physically, and they stand in need of drastic treatment. So it is as regards marriage and children. In a small group there may be good and sufficient explanations why the individual men and women have remained unmarried; and the fact that those that marry have no children, or only one or two children, may be cause only for sincere and respectful sympathy. But if, in a community of a thousand men and a thousand women, a large proportion of them remain unmarried, and if of the marriages so many are sterile, or with only one or two children, that the population is decreasing, then there is something radically wrong with the people of that community as a whole. The trouble may be partly physical, partly due to the strange troubles which accompany an over-strained intensity of life. But even in this case the root trouble is probably moral; and in all probability the whole trouble is moral, and is due to a complex tissue of causation in which coldness, love of ease, striving after social position, fear of pain, dislike of hard work and sheer inability to get life values in their proper perspective all play a part.

The fundamental instincts are not only the basic but also the loftiest instincts in human nature. The qualities that make men and women eager lovers, faithful, duty-performing, hard-working husbands and wives, and wise and devoted fathers and mothers stand at the foundations of all possible social welfare, and also represent the loftiest heights of human happiness and usefulness. No other form of personal success and happiness or of individual service to the state compares with that which is represented by the love of the one man for the one woman, of their joint work as home-maker and home-keeper, and of their ability to bring up the children that are theirs.

DOCUMENT 9.5: Paul Popenoe, *Modern Marriage* (New York: Grosset & Dunlap, 1925, pp. 175–177)

Paul Popenoe wrote extensively on population and the family. In the first selection presented here, taken from his book *Modern Marriage*, Popenoe's encouragement of parenthood appears limitless. However, in the second selection, from his book *The Child's Heredity* (Document 9.6), Popenoe gives a somewhat darker view. A proponent of eugenics and editor of the *Journal of Heredity*, Popenoe warned of the importance of good breeding.

The production of children is the goal of all life. From their offspring the parents derive tremendous advantages that they can get *in no other way*. Normal human beings do not have to be urged to have children, any more than they have to be urged to marry. Nevertheless, an examination of some of the reasons why the little ones fill the place they do in the human heart will make for clear thinking. In addition to the satisfaction of whatever pure instincts may be bound up with child-bearing, progeny are valued for such reasons as the following:

1. They give a unique experience and education to the parents. It is impossible to appreciate the extent and nature of this at second had: it must be felt. Man's personality and character (as well as woman's) is an incomplete—hopelessly and pathetically incomplete—thing unless it has included the joys, and the occasional sorrows, of bringing up a family of children. "Some, indeed," says John M. Cooper, "break under the test and training, but they are the exceptions. How frequently, in the case of the newly married couples, particularly after the birth of their first child, do we see the vital change that comes over both husband and wife—a putting away of the trivial and weakly sentimental, a deepening and enriching of the finer sentiments, a sobering sense of marital and parental responsibility, even the painted doll often grows into a woman and the callow stripling into a man."

2. They bind the parents together. Not only do husband and wife, separately, benefit from their children; but their community life is enriched and deepened as is possible in no other way.

3. They bring rejuvenation. Watching the development of his child, sharing its experiences, its pleasures and pains, the parent lives over again, in memory and imagination, his own boyhood. This process is normally repeated a second time, with his grandchildren. The best way to remain young is to live with children.

4. They give love in old age. One of the saddest things in life—so those say who are old enough to know—is to see one's friends gradually passing away, leaving one isolated, with none to care. This progressive bereavement, which casts a shadow over one's declining years, is safeguarded against only by a family of children, whose love and comradeship are dependable so long as life endures.

5. They give assistance in old age. No one anticipates being supported by his children in the future; nevertheless it is impossible to foresee the revolutions of the wheel of fortune, and those who have healthy and capable progeny never need fear to be left alone, friendless and impoverished, as a public charge.

6. They confer immortality—potentially at least. As to the continuation of personal existence after death, no one knows: it is a matter of belief, and each is entitled to believe what he finds most plausible and comforting. The only immortality of which one can speak with confidence is that derived from the continuation of the chain of life through one's offspring.

DOCUMENT 9.6: Paul Popenoe, *The Child's Heredity* (Baltimore: Williams & Wilkins Co., 1929, pp. 21–22)

Those who, for emotional reasons, believe in the literal equality of all men, often point to the fact that the child is heir of the whole race as evidence that all children must be born alike, and that any child with proper education can be made just like any other child,—the best or the worst of his kind, depending merely on the skill of the pedagogue.

Such an idea reflects a gross ignorance of the elementary facts of heredity.

So far as the fundamental traits go, it is true that every child possesses the possibility, if not the certainty, of developing them. Broadly speaking, every child is born with the possibility of having hair on his head.

But whether it shall be red, white, or black hair is a different question, the answer to which depends not on his remote ancestors who lived in the trees, but on his more recent ancestors who lived in Scotland, or Finland, or Bechuanaland, as the case might be.

It is not far wrong to say that the fundamental resemblances among men go back to the germ-plasm of the remote ancestry, which all share alike; the differences among men are mostly due to the germ-plasm of the more recent ancestry, which no two share alike—not even full brothers or full sisters, for the reasons pointed out in the discussion of the cell reduction division. . . .

And it is the differences in men that account for their differences in achievement.

If a man were breeding live-stock, he would never dream of following the equalitarian doctrine. . . .

What holds true of the influence of immediate ancestry in livestock holds equally true in man.

DOCUMENT 9.7: "The Children's Charter" (White House Conference on Child Health and Protection, 1931)

At the turn of the twentieth century, governments of western European nations and the United States implemented various programs intended to protect the health and welfare of women, infants, and children. At the onset of the Great Depression, there was some fear that governments could not afford to fund the programs. This selection from the Children's Charter of 1931 demonstrates the U.S. government's plan to continue support. Though intended for the United States, documents such as this would influence future legislation designed to protect the lives of women and children around the globe. Eventually, international population programs would be designed accordingly, attempting to meet expectations for global health and welfare.

III For every child a home and that security which a home provides; and for that child who must receive foster care, the nearest substitute for his own home

IV For every child full preparation for his birth, his mother receiving prenatal, natal, and postnatal care; and the establishment of such protective measures as will make child-bearing safer

V For every child health protection from birth through adolescence, including: periodical health examinations and, where needed, care of specialists and hospital treatment; regular dental examinations and care of the teeth; protective and preventive measures against communicable diseases; the insuring of pure food, pure milk, and pure water

VI For every child from birth through adolescence, promotion of health, including health instruction and a health program, wholesome physical and mental recreation, with teachers and leaders adequately trained

VII For every child a dwelling place safe, sanitary, and wholesome, with reasonable provisions for privacy, free from conditions which tend to thwart his development; and a home environment harmonious and enriching. . . .

IX For every child a community which recognizes and plans for his needs, protects him against physical dangers, moral hazards, and disease; provides him with safe and wholesome places for play and recreation; and makes provision for his cultural and social needs

X For every child an education which, through the discovery and development of his individual abilities, prepares him for life and through training and vocational guidance prepares him for a living which will yield him the maximum of satisfaction

XI For every child such teaching and training as will prepare him for successful parenthood, homemaking, and the rights of citizenship; and, for parents, supplementary training to fit them to deal wisely with the problems of parenthood. . . .

DOCUMENT 9.8: Ernest R. Groves, *Marriage* (New York: Henry Holt & Co., 1933, pp. 353–354)

Ernest R. Groves, professor of sociology at the University of North Carolina, examined the family as a social unit. To him and others in his field, a stable family was the foundation for a stable society. Here he expresses a number of modern notions regarding family size, the responsibilities of parenting, and contraception.

Contraception, if practiced by those who desire not to become parents or who wish to limit the number of their children, naturally raises the question whether men and whether women desire children or whether, once contraception is popularized, race suicide will be the inevitable result. In regard to this question literature abounds in dogmatism and emotional reaction. Commonly there is insistence upon a generalized answer and a reluctance to admit that just as there are various types of men and woman there are sure to be differences in the desire of children. It is at least usually admitted that there is no instinct that leads men and women irresistibly to parenthood. It is also clear that evidence cannot be gathered from the past regarding woman's wishes, because child bearing has formerly been one of the strongest of the traditions from which even the modern woman has not so thoroughly escaped as to make any declaration concerning the desire for children certain to be free from social coercion. . . .

Children are an increasing economic burden and to many parents a greater personal burden. Out of modern life are coming influences that tend to make them feel that children limit their freedom or pleasure more than has been commonly true in the past. . . . Society is rapidly coming to the new situation where there will be no effective pressure to make men and women accept parenthood unwillingly and when their determination not to become parents can be effectively carried out by an efficient contraceptive program. There are those who believe that under such circumstances we shall have to subsidize children as a necessary means of racial continuance.

DOCUMENT 9.9: D. V. Glass, *The Struggle for Population* (Oxford: Clarendon Press, 1936, pp. 87–88)

Pronatalism—the encouragement of births in a particular country—was implemented through various policies and programs. Some countries offered family allowances, tax deductions, or other economic incentives for having children. At times, such programs coincided with blatant rhetoric, particularly in fascist Germany and Italy, where women were told it was their duty to have babies for the good of the state. Other programs simply sought to replenish populations that were diminishing due to contraceptive practices and casualties of war. In his *The Struggle for Population*, eugenicist and professor of sociology at the London School of Economics D. V. Glass describes the changing role of the family in relation to government policies.

There has been a sharp rise in the birth-rate in [Germany], but the circumstances in which it occurred were so abnormal that we cannot tell how far it was influenced by external action, and how far it was due merely to the postponement of marriages during the economic depression of 1930 to 1932. On the negative side, however, we can arrive at some important conclusions. In the first place we can see the faults in some of the schemes which have been instituted. If, for example, the economic factor is really influential in keeping down the size of the family, then the family allowances given in France and Belgium cannot by themselves be very effective. Since they rarely cover more than 25 per cent of the cost of bringing up a child, they will only offer a real inducement to those people whose desire for children is relatively urgent. So far as we can tell from the size of the modern family, such people form a small proportion of the population. Nor, to take an Italian example, can we expect a significant change in the amount of marriage to result from a bachelor tax which, at its highest, is still far below the cost of a dog license in Italy. In Germany, on the other hand, a loan of £50 may well encourage marriage among relatively poor people. But here again, although the cancellation of a quarter of the loan on the birth of a child may tend to discourage abortion to some extent, it is unlikely to effect any profound change in people's desire to have children.

DOCUMENT 9.10: Rosamund McDougall, *The Human Multitude* (Hove, Sussex: Wayland Publishers, 1975, p. 68)

Warnings of the population explosion in developing regions of the world prompted examinations of attitudes toward family and children where birth rates were high. The following is an example of a report designed to inform the public of the severity of the situation, while attempting to provide some explanation for its causes. Here, McDougall points to a variety of reasons for differing cultural perspectives on family.

[T]he tradition of the family unit is still strong in Western countries. Religious beliefs still have a strong influence on marriage and childbearing, especially in Catholic countries. . . . Indeed, as far as attitudes to birth control are concerned, the Catholic countries of Europe and South America are well behind the developing countries of Asia and Africa. In Ireland *contraceptive aids* are illegal. Many practicing Catholics, however, now use contraceptives and some priests are trying to persuade the Church to change its attitude. In countries which are mainly Protestant or where religious influence is not so strong . . . there are more liberal attitudes to birth control, divorce and even illegitimacy, although marriage and children are still considered very important. In these countries there is not a great difference between the average family sizes of Catholic and non-Catholic families.

Family size in industrialized countries such as Britain is generally much smaller than in developing countries. But this has not always been the case. Before the Industrial Revolution, families were much larger than they are now. Parents at the top of the social scale were wealthy enough to have as many children as they wanted, and those at the bottom regarded a large family as an economic advantage. Many were sent down the mines and into factories at an early age. In this way the poverty of the whole family could be eased a little by the wages earned by the children.

Gradually laws were brought in to protect children from this sort of exploitation; and as they then became dependants (and a drain on the family budget until they were much older), family size began to drop. The children also began to lead much healthier and longer lives, so there was no longer the need to have so many of them.

DOCUMENT 9.11: Su Xiaokang, "The Humanitarian and Technical Dilemmas of Population Control in China," trans. Yuan Xue (*Journal of International Affairs* 49, winter 1996, pp. 343–344)

From the earliest discussions of the need for birth control on an international scale, China was the center of attention. The oft-cited yellow peril was perceived as a threat to the Western world, and there seemed to be no end in sight to expansion of China's population. However, the rise of communism in China paved the way for state-administered population control. By the 1960s, a stable planned economy that would serve the needs of all the people seemed to depend on greater control of birth rates and migration. Birth control policies, however, were confronted with strong traditions regarding reproduction, particularly the bearing of male children. The following article by Su Xiaokang explores some of the complex challenges posed by severe birth restriction mandated under Chinese population policy.

China does not have population theories like those in the West, but only a more traditional concept of child bearing that has become a custom for a thousand years or so. This custom regards carrying on the ancestral line as being the first priority of life, thus it is said, "of the three kinds of unfilial acts, having no descendants is the worst." Although it has been seriously challenged since China entered the modern period when traditional families began to disintegrate, this concept still remains today a basic value widely held among the people. The natural economy in the Chinese countryside sustains this basic value; that is, underdevelopment has been maintained mainly by the increase of labor. Therefore, both the rural economy and the concepts of the patriarchal family system stress to a great extent traditional customs such as having an extended family, valuing only the male child and raising children for old-age security. A thorough change of ethical practices before being able to change the rural economy will undoubtedly cause strong social instability.

The unprecedented ethical dilemma in human child-bearing behavior that exists in China stems from the following:

- people make the choice to bear children based on fear;
- for the first time in history, child-bearing has become an illegal action that makes many pregnant women flee from home in large numbers and hide in wild places to escape forced abortions;
- artificial distortions in demographics, that is, the practice of drowning infant females rages on, causing the numbers of female children proportionately less vis-à-vis those of males.

10

Gender and Sexuality

Legalized birth control is generally regarded as a fundamental component of the struggle for women's rights. While early birth control activists promoted voluntary motherhood and reproductive choice as liberating for women, legalization resulted from primarily social and economic concerns. But notions of gender and sexuality would not disappear from discussions of birth control.

Even the broadest of population debates took into account the role of women in population growth and decline. Notions of motherhood changed as families became smaller, and women could voluntarily space children. Notions of women changed when they could prevent pregnancy altogether. And notions of sexual intercourse changed when procreation was no longer a necessary end. The following documents highlight many of the concerns expressed as gender roles and ideas of sexuality were transformed.

DOCUMENT 10.1: Charles Knowlton, M.D., *Fruits of Philosophy. An Essay on the Population Question*, in "*A Dirty, Filthy Book*," ed. S. Chandrasekhar (Berkeley and Los Angeles: University of California Press, 1981, p. 97)

Physician Charles Knowlton is considered by many the founder of the birth control movement. He first printed his *Fruits of Philosophy* in 1832, which detailed various methods of birth control, and shocked society. The book sold widely but Knowlton was persecuted throughout his life. When Annie Besant and Charles Bradlaugh published Knowlton's work in 1877, it was described in court as material that was "likely to deprave or corrupt those whose minds are open to moral influences." Besant and Bradlaugh were sentenced to six months in prison, the sentence thrown out on appeal. In the following excerpt, Knowlton explains sexual desire and passion.

When an individual gratifies any of his instincts in a *temperate* degree, he adds an item to the sum total of human happiness, and causes the amount of human happiness to exceed the amount of misery, farther than if he had not enjoyed himself, therefore it is virtuous, or, to say the least, it is not vicious or sinful for him so to do. But it must ever be remembered, that this temperate degree depends on circumstances—that one person's health, pecuniary circumstances, or social relations may be such that it would cause more misery than happiness for him to do an act which, being done by a person under different circumstances, would cause more happiness than misery. Therefore it would be right for the latter to perform such act, but not for the former.

Again, owing to his *ignorance*, a man may not be able to gratify a desire without causing misery (wherefore it would be wrong for him to do it), but with knowledge of means to prevent this misery, he may so gratify it that more pleasure than pain will be the result of the act, in which case the act to say the least is justifiable. Now, therefore, it is virtuous, nay, it is the *duty* for him who has a knowledge of such means, to convey it to those who have it not; for, by so doing, he furthers the cause of human happiness.

Man by nature is endowed with the talent of devising means to remedy or prevent the evils that are liable to arise from gratifying our appetites; and it is as much the duty of the physician to inform mankind of the means of preventing the evils that are liable to arise from gratifying the reproductive instinct, as it is to inform them how to keep clear of the gout or the dyspepsia. Let not the cold ascetic say we ought not to gratify our appetites any farther than is necessary to maintain health, and to perpetuate the species. Mankind will not so abstain, and if means to prevent the evils that may arise from a farther gratification can be devised, they *need not*. Heaven has not only given us the capacity of greater enjoyment, but the talent of devising means to prevent the evils that are liable to arise therefrom; and it becomes us, "with thanksgiving, to make the most of them."

DOCUMENT 10.2: Annie Besant, "The Law of Population: Its Consequences, and Its Bearing upon Human Conduct and Morals," in "*A Dirty, Filthy Book*," ed. S. Chandrasekhar (Berkeley and Los Angeles: University of California Press, 1981, pp. 192–193)

Following her trial for the publication of Knowlton's *Fruits of Philosophy*, Annie Besant decided to publish her own birth control work, entitled *The Law of Population*. She spent her life working for school reform, labor issues, and women's suffrage. She saw contraception as beneficial to the lives of women and children. Here she discusses the morality of birth control.

What is morality? It is the greatest good of the greatest number. It is immoral to give life where you cannot support it. It is immoral to bring children into the world when you cannot clothe, feed, and educate them. It is immoral to crowd new life into already over-crowded houses. And to give birth to children wholesale, who never have a chance of healthy life. Conjugal prudence is most highly moral, and "those who endeavor to vilify and degrade these means in the eyes of the public, and who speak of them as 'immoral' and 'disgusting,' are little aware of the moral responsibility they incur thereby. As already shown, to reject preventive intercourse is in reality to choose the other three true population checks—poverty, prostitution, and celibacy. So far from meriting reprobation, the endeavor to spread the knowledge of the preventive methods, of the great law of nature which renders them necessary, is in my opinion the very greatest services which can at present be done to mankind" ("Elements of Social Science").

But the knowledge of these scientific checks would, it is argued, make vice bolder, and would increase unchastity among women by making it safe. Suppose that this were so, it might save some broken hearts and some deserted children; men ruin women and go scatheless, and then bitterly object that their victims escape something of public shame. And if so, are all to suffer, so that one or two already corrupt in heart may be preserved from becoming corrupt in act? Are mothers to die slowly that impure women may be held back, and wives to be sacrificed that the unchaste may be curbed? As well say that no knives must be used because throats may be cut with them; no pistols allowed because murders may be committed by them. Blank ignorance has some advantages in the way of safety, and if all men's eyes were put out none would ever be tempted to seduce a woman for her beauty. Let us bring for our women the veil to cover and the eunuch to guard, and so be at least consistent in our folly and our distrust! But this knowledge would *not* increase unchastity; the women who could thus use it would be solely those who only lack opportunity, not will, to go astray; the means suggested all imply deliberation and forethought.

DOCUMENT 10.3: J. Fizelle, "Decline of the Birthrate" (*Westminster Review* 170, September 1908, pp. 268–269)

Population trends in Australia paralleled those in England and the United States, as did the women's movement. In the following article, Australian women's rights activist J. Fizelle describes the relationship between changing women's roles and a lower birth rate.

In regard to the question of a declining birthrate it is well known that the uneasiness caused thereby is not confined to England alone, but is giving anxiety to statesmen in nearly all the most advanced and enlightened countries.

Here, in Australia, it has long been a matter of concern. In the state of New South Wales the falling off of births assumed such serious proportions that Mr. Carruthers, when Premier in the late Parliament, thought it necessary some three years ago to appoint a Royal Commission to inquire into the causes.

One would suppose that a problem that has manifested itself in countries so widely separated as Europe, America, Australia, and New Zealand would induce observers to ask whether what is regarded as an evil, and one so widely spread, might not have, like some diseases, a common origin. . . .

This decline in birthrate began in Australia, roughly speaking, twenty-five years ago or more, and has steadily continued ever since. Within the same period education, especially of women, has made enormous strides; medical publications have greatly increased, and within the same period sick nursing has been taken up by educated and go-ahead women, most of whom are the pick of their sex. Women of all ages and almost all classes have long taken an active share in the work of those various societies that labour for philanthropy and the promotion of social morality.

Questions and aspects of life are now known and freely discussed by old and young women, which thirty years ago would have been shunned as unfit for the ears and eyes of grandmothers. These various influences have combined to open the eyes of women to life as it is. The spread of education and the eager interest of women in politics has led them to the study of the questions affecting the welfare of women and children, and to those laws bearing upon them.

The knowledge thus gained from these different sources has resulted in an evolution of woman which is neither appreciated nor understood. As a proof I may point to this decline of birth rate in all the most advanced countries of the west, politically and educationally.

There has grown up in the minds of women a deep and bitter sense of injustice from the fact that they have come to realize that one-half humanity has been held in physical and mental subjection by the other half, and that freedom, the birthright of every human being, has been withheld from them by the accident of sex. . . .

DOCUMENT 10.4: Dr. F. W. Foerster, *Marriage and the Sex Problem*, trans. Meyrick Booth (New York: Frederick A. Stokes Company, 1912, 93–95)

Originally published in German, Dr. Friedrich Wilhelm Foerster's *Marriage and the Sex Problem* addresses changing attitudes toward the roles of husband and wife. He argues that contraception is not liberating for women, because it makes them more vulnerable to an unchecked sexual drive among men. Whereas the consequence of pregnancy would help to control men's passion, he warned women that sex without the fear of conception would make men sexually irresponsible.

We readily admit that the sphere of sex should be subjected to the human spirit; nay, we might go further and even define sexual ethics as the complete subordination of our sexual conduct to our life as a whole, with all its fundamental interests and responsibilities. But nothing could be more radically false than to imagine that the methods of Neo-Malthusianism mark an advance in the subordination of nature to the spirit. It must be obvious to every thinking person that precisely the opposite is the case. The perfection and popularization of these practices will not assist men to master their instincts and passions, but will on the contrary make it easier than has ever before been the case for man's sexual and animal self to dominate the will and spirit. For the artificial prevention of conception does not in the least control or discipline the sexual feeling itself. *It merely frees it from producing its normal results: and it is these very results which have, in the past, so powerfully contributed towards self-discipline and self-control.* Remove the proper and natural consequences of sexual intercourse, and a controlling factor of the first importance has been eliminated. We may therefore assume with the utmost confidence that the subjection of men and women to their sensual passions will rapidly increase with the increase of Neo-Malthusian practices. It will increase, moreover, for this further reason that the prevention of conception causes the sex instinct to concentrate itself, in a most unwholesome and dangerous manner, upon mere barren pleasure; here we have naked sensuality, stripped of all the nobility, sanctity, and responsibility which attach to the normally directed sexual impulse, associated as it is with *creation*. . . .

Is not the liberation of women from the burden of excessive motherhood a great success on the part of Neo-Malthusianism? It is only an apparent success. In reality it is women, in particular, who will be the sufferers through anything which increases sexual irresponsibility in men. Even the most excessive production of children could not endanger women so greatly or so deeply undermine the true necessities of their existence, as will the artificial restriction of the family. The male sex passion, when relieved from all sense of responsibility and from the necessity for periods of self-control, when artificially liberated from the natural consequences which lend it meaning and dignity and link it to the purpose of life as a whole, will necessarily become more pleasure-seeking and more recklessly selfish than it could be under normal conditions. The result will be an increase in every sort of disloyalty and irresponsibility.

DOCUMENT 10.5: Margaret Sanger, *The Woman Rebel* 1, no. 1, March 1914)

Margaret Sanger published her monthly newspaper *The Woman Rebel* beginning in 1914, to promote women's rights, socialist ideals, and so-called birth control, a phrase she coined when she began her movement. The following excerpts, taken from the first issue, illustrate a variety of ways in which contributing writers saw the connection between contraception and women's liberation.

EMMA GOLDMAN, "LOVE AND MARRIAGE"

The defenders of authority dread the advent of a free motherhood lest it rob them of their prey. Who would fight wars? Who would create wealth? Who would make the policeman, the jailer, if woman were to refuse the indiscriminate breeding of children? The race, the race! Shouts the king, the president, the capitalist, the priest. The race must be preserved, though woman be degraded to a mere machine,—and the marriage institution is our only safety valve against the pernicious sex-awakening of woman. But in vain these frantic efforts to maintain a state of bondage. In vain, too, the edicts of the Church, the mad attacks of rulers, in vain even the arm of the law. Woman no longer wants to be a party to the production of a race of sickly, feeble, decrepit, wretched human beings, who would have neither the strength nor moral courage to throw off the yoke of poverty and slavery. Instead she desires fewer and better children, begotten and reared in love and through free choice; not by compulsion, as marriage imposes. Our pseudo-moralists have yet to learn the deep sense of responsibility toward the child, that love in freedom has awakened in the breast of woman. Rather she forego [sic] forever the glory of motherhood than bring forth life in an atmosphere that breathes only destruction and death. And if she does become a mother, it is to give to the child the deepest and best her being can yield. To grow with the child is her motto; she knows but in that manner alone can she help build true manhood and womanhood.

MARGARET SANGER, "THE PREVENTION OF CONCEPTION"

Is there any reason why women should not receive clean, harmless, scientific knowledge on how to prevent conception? Everybody is aware that the old, stupid fallacy that such knowledge will cause a girl to enter into prostitution has long been shattered. Seldom does a prostitute become pregnant. Seldom does the girl practicing promiscuity become pregnant. The woman of the upper middle class has all available knowledge and implements to prevent conception. The woman of the lower middle class is struggling for this knowledge. She tries various methods of prevention, and after a few years of experience plus medical advice succeeds in discovering some method suitable to her individual self. The woman of the people is the only one left in ignorance of this information. Her neighbors, relatives and friends tell her stories of special devices and the success of them all. They tell her also of the blood-sucking men with M.D. after their names who perform operations for the price of so-and-so. But the working woman's purse is thin. It is far cheaper to have a baby, "though God knows what it will do after it gets here." Then, too, all other classes of women live in places where there is at least a semblance of privacy and sanitation. It is easier for them to care for themselves, whereas the large majority of the women of the people have no bathing or sanitary conveniences. This accounts too for the fact that the higher the standard of living, the more care can be taken and fewer children result. No plagues, famines or wars could ever frighten the capitalist class so much as the universal practice of the prevention of conception. On the other hand no better method could be utilized for increasing the wages of the workers.

As is well known, a law exists forbidding the imparting of information on this subject, the penalty being several years' imprisonment. Is it not time to defy this law? And what fitter place could be found than in the pages of the WOMAN REBEL!

DOCUMENT 10.6: Dr. Prabbu Dutt Shastri, "The Outlook in India," in *International Aspects of Birth Control*, ed. Margaret Sanger (New York: American Birth Control League, Inc., 1925, pp. 120–122)

Birth rates in India caused concern among neo-Malthusians in the early years of the twentieth century. At the same time, some progress was being made in the struggle for women's rights there, drawing further attention from birth control activists. Dr. Prabbu Dutt Shastri, professor at Presidency College in Calcutta, spoke to these issues at the Sixth International Neo-Malthusian and Birth Control Conference in 1925.

India at the present day is passing through a period of rapid transition, and a number of forces are at work with a view to bring about her social, economic and national regeneration. The chief interest of the country at the present moment, torn asunder by communal factions and sectarian frictions, centers round the question of political reform and advancement, consequently several movements which would otherwise have won the co-operation and interest of the people are now being shelved as of secondary importance. All the same the work of social reform is proceeding with as much vigor and success as is possible under the circumstances.

Hindu marriage is not a contract, but a religious institution with its religious duties. A good deal of superstition has accumulated round the ancient texts, so that it has been almost universally believed that the primary object of marriage is procreation, preferably of a male issue. In this light the use of any contraceptive would obviously be looked upon as "immoral" and "unnatural," and even "sinful." But this blind tradition is now rapidly losing its hold over the more educated classes, who, infused with a sense of freedom and the scientific spirit of enquiry, have begun to reflect for themselves on problems of such fundamental importance, apart from the tyrannical sway of any authoritative texts. Even the ancient Hindus had expounded sex knowledge in detail as "kokashastra," which not only contained their views on sex psychology, sex union, sex hygiene, but also methods to procreate male or female issues at will, as well as some psychological and mechanical devices of contraception. Again, many ancient Hindus and modern sages as well strongly recommend continence as the surest contraceptive. This is sufficient to indicate that the subject of Birth Control is not entirely alien to the mentality of Indian wisdom.

Some scattered individuals and societies are here and there working in India at present to enlighten and educate public opinion on the problems of eugenics, hygiene, sex love, etc. A Birth Control league was formed some time ago in Bombay, and a periodical was also issued on the subject, but outside the Bombay Presidency very little is so far known of the organisation. Its utility is bound to be extended when its secretary, Prof. Phadke, will co-ordinate its work with other workers in other parts of India. At Delhi and in the Punjab also, something is being done on the same lines, but there has no central organization come into being yet.

Indian women have been treated as slaves for centuries past. The greater bulk of the people are still ignorant and superstitious, and they have been taught by their orthodox tradition to look upon woman as an instrument of man's pleasure, as a machine for the propagation of the human species and the gratification of man's sex impulse. But this extremely narrow and purely selfish outlook is being speedily changed with the growth of Western institutions and the spread of Western education and culture, and a true revival of indigenous culture as well. Child-marriage is distinctly on the wane, widows are allowed and even encouraged and persuaded to re-marry, the age of consent is being raised from twelve to fourteen years in the case of married girls, and sixteen years in the case of unmarried girls, instruction in hygiene and sanitation is becoming more general; in short, with a more universal and liberal education coupled with the awakening of a higher consciousness of nationalism, social reform is being pushed in various directions. The higher classes are, in considerable numbers, already practicing Birth Control, as is the case in Western countries, while the poor are embarrassed with large families, when the keen struggle for existence hardly makes it possible for them to make their two ends meet. It is the poor

Indians as well as the middle classes in this country who badly need enlightenment on the subject of Birth Control and definite instruction in the use of scientific contraceptives. Such instruction seems to be the surest antidote to the very large number of cases of infanticide and secret abortions.

DOCUMENT 10.7: Charlotte Perkins Gilman, "Sex and Race Progress," in *Sex in Civilization*, ed. V. F. Calverton and S. D. Schmalhausen (Garden City, NY: Garden City Publishing Co., Inc., 1929, pp. 118–121)

Charlotte Perkins Gilman was a prolific writer of novels, essays, short stories, poems, and lectures. She supported women's rights and the peace movement but was most famous for her story "The Yellow Wallpaper," about a woman who suffers a nervous breakdown following the birth of her child. The story was modeled on her own experiences, after which she obtained a divorce and left her child with her ex-husband. Perkins Gilman seriously questioned society's expectations for women—in this essay she examines sexuality and gender roles in relation to the population question.

Instead of a normal social distribution which would ensure to all the nourishment essential to full production, we have had a world of struggling men trying to get away from one another the products of their industry, a world of destructive competition. It is no wonder that with socialist and communist theories there is associated in the popular mind the fear of sex promiscuity. Seeing women as possessions, and assuming common ownership of all property, it is natural, for minds accustomed to believe and not to think, to entertain this confused idea.

As a matter of fact promiscuity, such as was found in declining Rome, for instance, is no mark of communism, but of sex decay. Perhaps no better proof of our misuse of function can be shown than in this very tendency toward promiscuity which has accompanied the advance of civilization and contributed to its repeated ruin. . . .

As our history stands, we can see clearly enough how much this vital impulse has contributed to race progress, in so far as it improved the stock, or increased the value of individuals. We can see its lovely heights in types of undying love, in instances of parental devotion. No matter how wrongly we may conceive it, a natural force cannot be utterly thwarted even by our mistakes.

That we are still here, and on the whole advancing, shows that those mistakes have not been fatal. But when we look at our best progress, in the most advanced races, when we see the kind of people we produce and their manifold sufferings, it does seem as if we might do better in the way of progress.

DOCUMENT 10.8: Havelock Ellis, *On Life and Sex: Essays of Love and Virtue* (1921) (Garden City, NY: Garden City Publishing Co., Inc., 1937, pp. 106–113)

The medically trained writer and social psychologist Havelock Ellis is perhaps best known for his six-volume work entitled *Studies in the Psychology of Sex* (1897–1928), in which he challenges conventional mores regarding sex and promotes sexual freedom (even for women) and contraceptive use. Margaret Sanger embraced his work, and it became widely publicized due to battles with censors. He is credited with assisting in sexual liberation for women.

No doubt in its erotic aspects, as well as in its legal and economic aspects, the social order thus established was described, and in good faith, as beneficial to women, and even as maintained in their interests. Monogamy and the home, it was claimed, alike existed for the benefit and the protection of women. It was not so often explained that they greatly benefited and protected men, with, moreover, this additional advantage that while women were absolutely confined to the home, men were free to exercise their activities outside the home, even, with tacit general consent, on the erotic side. . . .

The social claims of women, their economic claims, their political claims, have long been before the world. Women themselves have actively asserted them, and they are all in process of realization. The erotic claims of women, which are at least as fundamental, are not publicly voiced, and women themselves would be the last to assert them. It is easy to understand why that should be so. The natural and acquired qualities of women, even the qualities developed in the art of courtship, have all been utilized in building up the masculine ideal of sexual morality; it is on feminine characteristics that this masculine ideal has been based, so that women have been helpless to protest against it. Moreover, even if that were not so, to formulate such rights is to raise the question whether there so much as exists anything that can be called "erotic rights." The right to joy cannot be claimed in the same way as one claims the right to put a voting paper in a ballot box. A human being's erotic aptitudes can only be developed where the right atmosphere for them exists, and where the attitudes of both persons concerned are in harmonious sympathy.

DOCUMENT 10.9: Simone de Beauvoir, *The Second Sex* (New York: Everyman's Library, Alfred A. Knopf, 1952, pp. 124–128)

The French writer and philosopher Simone de Beauvoir produced the influential *Le Deuxieme sexe* in 1949, translated and published as *The Second Sex* in 1953. The work inspired women's movements everywhere. In it she explores the origins of male patriarchy and the secondary position women have held through the ages. Here she discusses women's roles in reproduction and the politics of population.

One of the most basic problems of woman, as we have seen, is the reconciliation of her reproductive role and her part in productive labor. The fundamental fact that from the beginning of history doomed woman to domestic work and prevented her taking part in the shaping of the world was her enslavement to the generative function. In female animals there is a physiological and seasonal rhythm that assures the economizing of their strength; in women, on the contrary, between puberty and the menopause nature sets no limits to the number of her pregnancies. . . .

At certain epochs man has strongly felt the need to reduce the size of the population; but at the same time nations have feared becoming weak. In times of crisis and misery the birth rate may have been reduced by late marriage, but it remained the general rule to marry young and have as many children as the woman could produce; infant mortality alone reduced the number of living children.

In spite of prejudices, opposition, and the survival of an outdated morality, we have witnessed the passage from free fecundity to a fecundity controlled by the State or by individuals. Progress in obstetrical science has considerably reduced the dangers of confinement; and the pain of childbirth is on the way out. . . . During the nineteenth century woman in her turn emancipated herself from nature; she gained mastery of her own body. Now protected in large part from the slavery of reproduction, she is in a position to assume the economic role that is offered her and will assure her of complete independence.

DOCUMENT 10.10: *Memoranda Presented to the Royal Commission on Population* (London: His Majesty's Stationery Office, 1950, vol. 5, pp. 96–97)

Sir Roy Harrod, a student of John Maynard Keynes, went on to pioneer the economics of dynamic growth and macroeconomics. Here he considers the role of women in the economy in his report to the Royal Commission on Population in 1950. He acknowledges ways in which he believes the changing roles of women affect economics and population.

Many women now seek a college education, often with a view to pursuing occupations in life for which this education qualifies them. While it must be recognized that there is a minority of women temperamentally unfitted for family life, many of whom are highly qualified to do most valuable work as spinsters, it would be most undesirable if the majority of women who go to college were deflected from the tasks of motherhood. To some extent already they comprise the most gifted women in the nation and will come to do so more, as the education ladder is broadened. The arguments from stock and environment alike require that those women should in due course become mothers. Already on average they have to make a sacrifice in their standard of living to do so. The position will be worse if the system of "equal pay" is more widely adopted. Although this system may displace some women from their occupations, for others, presumably the more gifted, the sacrifice entailed by renouncing their profession in favour of motherhood will be still greater. . . . I suggest that in organized professions, opportunities should be given to women to return later in life. For instance, a young woman, having begun a career as a teacher, might get married after four or five years. Then after she had spent some twenty years on family duties, it should be open to her to return, say in the late forties, with suitable increments of pay and status. This project might wean away some who love their professional work and are reluctant to leave it, and at the same time might improve the lives of older women, who are apt to feel that, with their children already adolescent, the world has no more use for them.

DOCUMENT 10.11: Lee Rainwater, *And the Poor Get Children: Sex, Contraception, and Family Planning in the Working Class* (Chicago: Quadrangle Books, 1960, pp. 63–64)

Harvard professor of sociology and noted expert on poverty Lee Rainwater was among those who took the premise that the poor had more children than they could afford. This is most evident in his 1960 book *And the Poor Get Children*. In this excerpt from that work, Rainwater describes how sexual attitudes and practices differ in the lower classes, contributing to a higher rate of unwanted pregnancies.

Most working class men and women seem to marry in profound ignorance of family planning issues; many have bits and pieces of information, but most seem to feel ill-prepared for events and decisions about sex and its consequences. . . . The higher the status or the aspirations, the more likely it is that men or women will have something approaching adequate knowledge about sexual relations and conception. As might be expected, men generally tend to know more of the essential facts than women.

The typical lower class pattern among men includes at most the knowledge that men and women have sexual intercourse, that men enjoy it and women probably don't, that pregnancy results from having intercourse, and that contraception can be effected with a condom. The condom is useful especially before marriage to keep out of trouble if one is lucky enough to find a girl willing to have intercourse. Very little consideration seems to be given to family planning, and many lower class men seem to have thought of the condom before marriage mainly as an appliance to be used in premarital intercourse as a protection against disease and the proverbial shotgun.

Only infrequently do lower class couples discuss family planning or contraception before marriage. Sex is not discussed either; there may be some conflict over the man's desire for premarital intercourse, but it is an activity so surrounded with ambivalence and guilt that seldom does this problem lead to an explicit concern with sexuality or family planning. . . .

Working class women, particularly those in the lower-lower class, generally have even less information about sex and contraception than do the men, and the women seem to give relatively little thought to spacing and limiting their families until some time after marriage.

DOCUMENT 10.12: "Symposium on Law and Population, Text of Recommendations, June 17–21, 1974, Tunis," in *World Population Control: Rights and Restrictions*, ed. staff of Columbia University *Human Rights Law Review* (New York: Family Service Association of America, 1975, pp. 474–475)

While internal domestic studies of population were being conducted in a number of nations, international debates continued to unfold. By the 1970s, the women's movement had added new perspectives on gender roles in the developing world that would affect birth rates and the relationship between population and economics. Participants in the population symposium held in Tunis in June of 1974 recognized direct correlations between family size and opportunities for women. They subsequently recommended that population programs consider overall economic development in poorer regions as well as women's rights when funding birth control. This point of view would gain momentum in the next two decades.

Recognizing the vital relationship between the status of women and the overall social and economic development;

Realizing that the existing discrimination against women significantly limits their opportunity for free choice as to the number and spacing of their children, restricts their exercise of other human rights and prevents their full participation in the social and economic development in their own countries and in the international community;

Considering also that the discrimination against women works to the detriment not only of women but also directly or indirectly affects their children, their entire family as well as the society at large, and obstructs the implementation of population policies and the total development effort . . .

[The symposium recommends] that:

1. Governments give highest priority to the ratification of the above-mentioned Conventions and to the implementation of the international standards, contained in the international instruments, strategies and programmes, referred to above;

2. All people, men and women alike, be included in planning and policy-making in all questions concerning the entire development of a country, including questions of population, so that the exercise of individual rights may be harmonized with corresponding civic rights and responsibilities;

3. Governments and intergovernmental organizations pay full attention to the importance of technical and financial assistance through international cooperation to carry out local, national, regional and international plans, programmes and policies designed for the advancement of women and their full integration in the development process;

4. More concerted action be taken at local, national, regional, and international levels taking into account the assistance that can be offered by national and international non-governmental organizations; and,

5. Governments examine their laws, regulations and customs affecting the status of women with a view to bringing about their conformity with the basic principals of equality between men and women without discrimination as to sex.

11

Technology

Technology has affected population policy in a number of ways. Mainly, it has been embraced in order to develop new methods of contraception. Early records show that for millennia sexually active couples have used a variety of methods—some effective, some not—to avoid pregnancy. To a large extent, the modern world did not change attitudes toward childbearing as much as modern technology improved on ways to prevent conception.

In addition, advances in technology have given man greater power to breed what has been determined as a better population. Nineteenth-century scientific theories clarified categories of people based on new notions of race, heredity, and natural selection. Again, science did not necessarily change attitudes; rather, existing attitudes were often validated by science. Subsequent technological developments made it possible to control procreation among those deemed to be undesirables, and eventually to engineer fertilization for others.

At each step of the way, new technology would confront traditional teaching and raise additional religious and moral questions.

DOCUMENT 11.1: Francis Place, "To the Married of Both Sexes of the Working People," *Population, Evolution & Birth Control: A Collage of Controversial Ideas*, **2nd ed., ed. Garrett Hardin (London: W. H. Freeman & Co., 1969, pp. 192–193)**

The following passage by Francis Place speaks to the working class, who had long been criticized for having too many children. In that sense, it reflects issues previously explored. But it also includes a direct prescription for preventing pregnancy, which says much about nineteenth-century birth control technology. Birth control advocates generally preferred one form over another, in this case the contraceptive sponge. Place was a British radical reformer who fought for working-class rights.

When the number of working people in any trade or manufacture, has for some years been too great, wages are reduced very low, and the working people become little better than slaves.

When wages have thus been reduced to a very small sum, working people can no longer maintain their children as all good and respectable people wish to maintain their children, but are compelled to neglect them;—to send them to different employments;—to Mills and Manufactories, at a very early age.

The misery of these poor children cannot be described, and need not be described to you, who witness them and deplore them every day of your lives.

Many indeed among you are compelled for a bare subsistence to labour incessantly from the moment you rise in the morning to the moment you lie down again at night, without even the hope of ever being better off.

The sickness of yourselves and your children, the privation and pain and premature death of those you love but cannot cherish as you wish, need only be alluded to. You know all these evils too well.

And, what, you will ask is the remedy?

How are we to avoid these miseries?

The answer is short and plain: the means are easy. Do as other people do, to avoid having more children than they wish to have, and can easily maintain.

What is done by other people is this. A piece of soft sponge is tied by a bobbin or penny ribbon, and inserted just before the sexual intercourse takes place, and is withdrawn again as soon as it has taken place. Many tie a piece of sponge to each end of the ribbon, and they take care not to use the same sponge again until it has been washed.

If the sponge be large enough, that is, as large as a green walnut, or a small apple, it will prevent conception, and thus, without diminishing the pleasures of married life, or doing the least injury to the health of the most delicate woman, both the woman and her husband will be saved from all the miseries which having too many children produces.

By limiting the number of children, the wages both of children and of grown up persons will rise; the hours of working will be no more than they ought to be; you will have some time for recreation, some means of enjoying yourselves rationally, some means as well as some time for your own and your children's moral and religious instruction.

DOCUMENT 11.2: Alice Withrow Field, *Protection of Women and Children in Soviet Russia* (New York: E. P. Dutton & Co., Inc., 1932, pp. 78–80)

One of the most prevalent arguments for legalizing contraceptives was the claim that it would decrease the number of abortions. In that respect, birth control advocates of the 1920s were essentially anti-abortion. In the Soviet Union, however, the absence of a political/religious base facilitated the legalization of abortion as well. Twentieth-century technology brought safer contraceptives and safer abortions, shaping new debates where both were legal. Here Alice Withrow Field, sex researcher, criminologist, and social scientist, describes the status of abortion in the Soviet Union.

The law of 1920 which legalized abortion did so under the following conditions:

a) The operation known as abortion can only be performed by licensed surgeons.

b) Save in very exceptional circumstances, abortion must be the result of a surgical operation and not the result of medicine or drugs.

c) After every abortion performed, the woman concerned must stay in bed in the hospital, or other place of operation, for three full days.

d) After every abortion or miscarriage, the woman concerned must not be allowed to go to work for two weeks after said operation or illness.

e) An abortion must not be performed for the first pregnancy unless childbirth would seriously endanger the woman's life.

f) Abortion must not be performed if the pregnancy has been continued for more than two and one-half months.

g) Except as stated in paragraphs "e" and "f," no qualified doctor has the right to refuse abortion, although he is at liberty to discourage it in every way he thinks fit.

h) The State recommends that all abortions be performed in those State hospitals where there is a section definitely for that purpose. . . .

i) All midwives, and any other persons who are not licensed doctors, are strictly prohibited from performing abortions.

j) Private doctors or any other individuals who perform an abortion which results in death of the woman can be tried for manslaughter. Women who perform abortions on themselves are not subject to punishment. . . .

k) It is recommended that abortions be discouraged if the woman concerned has had less than three children; if she has adequate means for supporting another child; if her health would not be impaired by another pregnancy; if her living conditions make a good enough environment for children; and, if . . . there is not social, physical, or economic reason for the abortion.

DOCUMENT 11.3: Amram Scheinfeld, *The New You and Heredity* (Philadelphia: J. B. Lippincott Co., 1950, pp. 554–559)

Sterilization, in the form of both vasectomies and tubal ligations, were used widely as a eugenic measure in the United States before World War II. It was believed that so-called defectives should not be permitted to pass on their genes, and it became common to sterilize criminals, the mentally ill, and the mentally disabled. In the years following the war, eugenics became clearly identified with Hitler and the Nazis, raising complicated moral questions in the scientific community. Here, Amram Scheinfeld provides examples that demonstrate the complex dilemmas society faced.

How would *you* act in each case?

A young man in an eastern city lost an eye during childhood because of affliction with *retino-blastoma*, in some cases inherited through a *dominant* eye gene. He married and had two young children. The condition appeared in both. In 1949, the youngest, a boy baby 11 months old, was required to have both eyes removed. The other, a girl 2 ½ years old, had one eye removed and was threatened with the loss of another. If you had known of the threat beforehand, what would you have advised for this man? . . .

A widow in a western city in 1950 had *three hemophiliac sons,* aged 20, 16 and 13. The family has been on relief for years, receiving a large sum monthly, plus expensive free hospital and medical treatment because of the special needs. After the first hemophiliac son appeared, it might have been clear that the mother was a hemophilia-gene carrier, with a fifty-fifty chance that any subsequent son would be hemophiliac. Would you have advised sterilization under such circumstances? . . .

A delinquent girl in an institution in New England was turned loose without being sterilized because she was just over the borderline of "legal" feeble-mindedness (with an IQ of 72). Within a few years she had borne, illegitimately, first a feeble-minded child, then a pair of defective twins, who died in infancy. What would you have advised beforehand in such a case? . . .

In fact, when we look back over all the proposed curbs on human mating and reproduction for eugenic reasons, it seems pretty clear that any radical measures along these lines at this stage of our knowledge might invite more dangers than benefits, as was foreshadowed by the experience under Nazi rule.

DOCUMENT 11.4: John D. Rockefeller III, "Report of the President," in *The Population Council, Report for the Calendar Years 1962 and 1963* (New York, n.p., 1964, p. 13)

Here John D. Rockefeller III, founder of the Population Council, an international nongovernmental organization, reports on the successful implementation of birth control programs and the use of intrauterine contraceptive devices (IUDs) in the developing world. The Rockefeller Foundation served as a major donor for international population programs. The safety of IUDs was later challenged, but in 1964 they were accepted as modern and effective.

Devices of different sizes and shapes are being tried and the causes of discomfort studied. Research was also begun to determine exactly how the device prevents conception. Oddly enough, this most promising, convenient, and inexpensive method of fertility control remains a mystery in the way it works. Even though it is proving itself in more than fifty projects in America, and others abroad, full acceptance by the medical profession throughout the world will be facilitated when the mechanism of action becomes clearer. Therefore, while continuing to test the device's effectiveness, safety, and acceptability, the Council also supports research to gain an understanding of its mode of action.

With the financial support of the Council, the National Committee on Maternal Health was requested to accumulate statistical evidence from many of the research projects with which the Council is associated in the United States and Puerto Rico. Projects offering the device in foreign countries, each under the control of local doctors, scientists, and administrators, but with Council advice, were initiated in India and Pakistan, South Korea, and Taiwan. The birth control project in the Taichung area of Taiwan, under the sponsorship of the Joint

Commission on Rural Reconstruction (U.S. and Chinese Governments) and the Provincial Department of Health, is particularly promising.

Although it is too early to draw final conclusions about the intra-uterine devices, it is difficult now to feel other than optimistic. . . . There has been no other development in recent years that goes nearly so far in supplying a basis for optimism concerning man's ability to deal with the problems of the high rate of population growth.

DOCUMENT 11.5: Paul Ramsey, *Fabricated Man: The Ethics of Genetic Control* (New Haven, Conn.: Yale University Press, 1970, pp. 113–121)

In this chapter entitled "Parenthood and the Future of Man by Artificial Donor Insemination, Etcetera, Etcetera," theologian and bioethicist Paul Ramsey explores the possibilities provided by new fertilization techniques. He also notes some of the moral questions raised by such advancements.

Let us imagine that there can be developed an artificial placenta as good for the child as the womb—or better, because it abolishes the limits imposed by the human pelvis upon brain development, and makes the child accessible to "the management's" improvement. Even so, such a technical development skips over the crucial ethical question. Prescinding from the "good" ends in view, the decisive moral verdict must be that we cannot rightfully *get to know* how to do this without conducting unethical experiments upon the unborn who must be the "mishaps" (the dead and the retarded ones) through whom we learn how. It is amazing that, in discussions of man's self-modification of the future of his species by prenatal refabrication, this simple, decisive ethical objection is so seldom mentioned. This can only mean that our ethos is well prepared to make human waste for the sake of these self-elected goals. . . .

It may be unfair to attribute to geneticists, who write as if they are not to be deterred by a proper ethics of treating hypothetical children, the pro-natalist attitudes of past traditional societies. . . . A subtle but significant shift has taken place from doctoring primary patients to doctoring that nonpatient, the human race. For this reason, patients now alive or in the first and second generation may be passed over lightly, hypothetical children can be thought of as actualities to be improved at risk, and one can even contemplate permitting harm to come to them (with abortion as an escape prepared for the injured) for the sake of knowledge and learning the techniques ordered to the good to come.

DOCUMENT 11.6: James R. Sorenson, *Social Aspects of Applied Human Genetics—Series: Social Science Frontiers, Occasional Publications Reviewing New Fields for Social Science Development* (New York: Russell Sage Foundation, 1971, pp. 5–6)

While the nineteenth century introduced a new understanding of genetics, the twentieth century introduced a new practice called genetic counseling.

Couples were asked to examine their family histories and were advised to seek the expertise of medical geneticists to ensure healthy offspring. One of the most significant medical developments was the use of amniocentesis, which could diagnose a variety of conditions present in a developing fetus. The practice forced couples to make difficult decisions regarding abortion based on information gained from the procedure. James R. Sorenson, currently professor in the School of Public Health at the University of North Carolina, examined related questions in his early research.

There may be considerable economic advantages in developing mass screening programs of people likely to pass on specific genetic diseases to their offspring. Therapeutic abortion of fetuses afflicted with Down's Syndrome or other severely disabling diseases detectable in utero can save families much sorrow, and save both the state and the families from a severe financial burden. The development of intra-uterine detection techniques makes such screening programs feasible. The changing moral and legal climate surrounding abortion suggests that the number of therapeutic abortions will increase in the near future.

Increased application of genetics in medicine will not necessarily be automatic, however. The use of genetic knowledge in medical practice has given rise to many controversial issues in the recent past and continues to do so. How large a risk should prospective parents take? Should parents make the decision? Should abortion of a fetus be permitted on the grounds that it will be abnormal? Should carriers of severe genetic defects be forbidden to marry, or to have children? These questions are in every respect—ethically, morally, politically, emotionally, legally—difficult to answer. More questions will arise as knowledge of human heredity advances.

The increasing intervention in and control of genetic disease and the selection or avoidance of certain genetic constitutions have fostered debates within and between many different groups in society. Medical professionals, life scientists, lawyers, ministers, biologists, and philosophers are engaged in discussions concerning the proper use of such knowledge. . . . If man is to understand and to employ the potential good inherent in medical genetic advances, he must begin by determining by whom and how these advances are used. The social sciences, by providing such information, can make significant contributions to discussions on the use of genetic knowledge.

DOCUMENT 11.7: Julian L. Simon, "Birth-Control Market-Segmentation Strategy, or How to Increase Contraceptive Usage," in *The Economics of Population Growth* (Princeton, NJ: Princeton University Press, 1977, pp. 453–454)

Directors of population control programs sought the most effective and affordable contraceptive technology, but acknowledged that it was useless without widespread distribution. In order to ensure access, birth control advocates solicited the expertise of marketing strategists. One such expert was Julian Simon, professor of economics and business administration at the

University of Illinois, who describes here the structure of an effective marketing plan.

How should the marketer sell his product to a segment of the market that already uses modern, artificial contraceptive devices? In many places the marketing of contraceptives is (or has been until recently) illegal, for example, in Turkey, in the Arab countries, and in the state of Connecticut. In such circumstances, marketing is a matter of smuggling merchandise across the border. Retail marketing, in turn, is a compound of black-market selling and maintaining discrete behavior. In the United States in the past, condoms generally were marked "Sold only for the prevention of disease," and on the first day at the job, the druggist's assistant learned how to hand the pack of three to the customer in a turned-down palm. . . .

For the producer, marketing under such conditions seems to be a matter of (1) making a good product; (2) getting wide distribution; (3) in the case of condoms, pricing well, especially giving appropriate discounts to druggists; and (4) in the case of orals and I.U.D.'s, merchandising to doctors, especially "detailing" by drug salesmen.

Once contraception is accepted legally and socially, contraceptive manufacturers can employ the marketing strategies used in other industries, as is now the case in Japan, Sweden, and the United States. They can argue that a new product is more reliable or more convenient than another product, and they can compete with minor product improvements such as color and packaging. The most appropriate strategies for pricing and promotion will differ depending on the type of contraceptive product, the newness of the product, the market share of the brand, and other characteristics of the product and brand.

DOCUMENT 11.8: W. A. Hassouna, "Technologies and Organization for Sustainable Provision of Basic Health Needs in the Arab World," in *Basic Needs in the Arab Region: Environmental Aspects, Technologies and Policies* (Nairobi: United Nations Environment Programme, 1982, pp. 80–81)

In the following selection, W. A. Hassouna, with the Social Fund for Development in Cairo, describes population control as a fundamental necessity in ensuring successful development in the Arab world. He also describes the necessity of improved technology in health and sanitation. As such programs became more modern in countries outside the Arab world, they would often incorporate birth control as an issue of public health. In the Arab world, religion, politics, and resistance to policies of the Western world would influence debates over such programs.

Real gains in productivity are offset by uncontrolled population growth. Facing the facts of the population problem has implications for all social and industrial sectors. On the one had, greater attempts must be made to improve agricultural yields, to explore other resources for food production, and to increase the productivity of industry. On the other hand, health-sector plans must include comprehensive family-planning programmes which are national in scope, though they may be conducted under the auspices of a separate ministry.

The population growth rate has to be curbed. Improvement in the general socioeconomic conditions of families motivates the bearing of fewer children. This is just as true in the less industrialized situations as in the highly-industrialized countries. The level of health (health status) attained by man is dependent upon the interaction between man and his environment. This interaction involves a multiplicity of factors of a physical, economic, technological, social, cultural, political, mental and emotional nature. Health needs are thus complex in nature and their sustainable satisfaction is dependent upon the ability of man to manipulate these factors in order to affect the net outcome of the interaction between man and his environment positively. . . .

While health technology is important for the satisfaction of health needs, its success is conditioned by three basic factors:

a) nutrition;
b) environmental sanitation;
c) education.

Malnutrition can greatly affect health by rendering people more susceptible to disease and health hazards. The major environmental influence in developing countries is deficiency in basic sanitation, particularly the lack of an adequate pure water supply and satisfactory methods of disposal of human wastes. Environmental hazards have a profound effect on health and mortality. Hence, the provision of pure water and adequate sanitation services is essential for improving health. Education, both formal and informal, is fundamental for developing and sustaining behavioural patterns as well as for provision of economic needs for maintaining the level of health.

DOCUMENT 11.9: Glenn McGee, *The Perfect Baby: Parenthood in the New World of Cloning and Genetics*, 2nd ed. (Lanham, Md.: Rowman & Littlefield Publishers, Inc., 2000, pp. 148–150)

Perhaps the most difficult questions raised at the turn of the new millennium have resulted from cloning. Cloning confronts all conventional understanding of the origins of life, of population quality, of moral obligation, and of religion and science. In his book *The Perfect Baby*, Glenn McGee, professor of bioethics, philosophy, and history and sociology at the University of Pennsylvania, imagines the technology of cloning inspiring a world full of questions.

At one level, we need to know what sort of role individuals should be able to play in designing children; how far under the hood they should be allowed to go by our institutions. There surely are some negative rights against governmental interference in procreative activity, and these perhaps include some right to experiment with technologies like cloning. But more problematic is what it means to provide care for those who have a need to parent. . . .

More than 40 percent of those born after 1998, we now believe, will have more than one mother or father by age eighteen. The majority of American children are effectively raised in day care, while all three or four of their parents pursue careers. Many in our society have long believed that a critical role one can play in the life of a child is that of godparent, or coach, or foster parent, and many families in many ethnicities have well-articulated roles for these mentors.

New technologies will necessitate new stories. Octuplets and septuplets will be the first in our species to hear a story of the dogs and the cats, about being part of a litter. We need a story for a child whose entire first grade class, and soccer team, is composed of siblings. Children of postmenopausal pregnancy will need a new story more fitting than that of "the accidental" late-born child of yesterday. Children of sperm and egg donors will need a story. While today most parents do not tell their children of the presence of donor DNA, eventually it will not be optional.

But what story can one tell a clone?

12

Numbers

Some population theorists may continue to look at the global situation and see only numbers. As indicated thus far, population policymakers may have pointed to numbers, but a variety of factors influenced both their theories and their recommendations for solutions. Still the numbers are there. The following selections help to illustrate how the issue of numbers acted as a constant through the centuries.

DOCUMENT 12.1: John Hippisley, *Essays. I. On the Populousness of Africa. II. On the Trade at the Forts on the Gold Coast. III. On the Necessity of Erecting a Fort at Cape Appolonia* (London: T. Lownds, 1794, pp. 11–16)

According to John Hippisley, this essay on Africa's population sprang from his examinations of the slave trade, as numbers were clearly a concern when considering the profitability and future of slavery. By the late eighteenth century, Enlightenment philosophy addressing human rights had questioned the existence of slavery, and within decades, some nations would abolish the importation of slaves. With that in mind, examinations of numbers intensified. The following comes from Hippisley's report to "The Right Honourable Wills, Earl of Hillsborough, First Lord Commissioner of the Board of Trade and Plantations, and one of His Majesty's Most Honourable Privy Council, &c. &c."

A state of slavery [does not] prevent population, as it doubtless would in a civilized part of the world, where liberty is considered in so rapturous a light. A man or woman of sensibility,—that sensibility increased by reflection, and perhaps study, would under the yoke of slavery, be deaf to all the calls of inclination, and refuse giving going to wretches doomed to inherit the misery their parents feel in so exquisite a manner. (Did not the women of America make themselves miscarry to prevent their children having such cruel matters?) But the idea of slavery is different in Africa; for independent of the almost total absence of keen sensations, the slaves of a family are considered as no unrespectable part of it. Scarce one of them is ever [exiled from the] fold, unless for very great crimes; and then the rest of his fellows are consulted, and the case exactly laid before them. Should a master do otherwise, and dispose of one through mere ill humour or avarice, he stands in danger of the rest running away from him. Slaves also, if they have abilities, are permitted to make the most of them; by which they often become rich, and purchase slaves for themselves. In this they meet with no interruption, provided only that they acknowledge their subservience from time to time, and occasionally make some little presents to their master and his descendants. Nor are the less opulent slaves afraid of the burthn of a family, or that their offspring may want the assistance so absolutely requisite in their infant and tender state; it being a constant observation, in this as well as in every other country where slavery is allowed, that the masters and mistresses have almost the same fondness for the children of their slaves as for their own, and are equally careful in the bringing them up: a circumstance that ought to awaken our reverence of the Divine Providence, which in the default of parental love, or its inutility, supplies the want by an adventitious affection in one totally unconnected by the ties of blood to the poor helpless infant. . . .

The journeys made by the Africans are seldom or ever beyond the limits of their own countries, or just to the confines of a neighbouring one for the purposes of trade, never through curiosity, or for amusement; and even then their wives generally accompany them; so that few children are lost to these states by the absence of husbands from home. We may adhere, that child-birth is easier throughout all these countries than it is in Europe.

The[ir] wars are infinitely less bloody than ours. Scarce any of the prisoners taken in battle are put to death, but are almost all sold, and brought to some part of the coast.

Polygamy is universally allowed through Africa, and contributes vastly to its populousness. It would, however, be hurtful to that of Europe. Among us the number of males and females born is nearly equal, or at least differs only so much as about makes up for the multitudes of the former cut off by war, seavoyages, and other casualties attending their active state. Polygamy must in this case be certainly hurtful to population, for this plain and common reason, that ten women will not have so many children by one husband, as they might by ten; and if one man has ten wives, many others must go without any wives at all. But Africa is very differently circumstanced: and first with regard to trade.

Of all the slaves shipped from the coast, not a sixth part are women; consequently, the number of that sex remaining in the country, being greater than that of the other, polygamy becomes necessary. It ought, however, to be confessed, that this inequality, arising from the trade, is not of itself sufficient to show that propriety of polygamy's being allowed in a country, where scarce any man of opulence has less than two or three wives, and some of them have many hundreds. Some men must be cut off by war: and the male slaves sent from Africa, being five or six times more numerous than the females, is mere trifle in explaining such a case as this, where there is such a prodigious difference between the numbers of *wives* and *husbands*. Here, therefore, we must have recourse to another argument, if so we may call what is barely a recital of matter of fact. From the observations then of those Europeans who have long resided on the several parts of the African coast, and up the rivers, of those who so often visit them on account of trade, and by the strictest enquiries from the inland merchants, it appears that no man goes without a wife from a scarcity of women; that the richest men having many wives, does not prevent the poorest having one or two; in short, that an unmarried black man is seldom or ever seen. The number of women must, therefore, exceed that of the men; nor are we to look upon this as a singular case, the same happening in some places (exactly under the same latitudes as Africa) in the East-Indies.

Thus, of the many hindrances to population in Europe, not one takes place in Africa.

DOCUMENT 12.2: John Stuart Mill, *Principles of Political Economy, With Some of Their Applications to Social Philosophy* (1848) (London: Longmans, Green & Co., 1936, pp. 159–161)

Economist John Stuart Mill elaborated on Malthus's discussion of numbers, emphasizing the potential for limitless increase. He also extolled the benefits of having fewer children—that smaller families could enjoy better health and a higher degree of comfort. In so doing, he reflected the growing tendency toward smaller families. His work addressed population mainly in relation to economics.

It has been the practice of a great majority of the middle and poorer classes, whenever free from external control, to marry as early, and in most countries to have as many children, as was consistent with maintaining themselves in the condition of life which they were born to, or were accustomed to consider as theirs. Among the middle classes, in many individual instances, there is an additional restraint exercised from the desire of doing more than maintaining their circumstances—of improving them; but such a desire is rarely found, or rarely has that effect, in the labouring classes if they can bring up a family as they were themselves brought up, even the prudent among them are usually satisfied. Too often they do not think even of that, but rely on fortune, or on the resources to be found in legal or voluntary charity.

In a very backward state of society, like that of Europe in the Middle Ages, and many parts of Asia at present, population is kept down by actual starvation. The starvation does not take place in ordinary years, but in seasons of scarcity, which in those states of society are much more frequent and more extreme than Europe is now accustomed to. In these seasons actual want, or the maladies consequent on it, carry off numbers of the population, which in a succession of favourable years again expands, to be again cruelly decimated. In a more improved state, few, even among the poorest of the people, are limited to actual necessaries, and to a bare sufficiency of those: and the increase is kept within bounds, not by excess of deaths, but by limitation of births. The limitation is brought about in various ways. In some countries, it is the result of prudent or conscientious self-restraint. There is a condition to which the labouring people are habituated; they perceive that by having too numerous families, they must sink below that condition, or fail to transmit it to their children; and this they do not choose to submit to. The countries in which, so far as is known, a great degree of voluntary prudence has been longest practiced on this subject, are Norway and parts of Switzerland. Concerning both, there happens to be unusually authentic information; many facts were carefully brought together by Mr. Malthus, and much additional evidence has been obtained since his time. In both these countries the increase of population is very slow; and what checks it, is not multitude of deaths, but fewness of births. Both the births and the deaths are remarkable few in proportion to the population; the average duration of life is the longest in Europe; the population contains fewer children, and a greater proportional number of persons in the vigour of life, than is known to be the case in any other part of the world. The paucity of births tends directly to prolong life, by keeping the people in comfortable circumstances; and the same prudence is doubtless exercised in avoiding causes of disease, as in keeping clear of the principal cause of poverty. It is worthy of remark that the two countries thus honourably distinguished are countries of small landed proprietors. . . . But whatever be the causes by which population is anywhere limited to a comparatively slow rate of increase, an acceleration of the rate very speedily follows any diminution of the motives to restraint.

DOCUMENT 12.3: U.S. Census Bureau, *Five Civilized Tribes in Indian Territory: The Cherokee, Chickasaw, Choctaw, Creek, and Seminole Nations* (Washington, D.C.: United States Census Printing Office, 1894, p. 3)

This "Extra Census Bulletin" of the 1890 census taken in the United States estimates numbers among the so-called Five Civilized Tribes: the Cherokees, Chickasaws, Choctaws, Creeks, and Seminoles. These peoples had been moved west six decades earlier along the Trail of Tears and appeared to the United States government to be under control. The 1890 census paid particular attention to Native Americans, as that year marked what was considered the closing of the American frontier. Native Americans of the northern Plains had been put down one last time at Wounded Knee, South Dakota, placing in numbers whatever political influence remained among the entire Native American population.

Each of the Five Tribes takes a census very often; some every five years, some oftener. The peculiar method of government in the nations, whereby the authorities at the several capitals are kept advised by the Light Horse (police) or town, county, or district authorities of changes, enables them to keep fairly authentic lists of the population. This is done chiefly for the purpose of resisting the claims of persons desiring to be known as citizens of the tribes and participants in land divisions and the money to be divided between these Indians on account of sales of surplus lands. Such records as matters of proof will be invaluable in the future, as they will fix the date of settlement of many claimants.

The enumerators of The Five Civilized Tribes in the Indian territory for the United States census were mostly Indians, appointed on the recommendation of the governors or principal chiefs, but some changes were made, and almost all were changed in one of the tribes, for reason. Four special agents were sent to the Indian territory to supervise the work by an agreement with the governors or their representatives. The wisdom of this policy was apparent, when the peculiar nature of Indian political conditions became known.

Much opposition was shown to the census. The Creek and Seminole authorities aided it, however, by legislative action. They urged the residents to give information to the enumerators, but meetings were held to resist them. Under the circumstances, it was decided to ask as few questions as possible, and to get, as a rule, the general statistics of population. It was found difficult to obtain other statistics. The four special agents in charge visited the nations, and their reports give their observations in detail. The unsettled condition of the Indian territory and the constant clashing between the whites, called intruders, and the Indians or their authorities produced a prejudice against the census, which was hard to overcome.

The citizens of The Five Tribes watch with a jealous eye each movement of the United States or its agents, as questions of vast moment are pending. This made them chary of answering questions proposed by the enumerators or special agents.

A serious difficulty was met in the answer to "Are you an Indian?" Under the laws of The Five Tribes or nations of the Indian territory a person, white in color and features, is frequently an Indian, being so by remote degree of blood or by adoption. There are many whites now resident claiming to be Indians whose claims have not as yet been acted upon by the nations. Negroes are frequently met who speak nothing but Indian languages, and are Indians by tribal law and custom, and others are met who call themselves Indians, who have not yet been so acknowledged by the tribes. These circumstances necessarily produced some confusion as to the number of Indians separately designated. However, the total population as given is correct.

The difficulties surrounding the taking of this census were augmented by the fact that in enrolling the Indians it frequently occurred that it was necessary to equip two and sometimes three interpreters to accompany the enumerator to converse with Indians in the same locality. The residents of The Five Civilized Tribes, citizens or otherwise, pay no taxes on real or personal property, and there are no assessments for this purpose.

DOCUMENT 12.4: Halliday G. Sutherland, *Birth Control: A Statement of Christian Doctrine Against the Neo-Malthusians* (New York: P. J. Kennedy & Sons, 1922, pp. 9–13)

Halliday Sutherland was one of the most outspoken critics of the birth control movement that began in the first decades of the twentieth century. A Catholic physician, he essentially argued on religious grounds but used examples from various perspectives to support his position. Here he condemns Malthusian theory, attacking its numerical projections.

In a closed country, producing all its own necessities of life and incapable of expansion, a high birth-rate would eventually increase the struggle for existence and would lead to overpopulation, always provided that, firstly, the high birth-rate is accompanied by a low death-rate, and secondly, that the high birth-rate is maintained. For example, although a birth-rate was high, a population would not increase in numbers if the death-rate was equally high. Therefore, a high birth-rate does not of necessity imply that population will be increased or that overpopulation will occur. Again, if the birth-rate fell as the population increased, the danger of overpopulation would be avoided without the aid of a high death-rate. For a moment, however, let us assume that the Malthusian premise is correct, that a high birth-rate has led to overpopulation, and that the struggle for existence has therefore increased. Then obviously the death-rate would rise; the effect of the high birth-rate would be neutralized; and beyond a certain point neither the population nor the struggle for existence could be further increased. On these grounds Neo-Malthusians argue that birth-control is necessary precisely to obviate that cruel device whereby Nature strives to restore the balance upset by a reckless increase of births; and that the only alternative to frequent and premature deaths is regulation of the source of life. As a corollary to this proposition they claim that, if the death-rate be reduced, a country is bound to become overpopulated unless the births are artificially controlled. Fortunately it is possible to test the truth of this corollary, because certain definite observations on this very point have been recorded. These observations do not support the argument of birth controllers. . . .

During the past century the population of Europe increased by about 160,000,000 but it is utterly unreasonable to assume that this rate of increase will be maintained during the present century. It would be as sensible to argue that because a child is four feet high at the age of ten he will be eight feet high at the age of twenty. Moreover, there is evidence that, apart altogether from vice, the fertility of a nation is reduced at every step in civilization. The cause of this reduction in fertility is unknown. It is probably a reaction to many complex influences, and possibly associated with the vast growth of great cities. This decline in the fertility of a community is a natural protection against the possibility of overpopulation; but, on the other hand, there is a point beyond which any further decline in fertility will bring a community within sight of depopulation and of extinction.

DOCUMENT 12.5: Robert R. Kuczynski, *Population Movements* (Oxford: Clarendon Press, 1936, pp. 31–39)

In the following selection, Robert Kuczynski, from the Department of Social Biology of the London School of Economics, challenges the prevailing notion that it was civilization that brought smaller families. The assumption was based on evidence that nineteenth-century industrialization seemed to coincide with a lower birth rate. As industry denoted progress, and progress denoted civilization, with which came families with fewer children, experts concluded that any nonindustrialized society must have had a high birth rate. At the same time, authorities suggested that self-restraint was characteristic of a civilized person, and that lack of sexual control was characteristic of an uncivilized person, contributing to greater fecundity. Here Kuczynski reexamines assumptions through numbers.

How did the myth arise that in former times most families had very many children? Are the anthropologists and demographers by any chance to be blamed for it? This is certainly not the case. For uncivilized tribes, anthropologists have reported probably as often a scarcity of children as an abundance of children. . . .

The question whether fecundity has increased or decreased with progressing civilization is a controversial one. I am inclined rather to think that it has increased. But so far as the whites are concerned, the change in fecundity in the last centuries, whether it was an increase or not, must have been very small, and we may therefore assume that for them the upper limit of fertility was on the whole practically constant.

The upper limit would be reached only if all females, throughout their entire child-bearing period, had intercourse with procreative men and did nothing to prevent conception or to procure abortion. Since these conditions are never and nowhere fulfilled, fertility always and everywhere lags behind fecundity. But the degree to which fertility lags behind fecundity varies, of course, a great deal.

In England, till a few decades ago, abstinence of unmarried females was generally considered the most decisive factor in keeping fertility below fecundity. There were, to be sure, as early as the seventeenth century, writers who, in discussing population growth, pointed to practices preventing conception and procuring abortion, and also to differential fertility between urban and rural dwellers, between the well-to-do and the poor. But they referred merely to birth-control on the part of unmarried women, and they did not intimate that differential fertility of married women was due to any deliberate action, but rather to impotence of the husband, barrenness of the wife, the abuse of spirituous liquors, and luxurious and unwholesome manner of living.

DOCUMENT 12.6: Julian Huxley, "World Population," in *The Human Sum*, ed. C. H. Rolph (New York: Macmillan, 1957, pp. 14–15)

British biologist Julian Huxley, brother of Aldous Huxley, was invited to participate in a UN conference on world resources in 1949 as director general of UNESCO (the United Nations Educational, Scientific, and Cultural Organization). Huxley suggested that a discussion of resources should include a survey of the world's population. He warned that such a survey would meet with technical, political, and religious obstacles, but they were overcome, and a conference on population was held in 1954. According to Huxley, in the five years it took to arrange the conference, the world's population had increased by more than 130 million.

Let me begin by setting forth some of the facts—often surprising and sometimes alarming—which justify our calling the present a new and decisive phase in the history of mankind. The first fact is that the total world population has been increasing relentlessly, with only occasional minor setbacks, since before the dawn of history. The second fact is the enormous present size of the population—more than 2.5 billion. The third is the great annual increase: some 34 million people per year, nearly 4,000 per hour, more than one every second. The human race is adding to its numbers the equivalent of a good-sized town, more than 90,000 people, every day of the year. The fourth and most formidable fact is that the rate of increase itself is increasing. . . .

In short, the growth of human population on our planet has accelerated from a very slow beginning until it has now become an explosive process. Before the discovery of agriculture, about 6000 B.C., the total world population was probably less than 20 million. It did not pass the 100 million mark until after the time of the Old Kingdom of Egypt, and did not reach 500 million until the latter part of the seventeenth century. By the mid-eighteenth century it passed the billion mark, and in the 1920s it rose above two billion. That is to say, it doubled itself twice over in the period between 1650 and 1920. The first doubling took nearly two centuries, the second considerably less than one century. Now, at the present rate of acceleration, the population will have doubled itself again (from the 1920 figure) by the early 1980s—i.e., in the amazingly short space of 60 years.

DOCUMENT 12.7: Albert Gore, Jr., "International Conference on Population and Development" (*U.S. Department of State Dispatch* 5, September 19, 1994, p. 618)

> The following remarks were made by U.S. vice president Albert Gore at the opening session of the United Nations International Conference on Population and Development, in Cairo, Egypt, September 5, 1994. Before becoming vice president, Gore had written extensively on the global environment.

We would not be here today if we were not convinced that the rapid and unsustainable growth of human population was an issue of the utmost urgency. It took 10,000 generations for the world's population to reach 2 billion people. Yet over the past 50 years, we have gone from 2 billion to more than 5 ½ billion. And we are on a path to increase to 9 or 10 billion over the next 50 years. Ten thousand generations to reach 2 billion and then in one human lifetime—ours—we leap from 2 billion toward 10 billion.

These numbers are not by themselves the problem. But the startlingly new pattern they delineate is a symptom of a much larger and deeper spiritual challenge now facing humankind. Will we acknowledge our connections to one another or not? Will we accept responsibility for the consequences of the choices we make or not? Can we find ways to work together, or will we insist on selfishly exploring the limits of human pride? How can we come to see in the faces of others our own hopes and dreams for the future? Why is it so hard to recognize that we are all part of something larger than ourselves?

Of course, these are timeless questions that have always characterized the human condition. But they now have a new urgency, precisely because we have reached a new stage of human history—a stage defined not just by the meteoric growth in human numbers but also by the unprecedented Faustian powers of the new technologies we have acquired during these same 50 years—technologies which not only bring us new benefits, but also magnify the consequences of age-old behaviors to extremes that all too often exceed the wisdom we bring to our decisions to use them.

For example, warfare is an ancient human habit, but the invention of nuclear weapons so radically altered the consequences of this behavior that we were forced to find new ways of thinking about the relationship between nuclear states in order to avoid the use of these weapons. Similarly, the oceans have always been a source of food, but new technologies like 40-mile-long driftnets coupled with sophisticated sonar equipment to precisely locate fish have severely depleted or seriously distressed every ocean fishery on our planet. Thus, we have begun to curtail the use of driftnets.

But it is becoming increasingly clear that our margin for error is shrinking as rapid population growth is combined with huge and unsustainable levels of consumption in the developed countries, powerful new tools for exploiting the earth and each other, and a willful refusal to take responsibility for the future consequences of the choices we make. Economically, rapid population growth often contributes to the challenge of addressing persistent low wages, poverty, and economic disparity.

Population trends also challenge the ability of societies, economies, and governments to make the investments they need in both human capital and infrastructure. At the level of the family, demographic trends have kept the world's investment in its children—especially girls—unacceptably low. For individuals, population growth and high fertility are closely linked to the poor health and diminished opportunities of millions upon millions of women, infants, and children. And population pressures often put strains on hopes for stability at the national and international level. Look, for example, at the 20 million refugees in our world who have no homes.

The delegates to this conference have helped create a widely shared understanding of these new realities.

DOCUMENT 12.8: Malcolm Potts, "Too many people pose global risk" (*Forum for Applied Research and Public Policy* 12, summer 1997, pp. 6–15)

Malcolm Potts served as the first medical director of the International Planned Parenthood Federation. The observations made in the following excerpt parallel those made by Al Gore, Julian Huxley, and many others who supported population control at the international level in the last half of the twentieth century. At the time of publication, Potts was serving as Bixby Professor at the School of Public Health at the University of California, Berkeley.

Every 100 hours, one million more people are born than die. Such huge numbers make it difficult for most of us to appreciate the scale that this relentless trend represents. One macabre image that helps put the figures into perspective is this: If an atomic weapon as destructive as the one that fell on Hiroshima had been dropped each day on a major metropolitan area for the past 50 years, global population would still be increasing.

The rate at which people are having babies is falling, but the absolute increase in human numbers continues to rise. As a consequence of recent high birth rates, half the population in many developing countries is now below the age of marriage. Each year, many more young people enter their fertile years than the year before. The momentum in population growth caused by these demographic trends overshadows a notable rise in the acceptance and use of family planning. . . .

The Cairo conference estimated that by 2000, industrialized nations would need to give a minimum of $10.2 billion a year to support family planning initiatives and about $17 billion a year if all reproductive-health services are to be made available to the people who want them. Of this sum, conference attendees estimated that $5.7 billion would have to come from the international community.

The United States, which until the beginning of this decade provided nearly half of the foreign aid granted by Organization of Economic and Community Development (OECD) countries, has drastically reduced its level of aid, and, in 1996 and 1997, Congress threatened to cut it even further. In real terms, the United States spends about as much on international family planning as it does on kitty litter or that Proctor and Gamble spends on advertising laundry detergent each year.

Index

About the Author

KATHLEEN A. TOBIN is Assistant Professor of Latin American Studies at Purdue University. She is the author of *The Religious Debate over Birth Control* (2001).